D1507793

SOLVE YOUR CHILD'S MATH PROBLEMS

Quick and Easy Lessons for Parents

PATRICIA D. NORDSTROM

A Parachute Press Book
A FIRESIDE BOOK
Published by Simon & Schuster

New York London Toronto Sydney Tokyo Singapore

FIRESIDE
Rockefeller Center
1230 Avenue of the Americas
New York, New York 10020

DESIGNED BY BARBARA MARKS

Manufactured in the United States of America

10 9 8 7 6 5 4 3 2 1

Library of Congress Cataloging-in-Publication Data is available.

ISBN: 0-671-87026-2

CONTENTS

*In loving memory
of Virginia DeBerry,
my mother and
first spiritual director*

ACKNOWLEDGMENTS

I am very thankful to the individuals and communities who have sustained me with their love and support throughout the writing of this book:

My husband and best friend, Dr. Jeffrey Lee Nordstrom
Our children, Kurt, Trisha, Christina, and Alexander
My father, Percell DeBerry
My mother-in-law, Anita Nordstrom
My sisters, Maxine Hines, Yvonne Pinkard, and Vanessa Williams
My sister-in-law, Janice Nordstrom
The members of Morningside House Church of All Angels
    Episcopal Church in New York City
The members of my writing group, Matthew de Clercq, Peggy
    Harrington, Thea K. Hunter, Brother Paul Julian, and Mike
    Stone
The members of the Cambridge community who have shared their
    way of life, "without exception—no matter what."
The students, faculty, staff, and parents of Friends Seminary in
    New York City

I would also like to thank Dennis Riordan for his valuable help on the manuscript.

SOLVE YOUR CHILD'S MATH PROBLEMS

Solve Your Child's Math *Problems* was written for anyone who takes on the role of helping a child learn the basic skills for math, but it is especially written for parents.

Of all the curriculums, math is probably most unlike what parents today were taught as students. What was emphasized then is not emphasized now. How it was done then is not necessarily how it's done now. New names have been given to old procedures, and some procedures that took forever to master (such as finding the square root of a number) are no longer taught because a calculator can provide the answer at the push of a button.

Because today's math curriculum is so different from what you were taught, it's quite likely that one of these two scenes has been played out in your house at homework time:

Scene 1: It's 8:30 P.M. on a school night. You ask, for what seems like the umpteenth time, "Have you finished your homework?"

"No, I still have my math to do."

"Will you please get it done," you plead.

"I tried, Mom, but I don't understand it."

"Okay. Give me the book and let me see what I can do." You scan the problem and soon ask, "Why are you reducing fractions like this? I never learned to do it this way."

"I don't know, Mom. I'm just trying to do what the teacher said to do."

You find an example of working it out, but the explanation makes no sense to you. You feel the pressure of being on the spot and try to save face. Then math anxiety becomes a reality for you as these thoughts begin to compete with your figuring: "I hate this teacher. I hate this book. I hate math. I've always hated math."

Scene 2: Your child enters with a simple question: "Dad, how do you bisect an angle?"

You think, "I used to know how to do that. Let's see..." Using pencil and compass, you try a variety of strategies. You work frantically, but your lack of confidence in your ability is now very apparent. Your child, feeling bewildered and sorry for you, stands by.

"It's okay," your child says, "I'll ask my teacher when I get to school."

The fundamental goal of this book is to help you become a more effective helper for your child. It will:

- Introduce you to the skills emphasized today and give you background information on why these skills are taught and how they fit your child's overall math education;
- Refresh your memory by making connections between math as you learned it and how it is taught today; and
- Teach you the skills that you have forgotten or never learned at all.

Taking an active role in the learning process of your child is one of the greatest joys of parenting. We have a natural curiosity as we watch our children grow and discover the world around them. We want to be there, we want to help, we want to play an important part.

When our children were toddlers, teaching them was easy. They followed us around. They imitated us. We talked and read to them. They learned and this brought us joy because we saw ourselves as their first teachers.

As our children became older preschoolers, they began to pull away. Our learning relationship with them changed, but our confidence in our ability to teach them was still intact. We provided them with the learning tools: we bought the books, we chose the learning programs they watched, we set the curriculum.

Many of us feel that the real break occurred when our children reached school age. Unless we were among the minority who were "homeschool" parents or were involved in some type of parent-school cooperative, we didn't have a great influence on the choices for curriculum or how it was taught. We gradually lost confidence in our ability to play a major role in our children's education. Instead, our primary role was that of "homework helper."

For many of us, helping our middle school children with math homework does not become a "uniting" experience. On the contrary, it becomes one of the main sources of the "great divide." The role of parent as teacher can come to a screeching halt, as math homework becomes the focal point of constant frustration for both parent and child. But over and over again, studies show that students learn better when parents take an active role in their children's education.

The middle school grades of 5-8 are those during which children have the greatest potential of being turned off to math for a lifetime. Children at that age are growing in many ways—physically, emotionally, and intellectually. They question. They challenge. They insist upon relevancy and involvement. Until recently, these were the very behaviors that were discouraged in the math classroom. Math, for many, meant the meaningless memorization of facts and procedures that were seldom used. For these middle school children, the math classroom was anything but relevant—let alone exciting.

All of us are lucky that the way math is being taught is going through a dramatic change. In 1989, the National Council of Teachers of Mathematics published the *Curriculum and Evaluation Standards for School Mathematics*. This publication has been having a profound effect on the math curriculum in grades K-12. Children most likely learn math today by beginning with a real-life problem or situation that needs to be solved. They are given the freedom to use techniques that might be uniquely theirs. The premise is that children as well as adults are most likely to remember the things that they grapple with and resolve. In addition, children are more likely to be open to established ways of finding answers when the problems still remain after their own approaches have been exhausted.

Along with emphasizing problem solving, the new standards document urges teachers to introduce children to a broader range of mathematical topics. The seven chapters in this book reflect these recommendations. Two of the chapters—prealgebra and geometry—are fairly lengthy because they mirror an increased emphasis in your child's curriculum.

Solve Your Child's Math *Problems* is skills-based in its content. Regardless of how a topic is treated in the classroom, there is still a basic body of skills associated with the topic that students are expected to master. Since skills are easy to test, most teachers know that their students must be equipped for the reality of standardized tests.

The information in this book is organized to make it easily accessible to you. Keep in mind, though, that many schools no longer make such distinct demarcations as the names of the chapters in this book imply. Today, the trend in math is toward a more integrated approach wherein one chapter in your child's textbook might contain operations and concepts from several chapters in this book.

HOW TO USE THIS BOOK

Each chapter in *Solve Your Child's* Math *Problems* follows the same basic format. Each begins with an introduction, giving a general overview of the chapter and the topics that are included.

Next, you will find a section that has sample problems, followed by an answer section. The problems presented here are exactly like, or very similar to, the actual problems your child might have for homework or on a test. Use this section as an index. Skim through it to find the problem that is just like, or similar to, the one you are trying to solve with your child. Then look it up in the how-to guide, the last section of each chapter, to see how to solve it.

The how-to guide provides a simple step-by-step cookbook-style outline in the section entitled "How to Get the Answer" for each question in the sample problem section, fulfilling one of the most important goals of this book. It will show you how to solve the problem so that you can successfully help your child complete his or her homework assignment.

If you simply want to familiarize yourself with the math topics your child will be studying during his middle-grade education, you can read the sample problems section for a quick review or the "How-to Guide" for a more detailed description.

Following the seven chapters is a glossary in which you can find all the math terms and their definitions that were mentioned throughout the book.

The final section of this book is "At Your Fingertips", a collection of charts, tables, problem-solving tips, and strategies to be used for shortcuts when you are making extensive calculations.

Solve Your Child's Math *Problems* was not created to be a cure-all. Remember, you are the ones who are there—day in and day out, year in and year out—committed to trying still one more time to help your child become the very best he or she can be. This is a tremendous job. Every little bit helps, and your caring and love will offset a multitude of mistakes. But *Solve Your Child's* Math *Problems* can serve to encourage and remind you that there is, indeed, a workable solution and you don't have to go crazy while you are trying to find it. Welcome to *Solve Your Child's* Math *Problems,* the math homework manual for parents.

1 NUMBERS AND NUMERATION

If 500,000 one-dollar bills are stacked flat, one above the other, how high will the pile be? As high as Michael Jordan? Up to a third-floor window in an apartment building? About a mile high? How many is five hundred thousand anyway? What would it look like?

Getting a "number sense" for large numbers is the essence of "Numbers and Numeration". *Numbers* are the names of quantities that describe the things we count. *Numeration* is the act of counting things. Your children's introduction to the study of numbers and numeration started when they began to gather objects and form them into groups or sets. Soon, they needed a way to describe the numbers of objects in the sets. At first these descriptions were verbal—they counted by saying the names of numbers as objects were singled out (in math, this is called one-to-one correspondence). Symbols for numbers were eventually introduced, and once they could read, they learned to write numbers.

The middle-school math curriculum reflects this sequence of learning. Sometime during the school year, there is a review and extension of counting concepts. Much attention is focused on writing given numbers in different forms, so that your children can see and understand the numbers better. Throughout the study of this topic, which is the subject of this chapter, your children will learn and practice a lot of names for the same quantity. For example, they will come to understand that a numeral such as 293 can be written as $200 + 90 + 3$, 2.93×10^2, two hundred ninety-three, or CCXCIII, for example. When these skills have been mastered, children develop a real appreciation for numbers.

Rounding, another topic in "Numbers and Numeration", is a good example of how things have changed since most parents today were in school. Rather than being used just as a tool for estimating, it is used in today's curriculum to check the reasonableness of a calculation. This is especially important today because computation has moved toward calculators and computers and away from the paper and pencil (which has the small advantage of being able to trace an error because we can see where it was made). Technology has freed your children to try more elaborate procedures, but as procedures have gotten more elaborate, so have their mistakes. Bigger blunders can occur with just the slip of the finger. One safeguard against this is to use rounding to determine if a solution to a problem makes sense.

Writing numbers in different forms and rounding are just two of the topics your child will be learning about to achieve a "number sense." To help you make sense out of "number sense," you will find these topics along with the others listed below in this chapter.

By the way, just how high would that stack of 500,000 one-dollar bills reach? The answer is about 148 feet, or 12 stories high!

Topics in This Chapter

Writing numbers in standard form
Writing numbers in word form
Finding number values
Writing numbers in expanded form
Comparing numbers using the symbols > (greater than) and < (less than)
Ordering numbers from least to greatest
Rounding and estimating
Converting base ten numbers to other base systems

Writing Roman numerals
Using scientific notation

SAMPLE PROBLEMS

1. Write the standard form of two hundred nine million, four hundred sixty-five thousand, eight.
2. Write 51,708,020,091 in word form.
3. Write the value of the underlined digit in the following numeral: 781,2<u>9</u>1,001,421.
4. Write 632,487,020 in expanded form.
5. Show the relationship between the following two numerals by writing either < or > 872,421 _____ 872,241.
6. Order 5,050; 5,500; 5,005; and 5,550 from least to greatest.
7. Round 16,853 to the nearest thousand.
8. Round 59,652,313,017 to the greatest place value.
9. The attendance figures for the last five shows of the circus were 453, 281, 522, 621, and 749. Estimate the total attendance for these days.
10. Convert 45 in base ten to:
    (a) base two   (b) base eight.
11. Which decimal number is expressed by each of the following Roman numerals?
    (a) MDCLXVII   (b) MCMXXIX
12. Express 762,300,000 in scientific notation.

Answers

1. 209,465,008
2. Fifty-one billion, seven hundred eight million, twenty thousand, ninety-one.
3. 90,000,000
4. 600,000,000 + 30,000,000 + 2,000,000 + 400,000 + 80,000 + 7,000 + 20
5. 872,421 > 872,241

6. Starting with the "least" on the left, the order from least to greatest is: 5,005; 5,050; 5,500; 5,550
7. 17,000
8. 60,000,000,000
9. An estimate is 2,600.
10. (a) $45_{ten} = 101101_{two}$ (This is read, "one, zero, one, one, zero, one, base two".)
    (b) $45_{ten} = 55_{eight}$ (This is read, "five, five, base eight".)
11. (a) MDCLXVII = 1667
    (b) MCMXXIX = 1929
12. 7.623×10^8

How To Guide

PROBLEM 1

Write the standard form of two hundred nine million, four hundred sixty-five thousand, eight.

Answer
209,465,008

The *standard form* of a number is the regular way to write a numeral. For example, 17 is standard form, but "seventeen" is not. ("Seventeen" is in word form.) Most children have no difficulty translating "seventeen" to "17," but long, complex numbers like the one in this problem can be daunting. These kinds of problems—which are found on most standardized exams—test a child's understanding of our number system. Ten digits (0, 1, 2, 3, 4, 5, 6, 7, 8 and 9) are used to write all our numbers. We have a *place value* system, meaning that the position a digit holds in a number determines its value. In a base ten system, like ours, every place value is ten times greater than the place value directly to the right of it. A place-value chart helps to visualize these relationships better:

hundred billions	ten billions	billions	hundred millions	ten millions	millions	hundred thousands	ten thousands	thousands	hundreds	tens	ones
						6	4	1.	7	2	4

Beginning at the right, ten ones make one ten, ten tens make one hundred, ten hundreds make one thousand, and so on. Groups of three places make up a *period*. For example, ones, tens and hundreds make up the units, or ones, period; thousands, ten thousands and hundred thousands make up the thousands period.

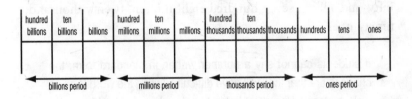

hundred billions	ten billions	billions	hundred millions	ten millions	millions	hundred thousands	ten thousands	thousands	hundreds	tens	ones

◄──── billions period ────► ◄──── millions period ────► ◄──── thousands period ────► ◄──── ones period ────►

How to Get the Answer

1. When a numeral is in word form, the word just before each comma denotes the name of the period. To translate a long numeral from word form to standard form, highlight these period names in the given word form:

   two hundred nine *million,* four hundred sixty-five *thousand,* eight

2. Then disregard the period names and translate the words before each period into symbols.

   Two hundred nine → 209

   Four hundred sixty-five → 465

   Eight →   8

3. Put the numbers together and insert commas between the periods. Don't forget to add zeros as place holders in the ones period: 265,465,008.

   If the word form of a number is not long enough for commas (that is, it has only one period), the word form translates word for word into the standard form. For example, two hundred ten becomes 210.

PROBLEM 2

Write 51,708,020,091 in word form.

Answer
Fifty-one billion, seven hundred eight million, twenty thousand, ninety-one.

If students cannot say a number written in standard form, the chances are that they will have difficulty writing the word form as well. A place-value chart helps translate the standard form of a number to its word form.

How to Get the Answer
1. Make a place-value chart.

hundred billions	ten billions	billions	hundred millions	ten millions	millions	hundred thousands	ten thousands	thousands	hundreds	tens	ones

2. Starting from the right side of the chart and the right side of the given standard numeral, write the digits in order in the place-value chart.

hundred billions	ten billions	billions	hundred millions	ten millions	millions	hundred thousands	ten thousands	thousands	hundreds	tens	ones
5	1	7	0	8	0	2	0	0	9	1

3. Notice that the first word in every group of three words from the right is a *period name*.

		period name ↓			period name ↓			period name ↓			period name ↓
hundred billions	ten billions	billions	hundred millions	ten millions	millions	hundred thousands	ten thousands	thousands	hundreds	tens	ones
5	1	7	0	8	0	2	0	0	9	1

4. Looking at the digits in each period, we can think of them as numbers in themselves:

		period name ↓			period name ↓			period name ↓			period name ↓
		billions			millions			thousands			ones
		51			708			20			91

5. Write the word form of each of these, along with the period names and commas:
   Fifty-one billion, seven hundred eight million, twenty thousand, ninety-one.

PROBLEM 3

Write the value of the underlined digit: 781,2<u>9</u>1,001,421.

Answer
90,000,000

How to Get the Answer
1. Put the given number in a place-value chart.

hundred billions	ten billions	billions	hundred millions	ten millions	millions	hundred thousands	ten thousands	thousands	hundreds	tens	ones
7	8	1	2	<u>9</u>	1	0	0	1	4	2	1

2. Find the underlined digit. Change the heading that it is under to a number in standard form. To find the value of the underlined digit, multiply the digit by this number.

$9 \times$ ten million $= 9 \times 10,000,000 = 90,000,000$

PROBLEM 4

Write 632,487,020 in expanded form.

Answer
600,000,000 + 30,000,000 + 2,000,000 + 400,000 + 80,000 + 7,000 + 20

When a number is in *expanded form,* it is written so that each digit shows its value. For example, 571 in expanded form is 500 + 70 + 1. Expanded form is also known as *expanded notation.*

How to Get the Answer
1. Show the value of each nonzero digit in the given numeral.

Specified Digit		Value
<u>6</u>32,487,020	$\rightarrow$	600,000,000
6<u>3</u>2,487,020	$\rightarrow$	30,000,000

$$632,\underline{4}87,020 \rightarrow 2,000,000$$
$$632,\underline{4}87,020 \rightarrow 400,000$$
$$632,4\underline{8}7,020 \rightarrow 80,000$$
$$632,48\underline{7},020 \rightarrow 7,000$$
$$632,487,0\underline{2}0 \rightarrow 20$$

2. Express the values as an addition phrase.

    $600,000,000 + 30,000,000 + 2,000,000 + 400,000 + 80,000 + 7,000 + 20$

PROBLEM 5

Show the relationship between the following two numerals by writing either < or >. 872,421 _____ 872,241

> means "is greater than"   < means "is less than"

Answer

872,421 > 872,241

Some students have difficulties when using the symbol for the words "is greater than" (>) and the symbol for the words "is less than" (<). Remind your child that mathematical expressions are read from left to right, in the same way that sentences are. The less than symbol (<) points left, or back, while the greater than symbol (>) points right, or forward.

How to Get the Answer

1. When comparing whole numbers that have the same number of digits, we must compare in stages. Start at the left in each numeral and compare digit by digit.

    ↓   ↓

    $\underline{8}72,421$? $\underline{8}72,241$ (Digits are the same.)

    ↓   ↓

    $8\underline{7}2,421$? $8\underline{7}2,241$ (Digits are the same.)

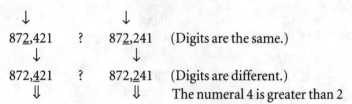

2. As you compare the digits from left to right, the numeral with
   the first greatest digit is the greater one. Therefore, 872,421
   > 872,241.

PROBLEM 6

Order 5,050; 5,500; 5,005; and 5,550 from least to greatest.

Answer
Starting with the "least" on the left, the order from least to greatest
is as follows:

    5,005   5,050   5,500   5,550

> To *order* a list of numerals means to arrange them in increasing
> (or decreasing) value.

How to Get the Answer
1. Compare the numerals digit by digit until a difference is
   found.

    ↓   ↓   ↓   ↓

  <u>5</u>,050   <u>5</u>,500   <u>5</u>,005   <u>5</u>,550 (Digits are the same.)

    ↓   ↓   ↓   ↓

  5,<u>0</u>50   5,<u>5</u>00   5,<u>0</u>05   5,<u>5</u>50 (Digits are different.)

    ⇓   ⇓   ⇓   ⇓

         These two are larger.

    ⇓   ⇓   ⇓   ⇓

       5,5<u>0</u>0   5,5<u>5</u>0 Digits are different.)
                             (This is largest.)

⇓   ⇓

These two are smaller.

5,0$\underline{5}$0   5,0$\underline{0}$5

(This is smallest.)

2. Check the problem for specific directions (i.e. "greatest to least" or "least to greatest"). Then write the numbers in the requested order: 5,005; 5,050; 5,500; 5,550.

PROBLEM 7

Round 16,853 to the nearest thousand.

Answer

17,000

> Rounding is a way of assigning a new name to a number to make it easier to work with.

How to Get the Answer

1. Find the place being "rounded to".

   1$\underline{6}$,853

   ↑

   thousands place

2. Note the digit directly to the right of this place. This digit becomes our "test digit." Our test digit in this example is 8.

3. If the test digit is 5 or more, the digit being "rounded" increases by 1.

   1$\underline{6}$,853

   ↑

   This digit becomes 7.

   If the test digit is 5 or less, the digit being rounded stays the same.

4. The test digit and all digits to the right of it become zeros.
   17,853
       ↑

   These digits become zeros.

5. All digits to the left of the rounded digit remain the same.
   17,000
   ↑

   This digit stays the same.

PROBLEM 8

Round 59,652,313,017 to the greatest place value.

Answer
60,000,000,000

How to Get the Answer

1. Determine the greatest place value. The *greatest place value* is the place value of the number's leading digit. In this example, the greatest place value is ten billion. The leading digit is 5.

2. Examine the test digit (the number directly to the right of the leading digit).

   leading digit
   ↓

   59,652,313,017
       ↑

   test digit

3. Because this digit is greater than 5, the leading digit will increase by 1. The test digit and all the digits to the right of it become zeros.
   60,000,000,000

PROBLEM 9

The attendance figures for the last five shows of the circus were 453, 281, 522, 621, and 749. Estimate the total attendance for these days.

Answer
The estimate is 2,600.

There are situations when time constraints do not allow one to make an exact calculation, but there remains a need for an intelligent numerical appraisal. (Think about being near the front of a long grocery checkout line with a basketful of items and a limited amount of cash.) This is when there is a deep sense of gratitude for the ability to estimate. *Estimation* is the process by which we first round the numbers involved and then use these rounded numbers to add, subtract, multiply, or divide.

Also, as calculators allow us to do faster and more complicated computations, we need a way to check the reasonableness of the answers we get. Estimation provides a means of determining whether an answer makes sense or not.

A good rule of thumb for rounding is to find the greatest place that is common to all the numbers on the list. Round all the numbers to this place. For example, if you were estimating the total of 253, 47, 82, 91, and 381, it would probably be best to round to the nearest ten.

How to Get the Answer

1. Determine the greatest place that is common to all the listed numbers.

   In this example, the greatest common place is hundreds.

2. Round all the numbers to this place.

Original number	Rounded number
453	500
281	300

$$522 \qquad 500$$
$$621 \qquad 600$$
$$749 \qquad 700$$

3. Add the rounded numbers.

$500 + 300 + 500 + 600 + 700 = 2,600$

The actual total is 2,626, so, as you can see, this method of estimation is quite efficient.

PROBLEM 10

Convert 45 in base ten to
   (a) base two   (b) base eight

Answer

(a) $45_{ten} = 101101_{two}$
   (This is read, "One, zero, one, one, zero, one, base two.")
(b) $45_{ten} = 55_{eight}$
   (This is read, "Five, five, base eight.")

Working with bases other than ten is confusing to many children—and absolutely mystifying to most parents! The best way to understand other base systems is to create a place-value chart. In our base ten system, all the numerals are made from ten digits (0, 1, 2, 3, 4, 5, 6, 7, 8, 9) and the value of each heading in the place-value chart (see p. 19) is ten times greater than the one to its right.

In a base two system, all the numerals are made from two digits (0, 1) and the value of each heading in the place-value chart is two times greater than the one to its right.

thirty-two	sixteen	eight	four	two	one
	1	0	1	1	0

In a base eight system, all the numerals are made from eight digits (0, 1, 2, 3, 4, 5, 6, 7) and the value of each heading in the place-value chart is eight times greater than the one to its right:

four thousand ninety-six	five hundred twelve	sixty-four	eight	one

Changing from one base to another is a matter of regrouping. We do this by dividing.

How to Get the Answer

(a) To convert 45 in base ten to base two:

1. Make a base two place-value chart.

sixty-four	thirty-two	sixteen	eight	four	two	one

2. Look for the greatest grouping of two that is contained in 45. Check the place-value chart headings for the one with the highest value that is not greater than 45. It is "thirty-two."
   Q. How many 32s are in 45?
   A. One with 13 left over.

$$\begin{array}{r} 1 \\ 32\overline{)45} \\ -32 \\ \hline 13 \end{array}$$

3. In the place-value chart under the heading "thirty-two,"
   place a 1.

sixty-four	thirty-two	sixteen	eight	four	two	one
	1					

4. Start the process with the 13 that is left over. Look for the
   greatest grouping of two that is contained in 13. (Check the
   headings for the highest value that is not greater than 13.)
   We find that it is "eight." We then ask:
   Q. How many 8s are in 13?
   A. One with 5 left over.

$$\begin{array}{r} 1 \\ 8\overline{)13} \\ \underline{-8} \\ 5 \end{array}$$

5. In the place-value chart under the heading "eight," place a 1.

sixty-four	thirty-two	sixteen	eight	four	two	one
	1		1			

6. We now start the process with the 5 "leftovers." Look for the
   greatest grouping of two that is contained in 5. (Check the
   headings for the highest value that is not greater than 5.) We
   find that it is "four." We then ask:
   Q. How many 4s are in 5?
   A. One with 1 left over.

$$4\overline{)5}^{\,1} \\ \underline{-4} \\ 1$$

7. In the place-value chart under the heading "four," place a 1.

sixty-four	thirty-two	sixteen	eight	four	two	one
			1	1		

8. Working with the 1 "leftover," we see that there is a heading called "one," so we place a 1 under the "one" heading. Finally, we place zeros underneath the headings that are blank.

sixty-four	thirty-two	sixteen	eight	four	two	one
0	1	0	1	1	0	1

Our conversion is complete: $45_{\text{ten}} = 101101_{\text{two}}$.

(b) To convert 45 in base ten to base eight:

1. Make a place-value chart for base eight.

four thousand ninety-six	five hundred twelve	sixty-four	eight	one

2. Find the greatest grouping of eight that is contained in 45. (Use the headings for guides.) It will be "eight."

    Q. How many 8s are in 45

    A. Five, with a 5 left over.

$$\begin{array}{r} 5 \\ 8\overline{)45} \\ -40 \\ \hline 5 \end{array}$$

3. Place the 5 in the chart under the heading "eight."

four thousand ninety-six	five hundred twelve	sixty-four	eight	one
			5	

4. The 5 leftovers are less than eight, so we put them in the last column.

four thousand ninety-six	five hundred twelve	sixty-four	eight	one
			5	5

    Our conversion is complete: $45_{ten} = 55_{eight}$.

PROBLEM 11

Which decimal number is expressed by the following Roman numerals?

(a) MDCLXVII   (b) MCMXXIX

Answer

(a) MDCLXVII = 1667   (b) MCMXXIX = 1929

When writing base ten numbers (also known as decimal numbers), we use a place-value system, wherein the value of a digit is dependent on its placement in the number.

The Romans used a system that employed addition. Symbols for the primary values were used to make all the other numbers:

I	→	1
V	→	5
X	→	10
L	→	50
C	→	100
D	→	500
M	→	1,000

When symbols were placed in descending order, the value of the number was obtained by adding the values of the symbols.

Whenever a symbol of lesser value was written to the left of one with greater value, its value was subtracted from the value of the symbol to the right.

How to Get the Answer

1. Translate the letters of the Roman numerals into their values. Combine the like symbols that are in direct succession (e.g., II = 2, XXX = 30).

   (a) M   D   C   L   X   V   II
       1,000 500   100   50   10   5   2
   (b) M   C   M   XX   I   X
       1,000 100   1,000 20   1   10

2. If the values are all descending, add them.
   (a) 1,000 + 500 + 100 + 50 + 10 + 5 + 2 = 1,667

3. If a symbol of lesser value is written to the left of one with greater value, its value is subtracted from the value of the symbol to the right.

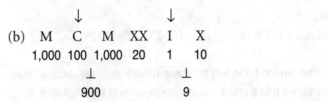

4. Write the values for the Roman numerals grouped in brackets in the preceding example.

   (b) M   CM XX IX
        1,000 900 20   9

5. Now add them together.

   (b) $1,000 + 900 + 20 + 9 = 1929$

   (a) MDCLXVII $= 1667$ b) MCMXXIX $= 1929$

PROBLEM 12

Express 762,300,000 in scientific notation.

Answer

7.623×10^8

Scientific notation is a method of expressing very large or very small numbers in a more compact manner. Because every whole number is understood to have a decimal point that follows the last digit, whole numbers also can be expressed using scientific notation.

The process involves moving the decimal point until the number is between 1 and 10. Moving the decimal point has the effect of multiplying or dividing by a power of 10.

How to Get the Answer

1. Make certain that the decimal is "showing" in the number.

decimal point
↓

762,300,000.

2. "Move" the decimal point so that it is just to the right of the leading digit (the one on the extreme left).

leading digit
↓

7.62300000. or 7.623

All zeros at the right end of the numeral can be dropped.

3. Count the number of places it took to make the move.

7.62300000.

The number of decimal point moves is eight.

4. The new number formed by moving the decimal point (from step 2) is expressed as a product of a power of 10, in which the number of moves (in step 3) becomes the exponent of 10:

new number • $10^{\text{number of decimal point moves}}$

7.623×10^8

2 NUMBER THEORY AND OPERATIONS

Problem

Peter and Randy are racing cars on a tabletop track. It takes Peter's car twelve seconds to make it around the track. It takes Randy's car fifteen seconds. If the cars start together, how much time will it take for the two cars to meet again at the starting line?

There are many ways to arrive at the answer to this problem. Multiples, a topic of study under number theory, offers a direct and relatively painless way to solve it. By making a table, we can chart the elapsed times it would take for each car to complete laps.

Elapsed Time in Seconds (marking a complete cycle)

	1 lap	2 laps	3 laps	4 laps	5 laps	6 laps	7 laps
Peter	12	24	36	48	60	72	84
Randy	15	30	45	60	75	90	105

Sixty seconds is the first elapsed time that both cars share—which answers the question.

Numbers, besides being practical, have fascinating properties. People have been observing their patterns and formulating theories about these observations for centuries. This is the basis for number theory. When we know more about the nature of a thing, we are usually less afraid of it. Number theory explores and explains many important characteristics about numbers. When students understand these characteristics, their apprehension about them decreases.

Addition, subtraction, multiplication, and division are the four major operations in math. These are operations that your child has mastered before middle school. At the middle-school level, students study number theory topics. From a study of number theory, children learn basic number properties, which give them a greater understanding of these four operations. With number theory knowledge, children discover certain shortcuts that can make the solution of math problems easier and more enjoyable.

In this chapter, we will explore the basic properties of addition, subtraction, multiplication, and division, and other number theory topics as well.

Topics in This Chapter
Divisibility
Factors
Greatest Common Factor
Lowest Common Factor
Prime and Composite Numbers
Sets
Associative, Commutative, and Distributive Properties

SAMPLE PROBLEMS

1. Decide which of the numbers below are divisible by 2, by 3, by 4, by 5, by 9, or by 10:
   (a) 18   (b) 120   (c) 2,070

2. List all the factors of:
   (a) 36   (b) 220
3. Find the GCF of 24 and 42.
4. Find the LCM of 24 and 42.
5. List all the prime numbers that are greater than 1 and less than 50.
6. Give the prime factorization of 420.
7. Use prime numbers to find the GCF and the LCM of 18 and 24.
8. Choose the correct symbol ($=, \approx, \in$, or $\subset$).
   (a) 76 ___ {456, 289, 76, 41}
   (b) {41} ___ {456, 289, 76, 41}
   (c) {1, 2, 3, 4, 5} ___ {43, 281, 17, 93, 22}
   (d) {14, 27, 92, 900, 12, 2} ___ {900, 14, 2, 27, 12, 92}
9. Perform the operation and find the answer set.
   (a) {22, 45, 361} $\cup$ {19, 37}
   (b) {36, 24, 91, 256} $\cap$ {36, 91, 400}
   (c) {36, 24, 91, 256} $\cap$ {25}
10. Simplify each expression:
    (a) $5 + (21\text{-}3) \div 6$
    (b) $10 + 6 \times 5$
    (c) $(6+3) \times 10 - 4$
11. Simplify the following: $2^3 \times 3^2$
12. State which property is illustrated by each of the following equations:
    (a) $(27+41) + (17+9) = (27+41) + (9+17)$
    (b) $(78+34)\,2 = (78)\,(2) + (34)\,(2)$
    (c) $14\,(25\times45) = (14\times25)\,45$

Answers

1. (a) 18 is divisible by 2, 3, 9
   (b) 120 is divisible by 2, 3, 4, 5, 10
   (c) 2,070 is divisible by 2, 3, 5, 9, 10
2. (a) {1, 2, 3, 4, 6, 9, 12, 18, 36}
   (b) {1, 2, 4, 5, 10, 11, 20, 22, 44, 55, 110, 220}
3. GCF = 6

4. LCM = 168
5. The prime numbers between 1 and 50 are 2, 3, 5, 7, 11, 13, 17, 19, 23, 29, 31, 37, 41, 43, and 47.
6. $2 \times 2 \times 3 \times 5 \times 7$ or $2^2 \times 3 \times 5 \times 7$
7. GCF = 6; LCM = 72
8. (a) $76 \in \{456, 289, 76, 41\}$
   (b) $\{41\} \subset \{456, 289, 76, 41\}$
   (c) $\{1, 2, 3, 4, 5\} \approx \{43, 281, 17, 93, 22\}$
   (d) $\{14, 27, 92, 900, 12, 2\} = \{900, 14, 2, 27, 12, 92\}$
9. (a) $\{19, 22, 37, 45, 361\}$
   (b) $\{36, 91\}$
   (c) $\{\ \}$ or ϕ
10. (a) 8
    (b) 40
    (c) 86
11. 72
12. (a) commutative property of addition
    (b) distributive property of multiplication over addition
    (c) associative property of multiplication

HOW-TO GUIDE

PROBLEM 1

Decide if each of the following numbers is divisible by 2, 3, 4, 5, 9 or 10:

    (a) 18   (b) 120   (c) 2,070

Answer

(a) 18 is divisible by 2, 3, 9
(b) 120 is divisible by 2, 3, 4, 5, 10
(c) 2,070 is divisible by 2, 3, 5, 9, 10

When a number can be divided by another number without a remainder, the first number is said to be *divisible* by the second.

Being able to recognize divisibility quickly is a great asset to your child—it allows many calculations to be done without pencil and paper.

These are the rules for divisibility:

All numbers . . .	Are divisible by
ending in 0, 2, 4, 6, 8	2
whose digits add up to a number that is divisible by 3	3
whose last two digits form a number that is divisible by 4	4
ending in 0 or 5	5
whose digits add up to a number that is divisible by 9	9
ending in 0	10

How to Get the Answer

1. 18 is divisible by 2, because it ends in 8.

    18 is divisible by 3, because its digits (1 and 8) add up to 9, which is divisible by 3.

    18 is divisible by 9, because its digits (1 and 8) add up to 9, which is divisible by 9.

2. 120 is divisible by 2, because it ends in 0.

    120 is divisible by 3, because its digits (1, 2, and 0) add up to 3, which is divisible by 3.

    120 is divisible by 4, because its last two digits form a number (20) that is divisible by 4.

    120 is divisible by 5, because it ends in 0.

    120 is divisible by 10, because it ends in 0.

3. 2,070 is divisible by 2, because it ends in 0.

    2,070 is divisible by 3, because its digits add up to 9, which is divisible by 3.

    2,070 is divisible by 5, because it ends in 0.

    2,070 is divisible by 9, because its digits add up to 9, which is divisible by 9.

    2,070 is divisible by 10, because it ends in 0.

PROBLEM 2

List all the factors of
(a) 36   (b) 220

Answer
(a) $\{1, 2, 3, 4, 6, 9, 12, 18, 36\}$
(b) $\{1, 2, 4, 5, 10, 11, 20, 22, 44, 55, 110, 220\}$

When you were in school, you might have learned that the parts of a multiplication problem were called the multiplier, the multiplicand, and the product.

Today, your child is taught that the answer to a multiplication problem is called the product, but the words multiplicand and multiplier have been replaced by a single word: factor. *Factors* are numbers that are multiplied together.

Old		New	
7	← multiplicand	7	
× 3	← multiplier	× 3	} ← factors
21	← product	21	← product

We sometimes talk about finding the factors of a number. To do this, it's helpful to think in terms of division. By dividing a number, we obtain two factors.

For example, $16 \div 8 = 2$

$$
\begin{array}{c}
2 \leftarrow \text{quotient} \\
8\overline{)16} \leftarrow \text{dividend} \\
\uparrow \\
\text{divisor}
\end{array}
\quad \text{or} \quad
\begin{array}{c}
\text{dividend} \\
\downarrow \\
16 \div 8 = 2 \leftarrow \text{quotient} \\
\uparrow \\
\text{divisor}
\end{array}
$$

8 and 2 are factors of 16, because $8 \times 2 = 16$.

When students are directed to list all the factors of a number, a common error is to leave out some of the factors. Outlined in the following section is a procedure that should be helpful in showing your child how to avoid this snare.

How to Get the Answer

1. Remember that 1 is a factor of every number. When listing all the factors, remember always to write 1 as the first factor. We use braces { } to enclose sets. When we have all the factors of 36, those factors will compose a set. (For more about sets, see p. 49)

   (a) $36 = \{1,$ (b) $220 = \{1,$

2. Find the other factors by testing every whole number larger than 1 to see if it will "go into" the given number. (If we ask, "Does 2 'go into' 14?", we mean "Is 14 divisible by 2", or "Can we divide 14 by two and not get a remainder?")

Test number	Does it "go into" 36?	Does it "go into" 220
2	yes	yes
3	yes	no
4	yes	yes
5	no	yes
6	yes	no
7	no	no
8	no	no
9	yes	no
10	no	yes

So far, the factors of 36 are $\{1, 2, 3, 4, 6, 9$

So far, the factors of 220 are $\{1, 2, 4, 5, 10$

3. When we reach this point, we have two options for finding the rest of the factors.

   Option 1: Continue in the same way, testing each successive number by using the divisibility rules. Remember that the last factor will always be the number itself.

   Option 2: Most students find this option faster and more efficient. It uses the idea of *factor pairs* (two factors that give a product equal to the original number).

   Looking at the list we have so far for the factors of 36, we can

think of 6 as being paired with itself because $6 \times 6 = 36$.
Also, 4 and 9 are factor pairs because $4 \times 9 = 36$.

$\downarrow$

The next factor will be the number that pairs with 3; this number is
12 because $3 \times 12 = 36$.
The next factor is the one that pairs with 2; this number is 18
because $2 \times 18 = 36$.
The last factor is 36. It pairs with 1 because $1 \times 36 = 36$.

$\downarrow$

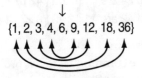

Looking at the list for the factors of 220, we have {1, 2, 4, 5, 10,
11, 20, 22, 44, 55, 110, 220}

PROBLEM 3

Find the GCF of 24 and 42.

Answer
GCF = 6

The letters GCF stand for the *greatest common factor*. The
greatest common factor of two or more numbers is exactly what
it says—the largest mutual factor of the given numbers. The
GCF is useful when simplifying fractions (see p. 77).

The procedure that follows is the first one that your child is
taught for finding GCF. (Another procedure will be presented later
in this guide.) Your child is usually taught to remember this first
procedure by reversing the letters for greatest common factor:

F - (for factor)   List all the factors for both numbers.
C - (for common) Point out the factors that are in common.
G - (for greatest) Choose the largest of these common factors.

How to Get the Answer

1. List all the factors of the given numbers, 24 and 42.
   The factors of 24 are $\{1, 2, 3, 4, 6, 8, 12, 24\}$
   The factors of 42 are $\{1, 2, 3, 6, 7, 14, 21, 42\}$
2. Point out the factors that are in common. (Some students find
   it helpful to draw a loop around the common factors.)

   The factors of 24 are {1, 2, 3, 4, 6, 8, 12, 24}
   The factors of 42 are {1, 2, 3, 6, 7, 14, 21, 42}

3. The largest of these common factors is 6. Therefore, the GCF
   of 24 and 42 is 6.

PROBLEM 4

Find the LCM of 24 and 42.

Answer
LCM = 168

LCM stands for *least common multiple*.

We generate multiples when we "count by" the number. For
example, counting by 2s (0, 2, 4, 6, 8, . . .) generates multiples of
2. Counting by 8s (0, 8, 16, 24, 32, . . .) generates multiples of 8.

The least common multiple of two numbers is referred to as
the LCM.

The LCM is useful when adding and subtracting fractions (p.
69).

How to Get the Answer

1. List the multiples of 24 and 42. (Use a calculator for this.)

   $24 \rightarrow 0, 24, 48, 72, 96, 120, 144, 168, 192, \ldots$

   $42 \rightarrow 0, 42, 84, 126, 168, 210, 252, 294, \ldots$

2. Find the first nonzero multiple that the two lists of multiples have in common. This number (168) is the LCM.

   $24 \rightarrow 0, 24, 48, 72, 96, 120, 144, \boxed{168}, 192, \ldots$

   $42 \rightarrow 0, 42, 84, 126, \boxed{168}, 210, 252, 294, \ldots$

PROBLEM 5

List all the prime numbers that are greater than 1 and less than 50.

Answer

The prime numbers between 1 and 50 are 2, 3, 5, 7, 11, 13, 17, 19, 23, 29, 31, 37, 41, 43, and 47.

A *prime number* is any number that has only two factors: 1 and itself. For example, of the numbers 2, 9, 17 and 91, the only prime numbers are 2 and 17. Both 9 and 91 are *composite numbers* (the opposite of prime), because they have more than two factors (1, 3, and 9 are factors of 9; 1, 7, and 13 are factors of 91). Your child can use the rules of divisibility to help determine if a number is prime or composite.

Another way to find primes was devised by Eratosthenes, a Greek mathematician who lived from 276-194 B.C. His procedure is known as the *sieve of Eratosthenes,* and is typically given to students when they are first introduced to primes. If your child is having trouble seeing the relationships among factors, multiples, and primes, working through this exercise helps. When children can "see" a definition, they are more likely to gain a deeper understanding of the concept.

Note: The numbers 0 and 1 are defined as being neither prime nor composite.

How to Get the Answer

To find the prime numbers that are greater than 2 and less than 50 using the sieve of Eratosthenes, follow these steps.

1. List the whole numbers between 1 and 50.

```
 1   2   3   4   5   6   7   8   9  10
11  12  13  14  15  16  17  18  19  20
21  22  23  24  25  26  27  28  29  30
31  32  33  34  35  36  37  38  39  40
41  42  43  44  45  46  47  48  49  50
```

2. Cross out 1 because it is defined as being neither prime nor composite. Circle 2 because it is the first prime number.

```
 ✗  (2)  3   4   5   6   7   8   9  10
11  12  13  14  15  16  17  18  19  20
21  22  23  24  25  26  27  28  29  30
31  32  33  34  35  36  37  38  39  40
41  42  43  44  45  46  47  48  49  50
```

3. Cross out all the multiples of 2 greater than 2. (These are all the even numbers after 2.)

```
 ✗  (2)  3   ✗   5   ✗   7   ✗   9  ✗
11  ✗  13  ✗  15  ✗  17  ✗  19  ✗
21  ✗  23  ✗  25  ✗  27  ✗  29  ✗
31  ✗  33  ✗  35  ✗  37  ✗  39  ✗
41  ✗  43  ✗  45  ✗  47  ✗  49  ✗
```

4. Circle the first number, now, that has not been crossed out or circled. This should be the number 3. Then, cross out all the multiples of three that are greater than three. (These will be every third number from the number three.)

$$\not{1} \enspace \circled{2} \enspace \circled{3} \enspace \not{4} \enspace 5 \enspace \not{6} \enspace 7 \enspace \not{8} \enspace \not{9} \enspace \not{10}$$

```
   X (2)(3) X   5  X   7  X  X  1Ø
  11 1Z 13 1A 1Ø 1Ø 17 1Ø 19 2Ø
  2X 2Z 23 2A 25 2Ø 2Z 2Ø 29 3Ø
  31 3Z 3Ø 3A 35 3Ø 37 3Ø 3Ø 4Ø
  41 4Z 43 4A 4Ø 4Ø 47 4Ø 49 5Ø
```

5. Circle the first number, now, that has not been crossed out. This should be the number 5. Then, cross out all the multiples of five that are greater than five. When this is complete, continue the process of circling and crossing out, as was described. When you have finished, the circled numbers will be the prime numbers.

PROBLEM 6

Give the prime factorization of 420.

Answer
$2 \times 2 \times 3 \times 5 \times 7$ or $2^2 \times 3 \times 5 \times 7$

When we express a number in terms of its factors, we have expressed a *factored form* of the number. For example, a factored form of 12 is 2×6. A factored form of 64 is $4 \times 4 \times 4$.

When the factored form of a number contains several of the same factors, these can be expressed as a power. For example,

<u>Factored form</u> <u>Power</u>

64 $4 \times 4 \times 4$ = 4^3 (This is read as "4 to the third power.")

The small raised number is called the *exponent* and the larger number is called the *base*.

It is possible to express all the factors of the factored form of a number as prime numbers. When we have done this, we have expressed the *prime factorization* of that number.

Number	A factored form	The prime factorization
24 →	4 × 6 →	2 × 2 × 2 × 3

What makes prime factorization special is that it is a unique factorization—no matter how you start, you'll always end up with the same factors.

Making a *factor tree* is a way of finding the prime factorization of a number. The process begins by putting the given number into factored form. Any primes in the factored form are then circled. Any composite numbers have "branches" drawn underneath them so that they can be factored. Each new factor is then factored until the result is the prime factorization.

How to Get the Answer

1. Express 420 in factored form. It is helpful to remember the rules of divisibility. Because 420 ends in 0, we know that it is divisible by 10. So one factored form of 420 would be 42×10

2. Check to see if any of the factors is prime. If so, circle each prime. For each factor that is not prime, draw a two-pronged branch under the number. (We are beginning to construct our factor tree.) At the ends of each prong, place any two numbers that, when multiplied, will form the number at the beginning of the prong. (They must be whole numbers that are greater than one.)

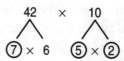

3. Repeat step 2 until there are no composite factors.

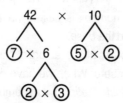

4. The circled factors are the prime factors of 420. Write these in factored form to express the factorization.

$2 \times 2 \times 3 \times 5 \times 7$ or $2^2 \times 3 \times 5 \times 7$

PROBLEM 7

Use prime numbers to find the GCF and the LCM of 18 and 24.

Answer
GCF = 6; LCM = 72

Prime numbers provide your child with a quicker way to find the GCF (greatest common factor), and the LCM (least common multiple).

How to Get the Answer

1. Use factor trees to find the prime factorization of the two numbers: 18 and 24.

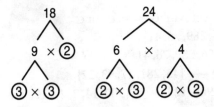

$18 = 2 \times 3 \times 3$ $24 = 2 \times 2 \times 2 \times 3$

2. Find the common factor pairs by drawing a loop around those factors that are present in both factored forms. (Note: This is not always possible, because there may be no common factors.)

Prime factors of 18 = ② × 3 × ③
Prime factors of 24 = ② × 2 × 2 × 3

3. From each loop, choose one of the factors and write it down.

2   3

4. Multiply these factors to get the GCF.

$2 \times 3 = 6 = GCF$

5. To find the LCM:

(a) Follow steps 1-3 above.

2×3

(b) To this group of factors, add all the factors that were not looped in step 2.

2×3 　　　　　　　　 $3 \times 2 \times 2$

from the looped pairs 　　 those that were not looped

6. Multiply these factors to get the LCM.

$2 \times 3 \times 3 \times 2 \times 2 = 72 = LCM$

PROBLEM 8

Choose the correct symbol: $=, \approx, \in,$ or $\subset$

(a) 76 ___ {456, 289, 76, 41}

(b) {41} ___ {456, 289, 76, 41}

(c) {1, 2, 3, 4, 5} —— {43, 281, 17, 93, 22}

(d) {14, 27, 92, 900, 12, 2} ___ {900, 14, 2, 27, 12, 92}

Answer

(a) $76 \in \{456, 289, 76, 41\}$

(b) $\{41\} \subset \{456, 289, 76, 41\}$

(c) $\{1, 2, 3, 4, 5\} \approx \{43, 281, 17, 93, 22\}$

(d) $\{14, 27, 92, 900, 12, 2\} = \{900, 14, 2, 27, 12, 92\}$

A *set* is a well-defined collection of objects. It is described by using words or by listing the individual objects that are contained in the set. A capital letter is used to name a set:

<u>By description</u>   <u>By listing</u>

A = {whole numbers less than 6} = {0, 1, 2, 3, 4, 5}

We use { } (called *braces)* to designate a set. When we see braces, we read the words "the set of." The objects of a set are called *elements,* or *members,* of the set. The symbol $\in$ is read "is an element of." An element is not enclosed in braces as shown in the example below:

$6 \in$ {5, 6, 7, 8} This is read "6 is an element of the set 5, 6, 7, 8."

A set with a limited number of members is called a *finite set.* An example of a finite set is {2, 4, 6}. A set with an unlimited number of members is called an *infinite set.* An example of an infinite set is {1, 2, 3, 4, . . .}. The three dots mean that the set continues according to the pattern indicated by the listed members.

The set that has no members is called the *empty* or *null* set. An example of a null set is the set of naturally purple cats. We indicate that a set is null by empty braces { } or ϕ. Do not indicate a null set by {0}, which is the set whose member is zero.

Two sets are *equal* if they have exactly the same members, even though the members may be listed in different orders:

{10, 20, 30} = {30, 10, 20}

Two sets are *equivalent* if they have the same number of members, regardless of the types of objects that make up the set. The symbol $\approx$ is read "is equivalent to." The example below shows equivalent sets:

{5, 9, 13, 21} $\approx$ {dog, cat, goat, rabbit}

When we make a set using the members of another set, we have made a *subset* of the original set. The symbol $\subset$ is read "is a subset of."

{a, e, u} $\subset$ {a, e, i, o, u}

Every set is a subset of itself.

When children need to picture a set, they use what are known as *Venn diagrams.* These diagrams allow them to visualize the relationship between sets. For example, the Venn diagram below shows that set *K* is a subset of set *J.*

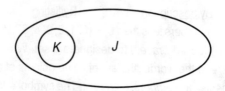

The study of sets is important, because it allows a group of objects to be thought of as a single object. Sets and their relationships will be referred to throughout your child's education in math.

How to Get the Answer

(a) 76 ____ {456, 289, 76, 41}

1. Starting with (a), we observe that 76 is not enclosed in braces. We also observe that it is a member of the set to the right of the answer blank. We conclude that 76 is an element of the set {456, 289, 76, 41} and choose the symbol ∈ for "is an element of."

(b) {41} ____ {456, 289, 76, 41}

2. Looking now at (b), we notice that 41 is enclosed in braces and is at the same time a member of the set to the right. By definition of subset, we conclude that {41} is a subset of the set {456, 289, 76, 41}. We choose the symbol ⊂ which means "is a subset of."

(c) {1, 2, 3, 4, 5} ____ {43, 281, 17, 93, 22}

3. Comparing the two sets in (c), we see that the only thing they seem to have in common is the number of elements (both have five elements). Thus, these two sets are equivalent by definition. We choose the symbol ≈ for "is equivalent to."

(d) {14, 27, 92, 900, 12, 2} ____ {900, 14, 2, 27, 92}

4. Both sets in (d) have exactly the same elements in them. By definition, they are equal sets. We choose the symbol = for "is equal to."

PROBLEM 9

Perform the operation and find the answer set for the following:
(a) {22, 45, 361} ∪ {19, 37}
(b) {36, 24, 91, 256} ∩ {36, 91, 400}
(c) {36, 24, 91, 256} ∩ {25}

Answer
(a) {19, 22, 37, 45, 361}
(b) {36, 91}
(c) { } or φ

> When the members of two or more sets are combined into one set, we have performed a *union* of the sets. The symbol ∪ denotes union:
>
> {5, 7, 9} ∪ {4, 6} = {4, 5, 6, 7, 9}
>
> The process of making a set of the common elements from two or more sets is known as the *intersection*. The symbol ∩ denotes intersection.
>
> {2, 3, 4, 5, 6, 7} ∩ {3, 6, 9, 12} = {3, 6}
>
> Union and intersection are called *operations* because they dictate a procedure based on a specific rule.

How to Get the Answer
1. In (a), we are dealing with a union of the two sets. By putting all the elements together into one set, we get {19, 22, 37, 45, 361}.
2. In (b), the operation is an intersection. We look for the elements that the two sets share.

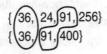

We place these common elements in a set and we get {36, 91}.

3. In (c), the operation is an intersection as well. They have no elements in common, so their intersection is the empty set or the null set and is designated by either { } or ϕ.

PROBLEM 10

Simplify each expression:
(a) $5 + (21-3) \div 6$
(b) $10 + 6 \times 5$
(c) $(6 + 3) \times 10 - 4$

Answer
(a) 8   (b) 40   (c) 86

The four basic operations that we perform on numbers are addition, subtraction, multiplication, and division. When more than one operation is to be performed on a group of numbers, we need a standard sequence to let us know which operation to do first. This standard sequence is known as the *order of operations*.

If there are no parentheses present, the order we follow is multiplication and division first (from left to right), followed by addition and subtraction (from left to right). Some students remember the order by saying, "My Dear Aunt Sally."

M—for multiplication
D—for division
A—for addition
S—for subtraction

If parentheses are present, however, the operation(s) contained inside them are *always* done first.

Later when your children study exponents, they will expand the order of operations and remember this order by using the acronym PEMDAS, which stands for parentheses, exponents, multiplication, division, addition, and subtraction.

A *numerical expression* is a way of naming a number using the symbols of operation (+, -, ÷, ×). For example, a numerical expression for 5 is (3 × 10) ÷ 6. To *simplify* a numerical expression means to determine the number it represents. This is done by performing the indicated operation(s).

How to Get the Answer

1. For $5 + (21-3) \div 6$, begin by doing the subtraction in the parentheses first. The expression becomes $5 + 18 \div 6$. The next operation in the order is division, $18 \div 6 = 3$, which makes the expression, $5 + 3$. Doing the addition, we get 8 for the answer.
2. For $10 + 6 \times 5$, we begin with multiplication, which changes the expression to $10 + 30$. We do the addition, and our answer is 40.
3. For $(6 + 3) \times 10 - 4$, we begin with the addition enclosed in the parentheses. This changes the expression to $9 \times 10 - 4$. The next operation is multiplication, which gives us $90 - 4$. Doing the subtraction, we find our answer is 86.

PROBLEM 11

Simplify the following:
$2^3 \times 3^2$

Answer
72

This type of problem illustrates *products of powers*. To simplify this expression, place the powers in factored form and then calculate the product.

How to Get the Answer

1. Write each power in factored form.

$$2^3 = 2 \times 2 \times 2$$
$$3^2 = 3 \times 3$$

2. Find the product of these factors.

$$2^3 \times 3^2 = 2 \times 2 \times 2 \times 3 \times 3$$
$$= 8 \times 9$$
$$= 72$$

PROBLEM 12

State which property is illustrated by each of the following equations:

(a) $(27+41) + (17+9) = (27+41) + (9+17)$
(b) $(78+34)\, 2 = (78)\, (2) + (34)\, (2)$
(c) $14\, (25 \times 45) = (14 \times 25)\, 45$

Answer

(a) commutative property of addition
(b) distributive property of multiplication over addition
(c) associative property of multiplication

A *property* is a statement made about the nature of a specified operation that gives your child permission to take shortcuts when performing them. There are six basic properties that your child is expected to know and use. They are as follows:

The commutative property
The associative property
The distributive property
The multiplication property of 1
The addition property of 0
The multiplication property of 0

The commutative property: When you add or multiply numbers, the order of the numbers does not matter. This is illustrated by the following examples when *a* and *b* stand for any numbers:

$a + b = b + a$ $a \times b = b \times a$

Example: $5 + 6 = 6 + 5$ Example: $9 \times 8 = 8 \times 9$

$11 = 11$ $72 = 72$

The Associative Property: When you add or multiply numbers, the grouping of the numbers does not matter. This is illustrated by the following examples when *a* and *b* stand for any numbers:

$(a + b) + c = a + (b + c)$ $(a \times b) \times c = a \times (b \times c)$

Example: Example:

$(4 + 3) + 5 = 4 + (3 + 5)$ $(6 \times 7) \times 8 = 6 \times (7 \times 8)$

$7 + 5 = 4 + 8$ $42 \times 8 = 6 \times 56$

$12 = 12$ $336 = 336$

In school, your child might have studied about the mathematician, Carl Gauss. One story students like concerns the time when Gauss stumped the teacher. As busy work, Gauss and his fellow students were asked to find the sum of the numbers from 1 to 100. While his classmates were adding $1 + 2 + 3 + 4 + \ldots$, Gauss grouped the numbers in a different order before adding. He paired the numbers as follows:

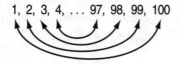

1, 2, 3, 4, ... 97, 98, 99, 100

and put the pairs in parentheses:

$(1 + 100) + (2 + 99) + (3 + 98) + \ldots$

Each pair of parentheses contained a sum of 101 and there were 50 of these pairs. In a very short time, he walked up to the teacher with the answer, which he had obtained by multiplying $101 \times 50 = 5050$.

When Carl Gauss regrouped the numbers, he was using the *associative property.*

The distributive property: There are two distributive properties:

(a) The distributive property of multiplication over addition states that when two numbers are added and then multiplied by a third number, the answer will be the same as multiplying each of the two numbers by the third one first, and then adding the products.

$a(b + c) = ab + ac$

Example: $7(5 + 4) = 7 \times 5 + 7 \times 4$

$7(9) = 35 + 28$

$63 = 63$

(b) The distributive property of multiplication over subtraction states that when two numbers are subtracted and then multiplied by a third number, the answer will be the same as multiplying each of the numbers by the third one first and then subtracting the products.

$a(b - c) = ab - ac$

Example: $7(5 - 4) = 7 \times 5 - 7 \times 4$

$7(1) = 35 - 28$

$7 = 7$

The distributive property helps when one is faced with a problem like the following:

$7(60 - 1)$

If you follow the normal order of operations, you would need to subtract $(60 - 1)$, because operations within the parentheses are done first. The problem now becomes

$7(59)$

This problem appears to be one that requires pencil and paper. However, with the distributive property, a shortcut can be used.

The distributive property: When *a, b* and *c* stand for real numbers:

$a(b + c) = ab + ac$ and $a(b - c) = ab - ac$

The distributive property allows you to multiply before doing the addition or subtraction that is contained within the parentheses. You are then able to "distribute" the multiplier over each term in the parentheses. The result is often easier to calculate mentally.

Each of these numbers can be multiplied by 7.

↓ ↓

$7(60 - 1) = 7(60) - 7(1)$
$7(59) = 420 - 7$
$413 = 413$

The three remaining properties that are covered at this level are as follows:

The multiplication property of 1: Any number multiplied by 1 equals the number.

$a \times 1 = a$

Example: $398 \times 1 = 398$

The addition property of 0: The sum (the answer in addition) of any number and zero equals the number.

$a + 0 = a$

Example: $91 + 0 = 91$

Because of these two properties, 1 is known as the *identity for multiplication,* and 0 is known as the *identity for addition.*

The multiplication property of 0: Any number multiplied by zero equals zero.

$a \times 0 = 0$

Example: $25 \times 0 = 0$

There is no logical way to give meaning to division by zero. Your child is taught that division by zero is not allowed and is undefined.

How to Get the Answer

When helping your children with these types of problems, encourage "detective work." Urge them to look for differences between how the numbers are expressed on the left side of the equation, and how they are expressed differently on the right side.

1. Compare the left and right sides of part (a):

    $(27 + 41) + (17 + 9) = (27 + 41) + (9 + 17)$

    Notice that the order of the numbers within the last parentheses has changed. On the left side of the equation, it is $(17 + 9)$; on the right, it is $(9 + 17)$. This illustrates the commutative property of addition.

2. In part (b), the equation involves both multiplication and addition:

    $(78 + 34)2 = (78)(2) + (34)(2)$

    (When a number is written directly beside parentheses, or is contained alone within parentheses, the operation being indicated is multiplication.) On the right side, we have distributed the multiplier over each number inside the parentheses. This is an example of the distributive property of multiplication over addition.

3. Comparing the left and right sides of part (c), we notice that the grouping has changed:

    $14(25 \times 45) = (14 \times 25)45$

    On the left, 25 and 45 are together within parentheses. On the right, 14 and 25 are together within parentheses. This different grouping illustrates the associative property of multiplication.

3 FRACTIONS

Take a minute right now. On a piece of scrap paper, draw an illustration that shows three-fourths of something.

Are you done? What did you draw? If you are a typical adult, you probably drew something like a circle divided into four sections, with three of them shaded—or perhaps you drew a long rectangle divided into four sections, with three of them shaded.

If your child was given this exercise, the drawings might be quite different. Children today learn that fractions deal with parts of a whole, but these parts are not restricted to just a "whole" that is one object. A fraction can also indicate a part of a set:

$$\begin{array}{cccc} * & * & * & * \\ * & * & * & * \\ * & * & * & * \\ * & * & * & * \end{array} = \frac{3}{4}$$

as well as a way to express division: $3 \div 4 = \frac{3}{4}$

The study of fractions, today, is rarely an isolated topic in the math curriculum. Nonetheless, your child is expected to know some basic how-tos. The working vocabulary for fractions includes the terms *numerator, denominator, equivalent fractions, LCD, lowest terms,* and *relatively prime.*

The sample problems will give you an overview of the fraction basics that are necessary for your child at this stage. After checking your answers, be sure to browse through the how-to guide that includes both traditional and newer procedures, along with the appropriate old and new vocabularies.

Topics in This Chapter

Finding equivalent fractions
Adding and subtracting fractions
Finding the least common denominator
Multiplying and dividing fractions
Comparing fractions using the symbols > (greater than) and
    < (less than)
Simplifying fractions
Working with improper fractions and mixed numbers

SAMPLE PROBLEMS

1. Complete by finding an equivalent fraction for each of the following:

    (a) $\frac{2}{3} = \frac{?}{27}$ (b) $\frac{8}{72} = \frac{1}{?}$

2. Add: Subtract:

    (a) $\frac{3}{7} + \frac{2}{7}$ (b) $\frac{9}{19} - \frac{6}{19}$

3. Find the least common denominator (LCD) of

    $\frac{5}{18}$ and $\frac{7}{24}$.

4. Add   Subtract:

   (a) $\frac{5}{6} + \frac{1}{12}$ (b) $\frac{8}{9} - \frac{3}{5}$

5. Multiply:

   $\frac{2}{3} \times \frac{5}{7}$

6. Divide:

   $\frac{3}{5} \div \frac{2}{3}$

7. Replace each ? with $<$, $>$, or $=$.

   (a) $\frac{2}{3}$? $\frac{5}{7}$ (b) $\frac{4}{9}$? $\frac{11}{37}$ (c) $\frac{17}{51}$? $\frac{1}{3}$

8. Simplify:

   $\frac{930}{2220}$

9. Change:

   (a) $3\frac{9}{10}$ to an improper fraction

   (b) $\frac{13}{9}$ to a mixed number

10. Add:

   $6\frac{7}{8} + 2\frac{1}{2}$

11. Subtract:

   (a) $3\frac{1}{2} - 1\frac{2}{3}$ (b) $7 - 1\frac{3}{4}$

12. Multiply: Divide:

   (a) $3\frac{6}{7} \times 9\frac{1}{3}$ (b) $3\frac{3}{10} \div 1\frac{7}{15}$

Answers

1. (a) $\frac{2}{3} = \frac{18}{27}$ (b) $\frac{8}{72} = \frac{1}{9}$

2. (a) $\frac{5}{7}$ (b) $\frac{3}{19}$

3. 72

4. (a) $\frac{11}{12}$ (b) $\frac{13}{45}$

5. $\frac{10}{21}$

6. $\frac{9}{10}$

7. (a) $\frac{2}{3} < \frac{5}{7}$ (b) $\frac{4}{9} > \frac{11}{37}$ (c) $\frac{17}{51} = \frac{1}{3}$

8. $\frac{31}{74}$

9. (a) $\frac{39}{10}$ (b) $1\frac{4}{9}$

10. $9\frac{3}{8}$

11. (a) $1\frac{5}{6}$ (b) $5\frac{1}{4}$

12. (a) 36 (b) $2\frac{1}{4}$

How-To Guide

PROBLEM 1

Complete by finding an equivalent fraction for each of the following:

(a) $\frac{2}{3} = \frac{?}{27}$ (b) $\frac{8}{72} = \frac{1}{?}$

Answer

(a) $\frac{2}{3} = \frac{18}{27}$ (b) $\frac{8}{72} = \frac{1}{9}$

Equivalent fractions are fractions of equal value. For example, $\frac{5}{10}$ and $\frac{1}{2}$ are equivalent fractions. Your child has learned to make equivalent fractions from given fractions by either multiplying or dividing the numerator and the denominator of these fractions by the same number.

$\underline{5}$ ← numerator
10 ← denominator

This works because we are essentially multiplying or dividing the fraction by 1.

$$\frac{5}{10} = \frac{1 \times \boxed{5}}{2 \times \boxed{5}}$$

$$\frac{1}{2} = \frac{5 \div \boxed{5}}{10 \div \boxed{5}}$$

This is equivalent to 1.   This is equivalent to 1.

How to Get the Answer

1. Remember that equivalent fractions are made by either multiplying or dividing the numerator and denominator of the original fraction by the same number.

$$\frac{3}{4} \rightarrow \frac{3 \times 7}{4 \times 7} \rightarrow \frac{21}{28}$$

$$\frac{15}{18} \rightarrow \frac{15 \div 3}{18 \div 3} \rightarrow \frac{5}{6}$$

2. When a part is missing in a pair of equivalent fractions, examine the parts that are not missing.

examine these
↓   ↓

(a) $\frac{2}{3} = \frac{?}{27}$ (b) $\frac{8}{72} = \frac{1}{?}$

↑   ↑
examine these

3. Ask yourself one of these questions:

Q. What did I multiply one number by to get the other?

(a) $\frac{2}{3} = \frac{?}{27}$

A. I multiplied by 9.

Q. What did I divide one number by to get the other?

(b) $\frac{8}{72} = \frac{1}{?}$

A. I divided by 8.

4. Multiply or divide the third number in the same manner to find the missing part.

(a) $\frac{2}{3} = \frac{?}{27}$　　Multiply 2 by 9 to get 18.

(b) $\frac{8}{72} = \frac{1}{?}$　　Divide 72 by 8 to get 9.

PROBLEM 2

Add

(a) $\frac{3}{7} + \frac{2}{7}$

Subtract

(b) $\frac{9}{19} - \frac{6}{19}$

Answer

(a) $\frac{5}{7}$

(b) $\frac{3}{19}$

When adding or subtracting fractions with the same denominator, most children find the procedure simple and straightforward. The answer will have the same denominator as the two given fractions. The numerator will be the sum (the result of adding) or the difference (the result of subtracting) of the given numerators.

How to Get the Answer

How to add fractions with the same denominators:

1. Add across the top.

    (a) $\frac{3}{7} + \frac{2}{7} = \frac{5}{7}$

2. *Do not* add across the bottom. The denominator will be the same as the fractions that are being added.

    (a) $\frac{3}{7} + \frac{2}{7} = \frac{5}{7}$

    ↑ ↑ ↑

    same denominator

How to subtract fractions with the same denominators:

1. Subtract across the top.

    (b) $\frac{9}{19} - \frac{6}{19} = \frac{3}{19}$

2. The denominator will be the same as the fractions that are being subtracted.

    (b) $\frac{9}{19} - \frac{6}{19} = \frac{3}{19}$

    ↑ ↑ ↑

    same denominator

PROBLEM 3

Find the least common denominator (LCD) of

$\frac{5}{18}$ and $\frac{7}{24}$.

Answer

72

Finding the least common denominator (LCD) involves changing the denominators of the given fractions to denominators that are the same. This is important because fractions cannot be added (or subtracted) until they have the same denominator.

You might remember finding the LCD by using a trial and error process that involved division. For example, if you were looking for the LCD of 12 and 18, you might have asked yourself, What is the smallest number that both 12 and 18 will divide into (without a remainder)? Eventually, you might have found that it was 36. This approach often involves a lot of "trials" and many "errors."

Your child uses a method that involves prime factorization (p. 47). This is the same procedure children use when finding the LCM (least common multiple).

How to Get the Answer

1. Give the prime factorization of each denominator.

   $18 \rightarrow 2 \cdot 3 \cdot 3$

   $24 \rightarrow 2 \cdot 2 \cdot 2 \cdot 3$

2. Loop the pairs of factors that are common to each.

   $18 \rightarrow 2 \cdot 3 \cdot 3$
   $24 \rightarrow 2 \cdot 2 \cdot 2 \cdot 3$

3. List all the numbers that were not looped.

   3, 2, 2

4. Multiply these numbers together with one number from each looped pair. This product is your LCD.

   a number from a looped pair
   ↓
   $3 \cdot 2 \cdot 2 \cdot 2 \cdot 3 = 72 = \text{LCD}$
   ↑
   a number from a looped pair

   The LCD is the LCM of the denominators.

PROBLEM 4

Add: Subtract:

(a) $\frac{5}{6} + \frac{1}{12}$ (b) $\frac{8}{9} - \frac{3}{5}$

Answer

(a) $\frac{11}{12}$ (b) $\frac{13}{45}$

Suppose there were five parrots and three canaries. Young children, describing them in terms of a single group, might say that there are eight birds. At some point in their thinking, they make this connection:

$$5 \text{ parrots} = 5 \text{ birds}$$
$$3 \text{ canaries} = 3 \text{ birds}$$
$$5 \text{ birds} + 3 \text{ birds} = 8 \text{ birds}$$

When your child adds fractions with unlike denominators, he or she goes through a similar process, replacing the given fractions with ones that are both equal in value to the original fractions, and, at the same time, connected to each other by a common denominator.

How to Get the Answer
How to add fractions with different denominators:
1. Write the problem vertically.

(a) $\frac{5}{6}$

  $+\frac{1}{12}$

  ⎯⎯⎯

2. Find the LCD of the fractions.

(a) $\frac{5}{6} = \overline{12}$ ← the LCD

  $+\frac{1}{12} = \overline{12}$ ← the LCD

  ⎯⎯⎯

3. Complete the fraction by finding an equivalent fraction.

(a) $\dfrac{5}{6} = \dfrac{10}{12}$

$+\dfrac{1}{12} = \dfrac{1}{12}$

$\overline{} \quad \overline{}$

4. Keep the LCD for the answer.

(a) $\dfrac{5}{6} = \dfrac{10}{12}$

$+\dfrac{1}{12} = \dfrac{1}{12}$

$\overline{} \quad \overline{}$

$\overline{12}$

5. Add the numerators.

(a) $\dfrac{5}{6} = \dfrac{10}{12}$

$+\dfrac{1}{12} = \dfrac{1}{12}$

$\overline{} \quad \overline{}$

$\dfrac{11}{12}$

How to subtract fractions with different denominators:

1. Write the problem vertically.

(b) $\dfrac{8}{9}$

$-\dfrac{3}{5}$

$\overline{}$

2. Find the LCD of the fractions.

(b) $\dfrac{8}{9} = \overline{45}$ ← the LCD

$-\dfrac{3}{5} = \overline{45}$ ← the LCD

$\overline{}$

3. Complete the fraction by finding an equivalent fraction.

(b) $\frac{8}{9} = \frac{40}{45}$

$-\frac{3}{5} = \frac{27}{45}$

———

4. Keep the LCD for the answer.

(b) $\frac{8}{9} = \frac{40}{45}$

$-\frac{3}{5} = \frac{27}{45}$

——   ——

$\overline{45}$

5.Subtract the numerators.

(b) $\frac{8}{9} = \frac{40}{45}$

$-\frac{3}{5} = \frac{27}{45}$

——   ——

$\frac{13}{45}$

PROBLEM 5

Multiply:

$\frac{2}{3} \times \frac{5}{7}$

Answer

$\frac{10}{21}$

Some students question why it is that one can multiply two fractions and end up with a smaller number. For example,

$\frac{1}{2} \times \frac{1}{2} = \frac{1}{4}$

To help your child see the answer to this, teachers might have given an illustration in school similar to the one that follows. Multiplication of fractions is explained as taking a subgroup of a subgroup:

X   X   X   X
X   X   X   X
X   X   X   X

Twelve books were on a library table.

One-half of these books were nonfiction.

One-half of these nonfiction books were math textbooks.

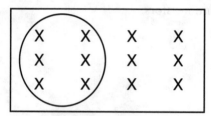

$\frac{1}{2}$ of $\frac{1}{2} = \frac{1}{4}$ means the same as $\frac{1}{2} \times \frac{1}{2} = \frac{1}{4}$

After adding and subtracting fractions and struggling with finding common denominators, many students embrace the ease of multiplying fractions.

How to Get the Answer

1. Multiply across the top.

$$\frac{2}{3} \times \frac{5}{7} = \frac{10}{}$$

2. Multiply across the bottom.

$$\frac{2}{3} \times \frac{5}{7} = \frac{10}{21}$$

PROBLEM 6

Divide:

$$\frac{3}{5} \div \frac{2}{3}$$

Answer

$$\frac{9}{10}$$

Division of fractions usually is introduced in the early grades through the use of fraction strips. At some point, your child might have been given a problem, such as $\frac{1}{2} \div \frac{1}{8}$, and was told to think of the problem in terms of how many $\frac{1}{8}$s are present in $\frac{1}{2}$. By placing the $\frac{1}{8}$ strip beneath the $\frac{1}{2}$ strip,

$\frac{1}{2}$							
$\frac{1}{8}$	$\frac{1}{8}$	$\frac{1}{8}$	$\frac{1}{8}$				

students can see that the answer is 4. Thus, $\frac{1}{2} \div \frac{1}{8} = 4$.

Through working with other problems, such as

$$\frac{1}{3} \div \frac{1}{6}, \ \frac{1}{2} \div \frac{1}{12} \ \text{or} \ \frac{1}{4} \div \frac{1}{8},$$

some students begin to see a relationship between multiplication and division.

$\frac{1}{3} \div \frac{1}{6}$ gives the same answer as $\frac{1}{3} \times \frac{6}{1} = 2$

$\frac{1}{2} \div \frac{1}{12}$ gives the same answer as $\frac{1}{2} \times \frac{12}{1} = 6$

$\frac{1}{4} \div \frac{1}{8}$ gives the same answer as $\frac{1}{4} \times \frac{8}{1} = 2$

Pairs of numbers such as $\frac{1}{6}$ and $\frac{6}{1}$, and $\frac{1}{12}$ and $\frac{12}{1}$ are called

reciprocals. When they are multiplied, their product is 1. The algorithm, or rule, for dividing fractions goes like this:

Division of fractions is traditionally done by multiplying by the reciprocal of the divisor. To put it plainly, we "flip" the fraction following the division sign, and then multiply.

How to Get the Answer

To divide $\frac{3}{5} \div \frac{2}{3}$

1. Solve an equivalent example by:
   (a) rewriting the first fraction,
   (b) replacing the division sign with a multiplication sign, and
   (c) replacing the second fraction with its reciprocal (i.e., by "flipping" it).

step (a)   step (c)
   ↓   ↓

$$\frac{3}{5} \times \frac{3}{2}$$

  ↑

  step (b)

2. Multiply across the top.

$$\frac{3}{5} \times \frac{3}{2} = \frac{9}{}$$

3. Multiply across the bottom.

$$\frac{3}{5} \times \frac{3}{2} = \frac{9}{10}$$

PROBLEM 7

Replace each ? with $<$, $>$, or $=$.

(a) $\frac{2}{3} ? \frac{5}{7}$ (b) $\frac{4}{9} ? \frac{11}{37}$ (c) $\frac{17}{51} ? \frac{1}{3}$

Answer

(a) $\frac{2}{3} < \frac{5}{7}$ (b) $\frac{4}{9} > \frac{11}{37}$ (c) $\frac{17}{51} = \frac{1}{3}$

When fractions have a numerator of 1, most children usually have little trouble determining which is bigger. They know that the larger the denominator, the smaller the fraction.

For comparing other fractions, the traditional method is to use the LCD (least common denominator) to express both fractions with the same denominator. Once they are expressed like this, it is clear that the larger fraction is the one with the larger numerator.

A faster way of comparing fractions is to use cross products (which are obtained by multiplying the numerator of one fraction by the denominator of the other fraction, and vice versa). Both strategies are presented here.

How to Get the Answer

How to compare fractions (traditional method):

1. Find the LCD of the fractions.

   (a) $\frac{2}{3} = \frac{}{21}$ and $\frac{5}{7} = \frac{}{21}$

2. Complete each fraction by finding its equivalent fraction.

   (a) $\frac{2}{3} = \frac{14}{21}$ and $\frac{5}{7} = \frac{15}{21}$

3. Determine which of the original fractions is larger or smaller or if they are the same by comparing the equivalent fractions.

   (a) $\frac{2}{3} < \frac{5}{7}$ because $\frac{14}{21} < \frac{15}{21}$

How to compare fractions (faster method):

1. Starting with the denominator on the left, multiply upward to the right. Write this number above the fraction on the right.

   (b)   answer to 9×11
                                           ↓
                                         (99)
                              $\frac{4}{9}$ ↗ $\frac{11}{37}$

2. Continuing with the denominator on the right, multiply upward to the left. Write this number above the fraction on the left.

   (b)   answer to 41×37
                        ↓   ↓
                     (148)   (99)
                   $\frac{4}{9}$ ↖ $\frac{11}{37}$

3. The larger fraction will be the one under the larger product.

   (b) $\frac{4}{9} > \frac{11}{37}$

   If these cross products are the same, then the fractions are equivalent.

(c)

$$\widehat{51}\ \widehat{51}$$

$$\frac{17}{51} \times \frac{1}{3}$$

$$\frac{17}{51} = \frac{1}{3}$$

PROBLEM 8

Simplify:

$\frac{930}{2220}$

Answer

$\frac{31}{74}$

One difficult aspect of fractions is that, as answers, they have to be "reduced" to the lowest terms. By "reducing" (called "simplifying" by your child), we put the fraction in a form in which 1 is the only number that can divide both the numerator and denominator.

You might remember reducing fractions by a succession of division trials. For example, if the problem was to reduce $\frac{32}{48}$, you would look for a number that would "go into" (i.e., divide) both 32 and 48 without a remainder:

Thought: 4 will work for 32 and 48. $\quad \frac{32 \div 4}{48 \div 4} = \frac{8}{12}$

Thought: 2 will work for 8 and 12. $\quad \frac{8 \div 2}{12 \div 2} = \frac{4}{6}$

Thought: 2 will work for 4 and 6. $\quad \frac{4 \div 2}{6 \div 2} = \frac{2}{3}$

Simplifying fractions in this way is a good strategy when the numbers are not very large. Remind your child to keep dividing until the numerator and the denominator are *relatively prime* (i.e., they have no common factors other than 1).

When numbers are very large, the strategy presented below, which uses prime factors, is probably more appropriate.

How to Get the Answer

1. Find the prime factors of the numerator and the denominator by making a factor tree (p. 48).

2. Write the prime factorization of the numerator and the denominator.

$$\frac{930}{2220} = \frac{2 \cdot 3 \cdot 5 \cdot 31}{2 \cdot 2 \cdot 3 \cdot 5 \cdot 37}$$

3. If a factor is in both the numerator and the denominator, cancel the pair.

$$\frac{930}{2220} = \frac{\not{2} \cdot \not{3} \cdot \not{5} \cdot 31}{\not{2} \cdot 2 \cdot \not{3} \cdot \not{5} \cdot 37}$$

4. Multiply the "leftovers" across the top. Multiply the "leftovers" across the bottom.

$$\frac{31}{2 \cdot 37} = \frac{31}{74}$$

PROBLEM 9

Change: (a) $3\frac{9}{10}$ to an improper fraction.

Change: (b) $\frac{13}{9}$ to a mixed number.

Answers

(a) $3\frac{9}{10} = \frac{39}{10}$ (b) $\frac{13}{9} = 1\frac{4}{9}$

A fraction in which the numerator is larger than the denominator is called an *improper fraction*. Some examples are $\frac{5}{3}$, $\frac{17}{2}$, and $\frac{14}{9}$. All of these fractions can be considered simplified, because the numerator and the denominator have no common factor other than 1. Your child might feel more comfortable, though, expressing them as *mixed numbers* (numbers like $13\frac{1}{2}$ or $21\frac{9}{14}$, that are part whole number and part fraction). This exercise reviews the procedure for converting from a mixed number to an improper fraction and vice versa.

How to Get the Answer

How to change a mixed number to an improper fraction:

1. The improper fraction will have the same denominator as the fraction part of the mixed number. Write this.

   (a) $3\frac{9}{10} = \frac{}{10}$

           ↑

   denominator for the improper fraction

2. To calculate the numerator of the improper fraction, first multiply the whole number of the mixed number by its denominator,

   (a) $3\frac{9}{10} = \frac{}{10}$

      ↑ ↑

   multiply these two numbers $3 \times 10 = 30$.

3. Then add the numerator of the mixed number to this product,
   (a) $9 + 30 = 39$.

     Add the product to this number.

     ↓

$$3\frac{9}{10} = \frac{30+9}{10}$$

4. This sum is the numerator of the improper fraction.

   (a) $3\frac{9}{10} = \frac{39}{10}$

How to change an improper fraction to a mixed number:

1. Divide the denominator into the numerator using long division.

   (b) To change $\frac{13}{9}$, divide 13 by 9.

$$\begin{array}{r} 1 \\ 9\overline{)13} \\ \underline{-9} \\ 4 \end{array}$$

2. Express the remainder in fraction form (i.e., place it over the divisor). Reduce this fraction to lowest terms.

   (b)

$$\begin{array}{r} 1\frac{4}{9} \leftarrow \text{mixed number} \\ 9\overline{)13} \\ \underline{-9} \\ 4 \leftarrow \text{remainder} \end{array}$$

PROBLEM 10

Add: $6\frac{7}{8} + 2\frac{1}{2}$

Answer

$9\frac{3}{8}$

A typical strategy for adding mixed numbers is to think of the problem in three parts:
(a) adding the whole numbers,
(b) adding the fractions, and
(c) changing any improper fractions to mixed numbers.

Most students find it easier to add and subtract mixed numbers when they are written vertically.

How to Get the Answer

1. Because the fractions of the mixed numbers have unlike denominators, use their least common denominators (LCD) to begin the renaming process (see p. 68).

$$6\frac{7}{8} = 6\frac{}{8}$$
$$+2\frac{1}{2} = 2\frac{}{8}$$
$$\overline{}$$

2. Complete the fraction by finding the equivalent fraction (see p. 65).

$$6\frac{7}{8} = 6\frac{7}{8}$$
$$+2\frac{1}{2} = 2\frac{4}{8}$$
$$\overline{}$$

3. Add the fractions. Add the whole numbers.

$$6\frac{7}{8} = 6\frac{7}{8}$$
$$+2\frac{1}{2} = 2\frac{4}{8}$$
$$\overline{}$$
$$8\frac{11}{8}$$

4. If the fraction is improper, change it to a mixed number. Add the whole number of this new mixed number to the whole number already present in the answer.

$$\frac{11}{8} = 1\frac{3}{8}$$

$$\begin{array}{r} 8 \\ +1\frac{3}{8} \\ \hline 9\frac{3}{8} \end{array}$$ ← this was the improper fraction part of the answer

---

PROBLEM 11

Subtract:

(a) $3\frac{1}{2} - 1\frac{2}{3}$ (b) $7 - 1\frac{3}{4}$

Answers

(a) $1\frac{5}{6}$ (b) $5\frac{1}{4}$

There are two popular strategies for subtracting mixed numbers. The first involves changing the mixed numbers into improper fractions before subtracting. The second involves "borrowing from" (i.e., renaming) the whole number to increase the fraction. Both strategies are presented here in the solution to this problem.

How to Get the Answers
Strategy 1

(a) Subtract: $3\frac{1}{2} - 1\frac{2}{3}$

1. Write the problem vertically. Change the mixed numbers to improper fractions.

$$3\frac{1}{2} = \frac{7}{2}$$
$$-1\frac{2}{3} = \frac{5}{3}$$
$$\overline{}$$

2. Rename the improper fractions so that the improper fractions have common denominators.

$$\frac{7}{2} = \frac{21}{6}$$
$$-\frac{5}{3} = \frac{10}{6}$$

3. Keep the denominator for the answer. Subtract the numerators. Change the improper fraction to a mixed number.

$$\frac{7}{2} = \frac{21}{6}$$
$$-\frac{5}{3} = \frac{10}{6}$$

$$\frac{11}{6} = 1\frac{5}{6}$$

Strategy 2

(b) Subtract: $7 - 1\frac{3}{4}$

1. "Borrow" 1 from the whole number in the top position.

Borrowing 1 decreases the whole number by 1
↓

$$7 = 6$$
$$-1\frac{3}{4} = -1\frac{3}{4}$$

2. Rename the "borrowed 1" as a fraction with the same denominator as the fraction in the mixed number.

$$1 = \frac{4}{4}$$

3. Place this fraction next to the decreased whole number.

$$7 = 6\frac{4}{4}$$
$$-1\frac{3}{4} = -1\frac{3}{4}$$

4. Subtract the fractions. Subtract the whole numbers. If
   necessary, reduce the fraction to lowest terms.

$$7 = 6\frac{4}{4}$$
$$-1\frac{3}{4} = -1\frac{3}{4}$$
$$\overline{} \quad \overline{}$$
$$5\frac{1}{4}$$

PROBLEM 12

Multiply: Divide:

(a) $3\frac{6}{7} \times 9\frac{1}{3}$ (b) $3\frac{3}{10} \div 1\frac{7}{15}$

Answers

(a) 36   (b) $2\frac{1}{4}$

Once mixed numbers have been rewritten as improper fractions,
they can be multiplied just as fractions were before.

How to Get the Answers

How to multiply mixed numbers:

1. Rewrite each mixed number as an improper fraction.

   (a) $3\frac{6}{7} \times 9\frac{1}{3} = \frac{27}{7} \times \frac{28}{3}$

2. Cancel out common factors. First, look diagonally from the
   first denominator to the second numerator, and ask
   yourself, What is the largest number that can 'go into' both
   these numbers?" Or, in other words, what is the greatest
   common factor (p. 43)?

$\frac{27}{7} \longleftarrow \times \longrightarrow \frac{28}{3}$ Q. What "goes into" both 7 and 28?
   A. 7

Second, cancel by dividing both these numbers by this factor.

$$\frac{\overset{}{\cancel{27}}}{\underset{1}{\cancel{7}}} \times \frac{\overset{4}{\cancel{28}}}{3}$$

Third, repeat the process by looking diagonally left, from the second denominator to the first numerator.

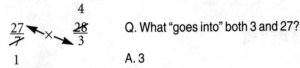

$$\frac{\overset{}{\cancel{27}}}{\underset{1}{\cancel{7}}} \times \frac{\overset{4}{\cancel{28}}}{3}$$

Q. What "goes into" both 3 and 27?

A. 3

Fourth, cancel by dividing both these numbers by their common factor.

$$\frac{\overset{9}{\cancel{27}}}{\underset{1}{\cancel{7}}} \times \frac{\overset{4}{\cancel{28}}}{\underset{1}{\cancel{3}}}$$

3. Multiply across the top. Multiply across the bottom. Simplify.

$$\frac{\overset{9}{\cancel{27}}}{\underset{1}{\cancel{7}}} \times \frac{\overset{4}{\cancel{28}}}{\underset{1}{\cancel{3}}} = \frac{36}{1} = 36$$

How to divide mixed numbers:

1. Rewrite each mixed number as an improper fraction.

(b) $3\frac{3}{10} \div 1\frac{7}{15} = \frac{33}{10} \div \frac{22}{15}$

2. Divide the improper fractions by "flipping" the second fraction and multiplying.

$\frac{33}{10} \div \frac{22}{15} = \frac{33}{10} \times \frac{15}{22}$

3. Cancel out common factors.

$$\overset{3}{\cancel{\underset{2}{35}}}\over{\cancel{\underset{}{10}}}} \times \overset{3}{\cancel{15}} \over {\cancel{\underset{2}{22}}}$$

4. Multiply across the top. Multiply across the bottom. Simplify.

$$\frac{\overset{3}{\cancel{35}}}{\underset{2}{\cancel{10}}} \times \frac{\overset{3}{\cancel{15}}}{\underset{2}{\cancel{22}}} = \frac{9}{4} = 2\frac{1}{4}$$

4 DECIMALS, PERCENTS, RATIOS, AND PROPORTIONS

Decimals, as numerical notations, are fairly new in comparison to many other mathematical notations. Decimal fractions, as they were called, were used in Persia, China, and India during the fifteenth century and did not become popular in Europe until late in the sixteenth century.

Decimals are a way to express fractions that have a denominator of ten or powers of ten. In the United States, we use a decimal point (as in 93.42). In France and Germany, a comma is used (as in 93,42) and in Britain, the decimal point is a raised dot (as in 93·42).

After struggling through fractions in the third and fourth grades, your child usually welcomes the study of decimals. They are easier to work with and follow many of the same procedures as whole numbers.

Your child's study of decimals usually begins with place value. The place-value chart is extended to the right and writing the word form of decimals is taught.

Next, your child learns about the relationships of decimals to decimals, of decimals to fractions, of fractions to ratios, of ratios to proportions, and of proportions to percents.

We will review all these relationships and show you how to calculate, using decimals, percents, ratios, and proportions.

Topics in This Chapter

Writing decimal numbers in word form
Finding equivalent decimals
Comparing decimals using the symbols > (greater than) and
    < (less than)
Rounding decimals
Adding, subtracting, multiplying, and dividing decimal numbers
Changing fractions to decimal numbers
Changing decimal numbers to fractions
Working with common and complex fractions
Writing ratios as fractions
Finding equivalent ratios
Solving proportions
Changing percents to fractions
Changing fractions to percents
Changing decimal numbers to percents
Writing percents as decimal numbers
Solving percent problems

SAMPLE PROBLEMS

1. Write the following in word form:
   (a) .0493   (b) 57.07
2. Choose the two decimals that are equivalent:
   0.26; 0.260; 0.026
3. Compare. Write < or >. 0.428 ____ 0.4028
4. Round 0.73825 to the nearest:
   (a) tenth
   (b) hundredth
   (c) whole number
5. Find the sum: 13.084 + 7.04 + 6.2 + 0.7125
6. Find the difference: 5 - 0.04971

7. Find the product: 93.712×423.8
8. Multiply mentally: $0.70193 \times 10,000$
9. Divide: $487.06 \div 343$
10. Divide: $39.44 \div 4.93$

11. Change $\frac{3}{8}$ to a decimal.

12. Change 0.24 to a common fraction.

13. Change $\frac{1}{6}$ to a decimal.

14. Divide mentally: $64.3 \div 1,000$

15. Change $0.66\frac{2}{3}$ to a common fraction.

16. Change these repeating decimals to common fractions:
    (a) $0.\overline{27}$ (b) $0.58\overline{3}$
17. Express each ratio as a fraction in lowest terms:
    (a) 7 days : 3 weeks   (b) 120 minutes to 4 hours
18. Complete: $3:2 = 21:\underline{}$
19. Give the unit price of each of the following:
    (a) 7 hours for $14.28
    (b) $1.79 for a 10 ounce package of cheese

20. Solve: $\frac{5}{30} = \frac{6}{n}$

21. Change to common fractions:

    (a) 15%   (b) $33\frac{1}{3}\%$

22. Change $\frac{1}{5}$ to a percent.

23. Change the following to percents:

    (a) .42   (b) $.16\frac{2}{3}$ (c) .135

24. Express these percents as decimals:
    (a) 9%   (b) 7.3%
25. What is 7.5% of 42?
26. 17% of a number is 31. What is the number?
27. What percent of 36 is 27?

Answers

1. (a) four hundred ninety-three ten thousandths
   (b) Fifty-seven and seven hundredths
2. 0.26 is equivalent to 0.260
3. 0.428 > 0.4028
4. (a) 0.7   (b) 0.74   (c) 1
5. 27.0365
6. 4.95029
7. 39,715.1456
8. 7,019.3
9. 1.42
10. 8
11. .375

12. $\frac{6}{25}$

13. $\frac{1}{6} = .166\frac{2}{3} = .166\ldots = .1\overline{6}$

14. .0643

15. $\frac{2}{3}$

16. (a) $.\overline{27} = \frac{3}{11}$ (b) $.58\overline{3} = \frac{7}{12}$

17. (a) $\frac{1}{3}$ (b) $\frac{1}{2}$

18. 3:2 = 21:14
19. (a) \$2.04/hour   (b) \$0.18/ounce

20. $\frac{5}{30} = \frac{6}{36}$

21. (a) $15\% = \frac{3}{20}$ (b) $33\frac{1}{3}\% = \frac{1}{3}$

22. $\frac{1}{5} = 20\%$

23. (a) 42%   (b) $16\frac{2}{3}\%$ (c) 13.5%

24. (a) .09   (b) .073

25. 7.5% of 42 = 3.15
26. 182.35
27. 75%

HOW-TO GUIDE

PROBLEM 1

Write in word form:
(a) .0493   (b) 57.07

Answer
(a) four hundred ninety-three ten thousandths
(b) Fifty-seven and seven hundredths

All the numbers in our system are called *decimal numbers.* Every decimal number has a *decimal point*—whether it "shows" or not. A decimal point separates the part of the number that is greater than 1 from the part that is less than 1. Therefore, 21 is the same as 21. or 21.0

When your child studied place value with whole numbers, the class created place-value charts in which each position in the chart is 10 times greater than the position to its right. (See page 19)

ten thousands	thousands	hundreds	tens	ones

Now the place value chart is extended to accommodate the decimal numbers that are less than one.

ten thousands	thousands	hundreds	tens	ones	.	tenths	hundredths	thousandths

The separating decimal point is to the right of the "ones" heading. The decimal point is followed to the right by a position that is 1/10 the value of one. This is the "tenths" position. The next position to the right is "hundredths," then "thousandths," and so on.

Writing the word form of a number is a way of testing if your child can read a number correctly.

How to Get the Answer

When the decimal number is less than 1:

Note: When a decimal number has all its digits to the right of the decimal point, it represents a number that is less than 1.

1. Place the decimal number in the place-value chart. Be certain to line up the decimal points. Make a note of the heading above the digit that is furthest to the right. This heading will be the final word in the word form.

ones	.	tenths	hundredths	thousandths	ten thousandths
	.	0	4	9	3

2. Cover up the decimal point and ask yourself:
   Q. How would I usually read this number?
   .0493 → 0493 → 493
   A. Four hundred ninety-three
3. Combine the answer in step 2 with the heading that is furthest to the right in step 1. You now have your answer.
   Four hundred ninety-three ten thousandths

When the decimal number is greater than 1:

1. Place the decimal number in the place-value chart. Be certain to line up the decimal points. Make a note of the heading

above the digit that is furthest to the right. This heading will be the final word in the word form.

tens	ones	.	tenths	hundredths
5	7	.	0	7

2. Cover up the decimal point and all the digits to the right and ask yourself:

Q. How would I usually read this number?

57.07 → 57.07 → 57

A. Fifty-seven

3. Cover up the decimal point and all the digits to the left and ask yourself:

Q. How would I usually read this number?

57.07 → 57.07 → 07 → 7

A. Seven

4. Write the responses in steps 2 and 3 in order and connect them with the word "and" (for the decimal point).

Fifty-seven and seven

5. Combine the answer in step 4 with the heading that is furthest to the right in step 1. You now have your answer.

Fifty-seven and seven hundredths

PROBLEM 2

Choose the two decimals that are equivalent:
0.26; 0.260; 0.026

Answer

0.26 is equivalent to 0.260

Decimal numbers that have the same value are called equivalent decimals. In a decimal number, any final zeros to the right of the decimal point can be deleted without changing the value of the number.

How to Get the Answer

1. Rewrite the decimals but leave off the final zero(s).

   0.26   0.260   0.026

   ↓   ↓   ↓

   0.26   0.26   0.026

2. By comparing the rewritten decimals, we can see that the first two have the same value.

PROBLEM 3

Compare. Write < or > . 0.428 _____ 0.4028

> Reminder: < means "is less than."
>
> > means "is greater than."

Answer

0.428 > 0.4028

This example asks us to compare decimal values. The strategy outlined below involves lining up the decimal points of the numbers and making a digit by digit comparison.

How to Get the Answer

1. Rewrite the decimals, one below the other. Be sure that the decimal points line up.

   0.428

   0.4028

2. Beginning with the first digit to the right of the decimal, compare digits until a difference is discovered.

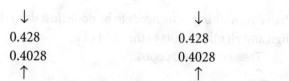

First comparison: no difference Second comparison: a difference

3. The decimal with the larger digit of the two being compared is the larger decimal.

0.428 > 0.4028

PROBLEM 4

Round 0.73825 to the nearest
(a) tenth
(b) hundredth
(c) whole number

Answers

(a) 0.7   (b) 0.74   (c) 1

All digits to the right of the rounded place are dropped when the number being rounded is not a whole number. The answer should reflect the place that was requested. For example, 5.437 rounded to the nearest tenth is 5.4 **not** 5.40.

Even though these two decimals are equivalent, only the first decimal is the correct answer, since the directions asked for the nearest tenth.

How to Get the Answer

1. Find the digit of the place being rounded to. (Use the place value chart if necessary.)
   (a) For 0.73825, this digit is 7.
2. If the next digit (the "test" digit) directly to the right is less

than five, nothing more needs to be done. Just drop the test
digit and all other digits to the right of it.

These will all be dropped.

(a) 0.73825 = 0.7 (rounded to the nearest tenth)
   ↑
Test digit is less than 5

3. To round to the nearest hundredth, find the hundredths place
   and the test digit will be directly to the right.

   hundredths place
   ↓
(b) 0.73825
      ↑
      test digit

Since the test digit is greater than five, you must increase the
hundredths place by one unit. Next, drop the test digit and
all other digits to the right of it.

(b) 0.73825 = 0.73 + one unit = 0.74 (rounded to the
                                    nearest hundredth)

4. When the directions say to "round to the nearest whole
   number," the place being rounded to is the ones place.

   ones place
   ↓
(c) 0.73825
       ↑
       test digit

Since the test digit is greater than five, the whole number must
be increased by one unit. Then drop the test digit and all
other digits to the right of it.

0.73825 = 0 + one unit = 1 (rounded to the nearest hundredth)

PROBLEM 5

Find the sum: 13.084 + 7.04 + 6.2 + 0.7125

Reminders
    –The *sum* is the answer in an addition problem.
    –*Addends* are the numbers being added together.

Answer
27.0365

How to Get the Answer
1. Write the problem vertically. Be very careful to line up the decimal points and to keep the digits in columns.

   13.084
     7.04
     6.2
  + 0.7125
  ————

2. The last decimal has the most digits to the right of the decimal point (four places). Add zeros to the other addends until they have four places behind the decimal point. (This will help your child avoid mistakes.) Bring down the decimal point in preparation for writing the answer.

   13.0840
     7.0400
     6.2000
  + 0.7125
  ————

      .
      ↑

The decimal point has been brought down.

3. Add the columns in the usual manner.

```
  13.0840
   7.0400
   6.2000
 + 0.7125
 _____
  27.0365
```

PROBLEM 6

Find the difference: 5 - 0.04971

> Reminder
> –The *difference* is the answer in a subtraction problem.

Answer
4.95029

How to Get the Answer

1. Write the problem vertically. Be very careful to line up the decimal points and to keep the digits in columns. (Note: When a decimal point is not showing, it is understood to follow the last digit to the right.

```
   5.
 - .04971
 _____
```

2. Make both decimals the same "length" by adding zeros. Bring down the decimal point in preparation for the answer.

```
   5.00000
 - 0.04971
 _____
   .
   ↑
```

The decimal point has been brought down.

3. Subtract column by column beginning from the right in the
   usual manner.

   5.00000
   - 0.04971
   ―――――
   4.95029

―――――――――――――――

PROBLEM 7

Find the product: 93.712×423.8

Reminder
–The *product* is the answer in a multiplication problem.

Answer
39,715.1456

Your child might question why a product is started directly below
the digit that is being used as a multiplier. For example,

      232
    × 97
    ―――
    1624
    2088   ← The 8 is shifted to be below the multiplier 9.
    ―――
    22504

One way to explain this shift to your child is to explain it in the
context of place value. In this example, multiplying by 9 is really
multiplying 232 by 90, which is 20880. Shifting the digits is a
shortcut notation.

How to Get the Answer
1. Write the problem vertically. Place the longer decimal above

and line up the digits that are furthest to the right in each number (**not decimal points**).

The two numbers are lined up by these digits.
↓

```
  93.712
× 423.8
————————
```

2. Multiply as if there were no decimal points. Each digit in the bottom number will be used as a multiplier. Add the resulting products.

```
  93.712
× 423.8
————————
  749696   ←   Zeros may be
  281136   ←   put in the spaces
  187424   ←   here to help
  374848   ←   avoid mistakes
————————
397151456
```

3. To determine the decimal placement in the final answer, ask this question:

Q. What is the total number of digits to the right of the decimal point for both factors?

A. The top factor has   3
    The bottom factor has   1
                    —
    The total is   4

The number of digits to place to the right of the decimal point in the final answer is 4.

4. Place the decimal point between the digits 5 and 1 so that there are four digits to the right of the decimal point in the answer.

39,715.1456

PROBLEM 8

Multiply mentally: $0.70193 \times 10,000$

Answer
7019.3

A *power of 10* is the result of repeated multiplication by 10. For example:

$$10 \times 10 = 100$$
$$10 \times 10 \times 10 = 1,000$$
$$10 \times 10 \times 10 \times 10 = 10,000$$

As was shown, 100 1,000 10,000 are all powers of ten.

Each time the decimal point is moved to the right in a number, it has the same effect as multiplying that number by 10. Multiplying by a power of 10, therefore, is easily accomplished by relocating the decimal point.

How to Get the Answer
1. Count the number of zeros in 10,000. There are four zeros in 10,000.
2. Move the decimal point to the right four times (the number of zeros.)

.7 0 1 9 3   or 7,019.3

The decimal point is moved 4 places to the right.

PROBLEM 9

Divide: 487.06 ÷ 343

Answer
1.42

Long division is a procedure for dividing without using a calculator. Some students hate long division because there are so many opportunities for error. The procedure involves not just the operation of division, but the operations of multiplication and subtraction as well.

Most errors can be avoided by keeping the numbers aligned in the appropriate columns. Using graph paper can help tremendously.

How to Get the Answer

1. Rewrite the example in the long division format. Place the decimal point directly above the decimal point in the dividend to prepare for the quotient.

Decimal point for quotient

↓

    .   ← Quotient goes here

Divisor → 343)‾4‾8‾7‾.‾0‾6‾   ← Dividend

2. Remember the steps in long division are *divide, multiply, subtract* and *bring down.*

3. *Divide:*

   Q. How many times does 343 "go into" 487?

   Note: By asking how many times 343 "goes into" 487, we are trying to determine how many groups of 343 there are in the number 487.

A. One time.

Place the "1" directly above the "7."

```
            ↓
            1.      ← Quotient goes here
    343 )487.06     ← Dividend
```

4. *Multiply:*

Multiply the divisor (343) by the partial quotient (1) and place this answer (343) underneath the 487.

```
divisor        partial quotient
   ↓                ↓
  343    ×    1    = 343    ← Place this underneath 487
                   Partial quotient
                        ↓

                 1.
       343 )487.06
           ↑  343
        divisor
```

5. *Subtract:*

Subtract the 343 from 487.

```
                 1.
       343 )487.06
Subtract →  - 343
           ─────
            144    ← (487-343 = 144)
```

6. *Bring down:*

Bring down the next digit (0) from the original dividend and place this beside the 144 to obtain the new dividend.

```
                 1.
       343 )487.06
          - 343 ↓
          ─────
           144 0
```

7. *Divide:*

Q. How many times does 343 "go into" 1,440?

A. Four times.

Note: To get an idea of how many times 343 will go into 1440, ask how many times 3 (the first digit of 343) will go into 14 (the first two digits of 1,440).

Place the "4" directly above the "0"
↓

$$343 \overline{)\begin{array}{r} 1.4 \\ 487.06 \end{array}}$$
$$- 343$$
$$\overline{144\ 0}$$

8. *Multiply:*

Multiply the divisor (343) by the partial quotient (4) and place the answer (1372) underneath the 1440.

divisor   partial quotient
↓   ↓

343   ×   4   = 1372   ← Place this underneath 1440.

partial quotient
↓

$$343 \overline{)\begin{array}{r} 1.4 \\ 487.06 \end{array}}$$
↑   - 343
divisor ‾‾‾‾‾
144 0
137 2

9. *Subtract:*

Subtract 1372 from 1440.

$$343 \overline{)\begin{array}{r} 1.4 \\ 487.06 \end{array}}$$
- 343
‾‾‾‾‾
144 0

Subtract → - 137 2
‾‾‾‾‾
6 8   ← (1440 - 1372 = 68)

10. *Bring down:*

Bring down the next digit (6) from the original dividend and place this digit beside the 68 to obtain the new dividend.

$$
\begin{array}{r}
1.4 \\
343 \overline{\smash{\big)}\ 487.06} \\
-343 \\
\hline
144\ 0 \\
-137\ 2 \\
\hline
6\ 86
\end{array}
$$

11. *Divide:*

    Q. How many times does 343 "go into" 686?

    A. Two times.

    Place the "2" directly above the "6."
    ↓

$$
\begin{array}{r}
1.42 \\
343 \overline{\smash{\big)}\ 487.06} \\
\underset{\text{divisor}}{\uparrow}\ -343 \\
\hline
144\ 0 \\
-137\ 2 \\
\hline
6\ 86
\end{array}
$$

12. *Multiply:*

    Multiply the divisor (343) by the partial quotient (2) and place the answer (686) underneath the 686.

    divisor   partial quotient
    ↓   ↓

    343 × 2 = 686   ← Place this underneath 686.

$$
\begin{array}{r}
1.42 \\
343 \overline{\smash{\big)}\ 487.06} \\
\underset{\text{divisor}}{\uparrow}\ -343 \\
\hline
144\ 0 \\
-137\ 2 \\
\hline
6\ 86 \\
6\ 86
\end{array}
$$

13. *Subtract:*

    Subtract 686 from 686.

$$
\begin{array}{r}
1.42 \\
343 \overline{)487.06} \\
-343 \\
\hline
144\ 0 \\
-137\ 2 \\
\hline
6\ 86 \\
\text{Subtract} \rightarrow \quad -6\ 86 \\
\hline
0 \quad \leftarrow (686 - 686 = 0)
\end{array}
$$

The problem ends at this point because there are no more digits to bring down. The answer is 1.42.

PROBLEM 10

Divide: 39.44 ÷ 4.93

Answer

8

The process of dividing a decimal by a decimal involves multiplying both the divisor and the dividend by a power of 10. This makes the number easier to handle and does not change the value of the answer. To multiply by a power of 10 move the decimal point of the divisor until it is a whole number. Then move the decimal point of the dividend the same number of places.

Once the divisor and the dividends are whole numbers (as a result of this process), we use the same procedure that was used in problem 9. We place a decimal point directly above the decimal point in the adjusted dividend. We then follow the procedure for long division.

How to Get the Answer

1. Rewrite the example in the long division format.

$$4.93 \overline{)39.44}$$

2. Move the divisor's decimal point to the end of the number. Count the number of "jumps" that it took.

$$4\,93. \overline{)39.44}$$

2 jumps

3. Move the decimal point of the dividend the same number of "jumps" in the same direction. Place a decimal point directly above this new location, to be part of the quotient.

$$493. \overline{)39\,44.}$$

2 jumps

4. Follow the procedure for long division: divide, multiply, and subtract.

$$
\begin{array}{r}
8. \\
493. \overline{)3944.} \\
-3944 \\
\hline
0
\end{array}
$$

PROBLEM 11

Change $\frac{3}{8}$ to a decimal.

Answer

.375

A fraction is another way to write division. So, $\frac{3}{8}$ can be thought of as 3 divided by 8. Some kids remember this by the word "bit," which stands for "bottom into top." To carry out the long division, first express 3 with its decimal point and add zeros to the right of the decimal point. Then follow the steps in long division: divide, multiply, subtract, and bring down.

How to Get the Answer

1. Express the fraction in terms of division. Rewrite it in long division format.

$$\frac{3}{8} = 3 \div 8 = 8\,\overline{)3}$$

2. Place the decimal point in the dividend and add zeros.

$$8\,\overline{)3.000}$$

3. Place a decimal point in the quotient directly above the decimal point in the dividend. Follow the steps for long division. Add more zeros if necessary.

$$
\begin{array}{r}
.375 \\
8\,\overline{)3.000} \\
-2\,4\downarrow \\
\hline
60\downarrow \\
-56 \\
\hline
40 \\
-40 \\
\hline
0
\end{array}
$$

PROBLEM 12

Change 0.24 to a common fraction.

Answer

$$\frac{6}{25}$$

Once a child can say a decimal correctly they have little or no trouble changing a decimal into a fraction. A decimal and its equivalent fraction form are read in the same way:

$0.7 = \frac{7}{10}$ These are both read, "seven tenths."

How to Get the Answer

1. Ask yourself the following question:

   Q. How would I read the decimal?

   A. .24 is read "twenty-four hundredths."

2. Express what you read as a fraction.

   $\frac{24}{100}$

3. Use prime factors (p. 47) to reduce the fraction to the lowest terms.

$$\frac{24}{100} = \frac{2 \cdot 2 \cdot 2 \cdot 3}{2 \cdot 2 \cdot 5 \cdot 5} = \frac{\cancel{2} \cdot \cancel{2} \cdot 2 \cdot 3}{\cancel{2} \cdot \cancel{2} \cdot 5 \cdot 5} = \frac{6}{25}$$

PROBLEM 13

Change $\frac{1}{6}$ to a decimal.

Answer

$$\frac{1}{6} = .166\frac{2}{3} = .166\ldots = .1\overline{6}$$

When a fraction is changed to a decimal and the quotient comes out exactly, the resulting decimal is known as a *terminating decimal*. For example, $\frac{3}{4}$ changed to a decimal results in a terminating decimal, because the division process leaves no remainder.

$$\frac{3}{4} = 3 \div 4 = 4\overline{\smash{)}3.00} \quad .75$$

$$
\begin{array}{r}
.75 \\
4\overline{\smash{)}3.00} \\
-2\,8 \\
\hline
20 \\
-20 \\
\hline
0
\end{array}
$$

When a fraction is changed to a decimal and, regardless of how many zeros are added, the quotient does *not* come out exactly, the result is a *nonterminating decimal*. For example,

$$
\frac{22}{7} = 22 \div 7 = 7\overline{\smash{)}22.0000000}
$$

$$
\begin{array}{r}
3.1428571 \\
7\overline{\smash{)}22.0000000} \\
-21 \\
\hline
1\,0 \\
-\ 7 \\
\hline
30 \\
-28 \\
\hline
20 \\
-14 \\
\hline
60 \\
-56 \\
\hline
40 \\
-35 \\
\hline
50 \\
-49 \\
\hline
10 \\
-\ 7 \\
\hline
3 \quad \leftarrow \text{A remainder keeps} \\
\text{occurring.}
\end{array}
$$

Sometimes a nonterminating decimal has digits or groups of digits that keep repeating. These are called *repeating decimals.* For example, $\frac{1}{22}$ changed to a decimal results in a repeating decimal.

$$
\begin{array}{r}
.0454545 \quad = .0\overline{45} \\
22\,\overline{\big)\,1.0000000} \\
-88 \\
\hline
120 \\
-110 \\
\hline
100 \\
-88 \\
\hline
-120 \\
-110 \\
\hline
100 \\
-88 \\
\hline
120 \\
-110 \\
\hline
10 \quad \leftarrow \text{A remainder keeps occurring.}
\end{array}
$$

Note: In a repeating decimal, the group of repeating digits is called the *repetend.*

How to Get the Answer

1. Begin changing the fraction to a decimal by dividing the denominator into the numerator.

$$
\frac{1}{6} = 1 \div 6 = 6\,\overline{\big)\,1.000}
$$

$$
\begin{array}{r}
.166 \\
-6 \\
\hline
40 \\
-36 \\
\hline
40 \\
-36 \\
\hline
4 \quad \leftarrow \text{The same remainder keeps occurring.}
\end{array}
$$

2. There are several ways we can express this decimal:
   (a) The remainder (4) can be placed over the divisor (6) as a fraction. In this form, the decimal is known as a *complex decimal*.

   $$\frac{1}{6} = .166\frac{4}{6} = .166\frac{2}{3}$$

   (b) Three dots can be placed behind the quotient indicating a *repeating decimal*.

   $$\frac{1}{6} = .166\ldots$$

   (c) A bar can be placed over the digit(s) that repeats.

   $$\frac{1}{6} = .1\overline{6}$$

PROBLEM 14

Divide mentally: $64.3 \div 1,000$

Answer
.0643

Each move of the decimal point to the left in a number has the effect of dividing the number by a power of 10 (see problem 8). Dividing by 1,000 means moving the decimal point three places to the left. Because there are only two places to move in the number as it is presently written, you must place a zero to the left of the six to indicate place value.

How to Get the Answer
1. Because there are three zeros in 1,000, you will need to move the decimal point three places to the left. Since there are only two places available, create another place by writing a zero just before the digit 6. This will not change the value of the decimal.

Write a zero in the hundreds place.

$\downarrow$

64.3 = 064.3

$\uparrow\uparrow$

Places available in the original format.

2. Place the decimal point before the zero (a move of three places) to indicate that division by 1,000 has occurred.

$\underset{\smile\smile\smile}{0\,6\,4}\,.\,3 = .0643$

PROBLEM 15

Change $0.66\frac{2}{3}$ to a common fraction.

Answer

$\frac{2}{3}$

A *common fraction* is one in which the numerator and the denominator are whole numbers.

$\frac{13}{8}$ and $\frac{7}{23}$ are examples of common fractions.

A *complex fraction* has mixed numbers or another fraction in its numerator or denominator.

$\frac{1\frac{1}{2}}{14}$ and $\frac{\frac{3}{2}}{11}$ are examples of complex fractions.

To change the complex decimal $0.66\frac{2}{3}$ to a common fraction, follow this sequence:

1. Change the complex decimal to a complex fraction.
2. Rewrite the complex fraction as a division problem.
3. Divide to get a common fraction.

How to Get the Answer

1. Ask yourself the following question:

   Q. How would I read the decimal, $0.66\frac{2}{3}$?

   A. Sixty-six and two-thirds hundredths.

2. As a fraction, this is $\dfrac{66\frac{2}{3}}{100}$.

3. Recalling that a fraction can mean division, we can think of the complex fraction in terms of division. In this way,

   $\dfrac{66\frac{2}{3}}{100}$ means $66\frac{2}{3}$ divided by 100,

   which can be written as $66\frac{2}{3} \div 100$.

4. We then change the mixed number $66\frac{2}{3}$ into an improper fraction by multiplying 66 by 3 and adding 2:

   $66\frac{2}{3}$ becomes $\dfrac{200}{3}$.

   We also change 100 into a fraction by placing it over 1. The division format then changes:

   $66\frac{2}{3} \div 100$ becomes $\dfrac{200}{3} \div \dfrac{100}{1}$.

5. Following the procedure for dividing fractions (p. 74), we replace the divisor, $\dfrac{100}{1}$, by its reciprocal, $\dfrac{1}{100}$, and we multiply:

   $$\frac{200}{3} \div \frac{100}{1} \text{ becomes } \frac{200}{3} \times \frac{1}{100} = \frac{\overset{2}{\cancel{200}}}{3} \times \frac{1}{\underset{1}{\cancel{100}}} = \frac{2}{3}$$

PROBLEM 16

Change these repeating decimals to common fractions:
(a) $0.\overline{27}$ (b) $0.58\overline{3}$

Answer

(a) $.\overline{27} = \frac{3}{11}$ (b) $.58\overline{3} = \frac{7}{12}$

These examples reflect the two types of repeating decimals. In (a), the repeating digits (the *repeten*d) follow the decimal point directly. In (b), there are other digits between the decimal point and the repetend. The method for changing them to fractions are similar, except that in (b) there is an additional step.

How to Get the Answer

Solving (a):

1. Let any variable represent the repeating decimal that needs to be changed. In this example we are using x. This is your primary equation.

   $x = 0.\overline{27}$

2. Because the number of digits in the repetend is two, multiply both sides of the primary equation by the second power of 10. The second power of 10 is 100 (Think: 1 followed by 2 zeros).

   $x = 0.\overline{27}$ ← primary equation
   $100x = 27.\overline{27}$ ← both sides of the primary equation
                       multiplied by 100

   Note: We are preparing to eliminate the repetend.

3. Subtract the primary equation from this newer one.

   $100x = 27.\overline{27}$
   $-x = 0.\overline{27}$
   _____
   $99x = 27.00 = 27$

We now have an equation equivalent to the decimal that does not have the repetend.

4. The number on the right, in $99x = 27$, placed over the number that is before the x on the left, will give us the fraction we need.

$$x = \frac{27}{99}$$

5. Reduce this fraction to its lowest terms.

$$\frac{27}{99} = \frac{\cancel{3} \cdot \cancel{3} \cdot 3}{\cancel{3} \cdot \cancel{3} \cdot 11} = \frac{3}{11}$$

Solving (b):

1. Let any variable represent the repeating decimal that needs to be changed. In this example, we are using an n.

$n = .58\overline{3}$

2. Multiply both sides of the equation by the power of 10 that will "move" the decimal point to a place that is just before the repetend. This is your primary equation.

$100n = 58.\overline{3}$

3. Since the number of digits in the repetend is one, multiply both sides of the primary equation by 10, which is 1 followed by *one* zero.

$1000n = 583.\overline{3}$

4. Subtract the primary equation from this new equation.

$$1000n = 583.\overline{3}$$
$$- \ 100n = \ \ 58.\overline{3}$$
$$\overline{}$$
$$900n = 525.0 \ \ (525.0 = 525)$$

5. The number on the right placed over the number that is before the n on the left will give the fraction we need.

$$n = \frac{525}{900}$$

6. Reduce this fraction to its lowest terms.

$$\frac{525}{900} = \frac{\cancel{5} \cdot \cancel{5} \cdot \cancel{3} \cdot 7}{2 \cdot 2 \cdot \cancel{5} \cdot 3 \cdot \cancel{5} \cdot \cancel{3}} = \frac{7}{12}$$

PROBLEM 17

Express each ratio as a fraction in lowest terms:
(a) 7 days : 3 weeks   (b) 120 minutes to 4 hours

Answer

(a) $\frac{1}{3}$ (b) $\frac{1}{2}$

A *ratio* is a way to compare two quantities. We can express a ratio in any of three ways : (a) by using the word "to", (b) by using a colon, and (c) by using a fraction. The object that is stated first in the verbal description always becomes the first component in the symbolic representation. For example, in a class of 13 girls and 11 boys, the three ratio expressions for the number of *girls* to *boys* are:

(a) 13 to 11   (b) 13:11   (c) $\frac{13}{11}$

These are all read the same way, "thirteen to eleven." The three ratio expressions for *boys* to *girls* are:

(a) 11 to 13   (b) 11:13   (c) $\frac{11}{13}$

When asked to express a ratio as a fraction in lowest terms, we must first change the quantities so that they are expressed in the same unit of measure. For example, to compare 3 inches to 1 foot, first change the foot to 12 inches.

How to Get the Answer

1. Express the two quantities by using the same units of measure.
     (a) 7 days:3 weeks   becomes   1 week:3 weeks
     (b) 120 minutes to 4 hours   becomes   2 hours to 4 hours
2. Write a fraction. The first stated quantity becomes the numerator. The second becomes the denominator.
     (a) $\frac{1 \text{ week}}{3 \text{ weeks}} = \frac{1}{3}$ This fraction is in its lowest terms.

(b) $\dfrac{2\text{ hours}}{4\text{ hours}} = \dfrac{2}{4}$ This fraction is not in its lowest terms, so it must be reduced.

3. If needed, reduce the fraction to lowest terms.

(b) $\dfrac{2}{4} = \dfrac{2}{2 \cdot 2} = \dfrac{1}{2}$

PROBLEM 18

Complete: 3:2 = 21:___

Answer
3:2 = 21:14

> *Equivalent ratios* are ratios that have the same value. Your children find equivalent ratios by expressing the ratios as fractions and following the same procedure that they learned in the previous chapter on equivalent fractions.

How to Get the Answer
1. Write the ratios in their fraction form.

$$\frac{3}{2} = \frac{21}{?}$$

2. Remember that equivalent fractions are made by multiplying or dividing the numerator and the denominator of the original fraction by the same number. When a part is missing in a pair of equivalent fractions, examine the parts that are not missing in order to determine whether multiplication or division is to be used to find the missing parts.

$\dfrac{3}{2} = \dfrac{21}{?}$ To get 3 to 21, I must multiply by 7.

3. Multiply 2 by 7 to find the missing number. That number is 14.

PROBLEM 19

Give the unit price of each of the following:
(a) 7 hours for $14.28
(b) $1.79 for a 10 ounce package of cheese

Answer

(a) $2.04/hour
(b) $0.18/ounce

> A *rate* is a ratio that compares two quantities that are expressed in different units of measure.
> rate → $4.80 per 4 gallons
> The rate for one item or unit is called the *unit price.*
> unit price → $1.20 per gallon

How to Get the Answer

1. Write a fraction using the money as the numerator and the other given quantity as the denominator.

(a) $\dfrac{14.28}{7 \text{ hours}}$

(b) $\dfrac{1.79}{10 \text{ ounces}}$

2. Follow the procedure for changing a fraction to a decimal.

(a)
$$
\begin{array}{r}
2.04 \\
7\,\overline{)14.28} \\
-14 \\
\hline
28 \\
-28 \\
\end{array}
$$

$$\begin{array}{r} .179 = .18 \\ 10\overline{)1.790} \\ \end{array}$$

(b)

$$
\begin{array}{r}
.179 = .18 \\
10\,\overline{)1.790} \\
-1\,0 \quad\;\; \\
\hline
79 \quad \\
-70 \quad \\
\hline
90 \\
-90 \\
\hline
\end{array}
$$

3. Express the answer per unit, using the measurement named in the denominator.
   (a) $2.04 per hour
   (b) $.18 per ounce

PROBLEM 20

Solve: $\dfrac{5}{30} = \dfrac{6}{n}$

Answer

$$\frac{5}{30} = \frac{6}{36}$$

A *proportion* is an equation made up of two ratios. All the following are examples of proportions:

$$\frac{9}{15} = \frac{15}{25} \qquad 1:2 = 8:16 \qquad 3 \text{ to } 8 = 24 \text{ to } 64$$

The parts of a proportion are the *means* and the *extremes*. These parts can be distinguished more easily when the proportion is not written in the fraction form. Most children remember the phrases "middle for means" and "end for extremes." The means and the extremes are shown below.

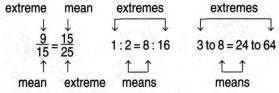

Your child has learned that multiplying the means of a proportion together will give the same answer as multiplying the extremes together. This product is called the *cross product*.

For example, in 3 to 8 = 24 to 64, the cross product is 192, because 8×24 (means) = 192, and 3×64 (extremes) = 192.

The cross product is used to find the missing part of a proportion.

How to Get the Answer

1. In a proportion, the product of the means is equal to the product of the extremes. Using this fact, we can write an equation that is equivalent to the proportion and that will help us to find the missing part.

$$\frac{5}{30} = \frac{6}{n}$$

$5 \times n = 30 \times 6 \leftarrow$ This equation was made by multiplying the extremes and then multiplying the means.

$5 \times n = 180$

2. Find the missing number by dividing 180 by 5.

$$
\begin{array}{r}
36 \\
5 \overline{\smash{\big)}\,180} \\
-15 \\
\hline
30 \\
-30 \\
\hline
0
\end{array}
$$

$n = 36$

PROBLEM 21

Change the following to common fractions:

(a) 15%   (b) $33\frac{1}{3}\%$

Answer

(a) $15\% = \frac{3}{20}$ (b) $33\frac{1}{3}\% = \frac{1}{3}$

A *percent* is the numerator of a fraction whose denominator is 100. "Per cent" means literally "for each one hundred." The symbol for percent is %. For example, $\frac{71}{100}$ is the same as 71%.

How to Get the Answer

1. Drop the percent sign and place the number over 100.

(a) 15% becomes $\frac{15}{100}$

(b) $33\frac{1}{3}\%$ becomes $\frac{33\frac{1}{3}}{100}$

2. Reduce all common fractions to their lowest terms.

(a) $\frac{15}{100} = \frac{3 \cdot 5}{2 \cdot 2 \cdot 5 \cdot 5} = \frac{3}{20}$

3. Express all complex fractions as common fractions.

$$\frac{33\frac{1}{3}}{100} = 33\frac{1}{3} \div 100 = \frac{100}{3} \times \frac{1}{100} = \frac{\cancel{100}^{1}}{3} \times \frac{1}{\cancel{100}_{1}} = \frac{1}{3}$$

PROBLEM 22

Change $\frac{1}{5}$ to a percent.

Answer

$\frac{1}{5} = 20\%$

One way to change a fraction to a percent is to use a proportion to help rewrite the fraction with a denominator of 100. The numerator, then, is the percent.

How to Get the Answer

1. Set up a proportion to find a fraction that is equivalent to the given fraction and has a denominator of 100.

$$\frac{1}{5} = \frac{x}{100}$$

2. Use cross products to find the missing denominator.

$5 \cdot x = 100$

$x = 20$

Thus, $\frac{1}{5} = \frac{20}{100} = 20\%$

PROBLEM 23

Change the following to percents:

(a) .42   (b) .$16\frac{2}{3}$ (c) .135

Answer

(a) 42%   (b) $16\frac{2}{3}\%$ (c) 13.5%

A decimal can be changed to a percent by being changed to an equivalent fraction with a denominator of 100 and then being changed from a fraction to a percent (see problem 22).

How to Get the Answer

1. Read each decimal aloud to identify the place value.
2. Express each decimal as a fraction.

(a) $.42 = \dfrac{42}{100}$

(b) $.16\frac{2}{3} = \dfrac{16\frac{2}{3}}{100}$

(c) $.135 = \dfrac{135}{1000}$

3. Since both (a) and (b) already have denominators of 100, the percent will be the numerator.

(a) $\dfrac{42}{100} = 42\%$

(b) $\dfrac{16\frac{2}{3}}{100} = 16\frac{2}{3}\%$

4. A proportion can be used in (c).

(c) $\dfrac{135}{1000} = \dfrac{x}{100}$

$1000 \cdot x = 13{,}500$

$x = 13.5$ (This was found by dividing 13,500 by 1000.)

Thus, $\dfrac{x}{100} = \dfrac{13.5}{100} = 13.5\%$

PROBLEM 24

Express these percents as decimals:

(a) 9%   (b) 7.3%

Answer

(a) .09   (b) .073

A percent can be written as a fraction by deleting the percent sign and placing the number over 100.

A fraction can be thought of in terms of division. Therefore, $\frac{29}{100}$ is the same as 29 ÷ 100, which is the same as moving the decimal point two places to the left.

How to Get the Answer

1. If the decimal point is not already showing, put in the decimal point.

   9 % becomes 9. %

2. Delete the percent sign and move the decimal point two places to the *left* so the 9 is in the hundredths place. (Add zeros if necessary.)

   (a) 9.% = .09 = .09

   (b) 7.3% = .073 = .073

PROBLEM 25

What is 7.5% of 42?

Answer
7.5% of 42 = 3.15

Solving percent problems becomes less confusing when your child learns to translate certain words into mathematical symbols. After the words have been changed in this way, your child will be able to see how to find the answer more clearly.

Two very common English words, "is" and "of," are often translated into mathematical symbols. "Is" can be replaced by =, and "of," which implies multiplication, can be replaced by one of the multiplication symbols, either × or •.

A *variable* is a letter or symbol that represents an unknown quantity. In questions that begin with "What is . . . ," the word "what" can be replaced by a variable.

How to Get the Answer

1. Translate the words of the problem into mathematical symbols.

   What is   7.5%   of   42?
   ↓   ↓   ↓
   n =   7.5%   ×   42

2. Change 7.5% into either a fraction or a decimal (see problem 24).

   $n = .075 \times 42$

3 Multiply $.075 \times 42$, and you will get 3.15 as your answer.

PROBLEM 26

17% of a number is 31. What is the number?

Answer

182.35

In problems like this, the words "a number" can be replaced by a variable. One strategy for solving this problem is first to solve a simpler problem, then apply the same procedure to the problem at hand.

How to Get the Answer

1. Translate the words of the problem into mathematical symbols.

$$
\begin{array}{cccc}
17\% & \text{of} & \text{a number} & \text{is} \quad 31 \\
\downarrow & & \downarrow & \downarrow \\
17\% & x & n & = \quad 31
\end{array}
$$

2. Change 17% to a fraction or a decimal (see problem 24).

   $.17 \times n = 31$

3. Think of a simpler problem to help find the value of n. For example,

   $7 \times n = 21$

   is an equation that is in the same form as the equation in step 2. If we didn't know that $n = 3$, we could find it by dividing 21 by 7.

   To find the value of n in the equation in step 2 ($.17 \times n = 31$), we should use the same procedure. Therefore, we should divide 31 by .17

$$
\begin{array}{r}
1\,82.352 = 182.35 \\
.17.\overline{)31.00.000} \\
-17 \\
\hline
14\,0 \\
-13\,6 \\
\hline
40 \\
-34 \\
\hline
6\,0 \\
-5\,1 \\
\hline
90 \\
-85 \\
\hline
50 \\
-34 \\
\hline
16
\end{array}
$$

PROBLEM 27

What percent of 36 is 27?

Answer
75%

> Children are taught to translate the word "what" to n (or any other variable). In this problem, they translate the words "what percent" to $n\%$. This may seem like a very long and roundabout way to solve this problem—and it is. But current thinking in math is to try to get children to think in terms of equations whenever possible. This helps develop logic and problem-solving skills, and, of course, it helps when they encounter algebra in the later grades.

How to Get the Answer

1. Translate the words of the problem into mathematical symbols.

   What percent of 36 is 27 ?

   $$n\% \times 36 = 27$$

2. Change the $n\%$ into a fraction.

   $$\frac{n}{100} \times 36 = 27$$

3. Since the variable is part of a fraction, represent the other parts of the problem as fractions for a uniform format.

   $$\frac{n}{100} \times \frac{36}{1} = \frac{27}{1}$$

4. Reduce the fractions so they are easier to handle. Now multiply the fractions on the left side of the equation.

   $$\frac{n}{\cancel{100}_{25}} \times \frac{\cancel{36}^{9}}{1} = \frac{27}{1}$$

$$\frac{9n}{25} = \frac{27}{1}$$

5. Use cross products (see p. 121) to eliminate the fraction.

$9n \times 1 = 25 \times 27$

$9n = 675$

6. Divide 675 by 9 to find the value of n. The answer is 75%.

5 GEOMETRY AND MEASUREMENT

Problem

> Margaret wants to make a two-flavor ice cream cone. How many different flavor combinations can she make if she has four flavors to choose from?

Could you use geometry to solve this problem? Chances are that your child could. He or she might draw four points and count the number of line segments it would take to connect every pair of points.

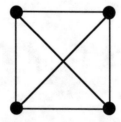

In this way, he or she would find that Margaret could make six different flavor combinations.

Once geometry meant memorizing vocabulary and facts. Today students are taught to "see" geometry as it relates to the world around them. From this, they move to defining, relating, and connecting these observations and using what they learn to solve problems.

Topics in This Chapter

Part I: Point, Lines, and Planes
Identifying collinear points, planes, lines, line segments, rays, and
  endpoints
Finding acute angles, right angles, and obtuse angles
Measuring angles with a protractor
Identifying triangles by types of angles (acute, right, obtuse,
  equilateral, isosceles, and scalene) and congruent sides
Identifying intersecting, parallel, and perpendicular lines
Identifying closed and open figures (simple and complex)
Identifying polygons: regular polygon, rectangle, parallelogram,
  quadrilateral, rhombus, pentagon, hexagon, and octagon
Finding the unknown measurement of an angle when all other
  angles are known
Finding supplementary and complementary angles
Identifying vertical angles, corresponding angles, adjacent angles,
  and alternate interior angles
Defining a circle
Identifying areas within a circle: chord, diameter, radius, central
  angles, inscribed triangle, and isosceles triangle
Describing figures: rotation, reflection, and translation
Drawing lines of symmetry
Identifying corresponding parts, angles, and sides of congruent
  figures
Calculating measurements of similar figures

Part II: Constructions
Constructing congruent line segments
Bisecting a line segment
Copying an angle

Bisecting an angle
Constructing perpendicular line segments
Constructing parallel lines
Constructing congruent triangles

Part III: Measurement
Standard metric units of measure
Operations using metric measures and customary units

Part IV: Perimeters, Areas, and Volumes
Calculating the perimeters of polygons
Calculating the circumference of a circle
Calculating the area of rectangles, squares, and circles
Calculating the area of triangles, parallelograms, and trapezoids
Identifying three-dimensional figures
Calculating the surface area of three-dimensional figures
Calculating the volume of rectangular prisms, cubes, cylinders,
    cones, and pyramids
Calculating the surface area and volume of a sphere

PART I: POINTS, LINES AND PLANES

SAMPLE PROBLEMS

1. Using the figure below, identify the following:
   (a) three collinear points
   (b) four different lines
   (c) four different line segments
   (d) four rays that have endpoint *L*.

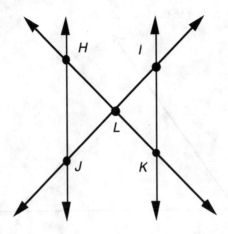

2. Using the figure below, name all
   (a) acute angles
   (b) right angles
   (c) obtuse angles

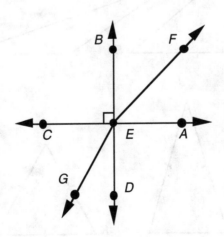

3. Use a protractor to measure ∠XYZ.

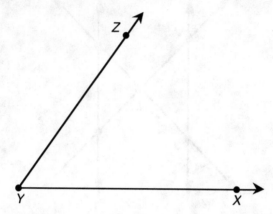

4. Using the figures below, name all the triangles that are
   (a) acute   (b) equilateral   (c) isosceles
   (d) obtuse   (e) right   (f) scalene

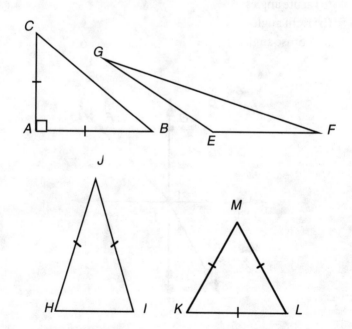

5. Using a straightedge, draw, label, and identify
   (a) a pair of intersecting lines
   (b) a pair of parallel lines
   (c) a pair of perpendicular lines
6. Match the terms for different types of figures below with all of the characteristics that apply from the second list (There may be more than one answer.):
   A. hexagon _____
   B. octagon _____
   C. parallelogram _____
   D. pentagon _____
   E. quadrilateral _____
   F. rectangle _____
   G. regular polygon _____
   H. rhombus _____
   I. square _____
   J. trapezoid _____
   1. has four sides
   2. has five sides
   3. has six sides
   4. has eight sides
   5. has only one pair of parallel sides
   6. opposite sides parallel
   7. opposite sides congruent
   8. all sides congruent
   9. all angles congruent
7. Complete the following statements:
   (a) The measure of the third angle of a triangle is ____ when the other two angles measure 59° and 17°.
   (b) If three angles of a quadrilateral measure 42°, 98° and 75°, the measure of the fourth angle is ____.
8. If an angle measures 78°, what is the measure of its
   (a) supplement?   (b) complement?
9. Transversal *KN* intersects the parallel lines *JL* and *PM*. If m∠5 = 32°, what is the measure of:

(a) ∠1   (b) ∠2   (c) ∠3   (d) ∠4
(e) ∠6   (f) ∠7   (g) ∠8

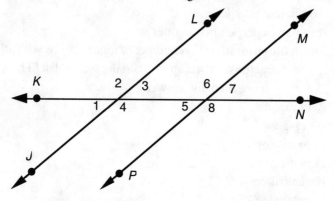

10. *M* is the center of the circle below. Identify the following:
   (a) the chords
   (b) the diameter
   (c) the radii (plural of radius)
   (d) one inscribed triangle
   (e) one central angle
   (f) one isosceles triangle

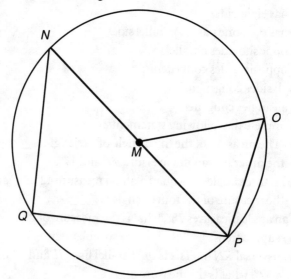

11. Choose either the term *rotation, translation,* or *reflection* to describe the change from *A* to *B* for each figure below:

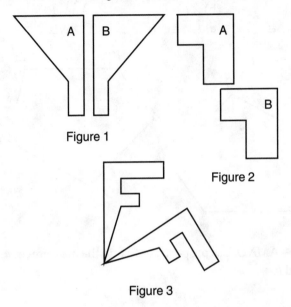

Figure 1

Figure 2

Figure 3

12. Draw in the lines of symmetry for each figure below:

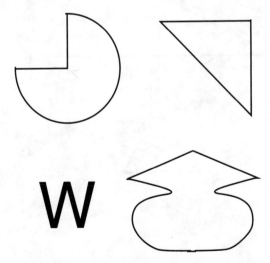

13. The following two pentagons are congruent. Complete each
    statement about their corresponding parts.
    (a) $\overline{JK} \cong$ (b) $\angle F \cong$ (c) m$\angle L =$
    (d) $\overline{HG} \cong$ (e) $\overline{LM} \cong$ (f) $\angle N \cong$

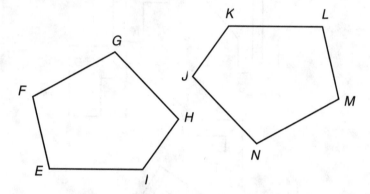

14. $\triangle JKL \sim \triangle MNO$. Use proportions to find the measures of a
    and b.

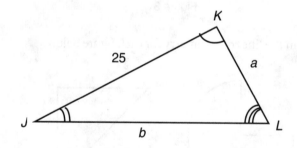

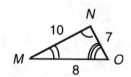

Answers

1. (a) *J, L, I* or *H, L, K*

   (b) $\overleftrightarrow{JI}, \overleftrightarrow{HK}, \overleftrightarrow{HJ}, \overleftrightarrow{IK}, \overleftrightarrow{JL}, \overleftrightarrow{LI}, \overleftrightarrow{HL}, \overleftrightarrow{LK}$

   (c) $\overline{JI}, \overline{HK}, \overline{HJ}, \overline{IK}, \overline{JL}, \overline{LI}, \overline{HL}, \overline{LK}$

   (d) $\overrightarrow{LH}, \overrightarrow{LJ}, \overrightarrow{LI}, \overrightarrow{LK}$

2. (a) acute angles: $\angle AEF$, ($\angle FEA$), $\angle FEB$, ($\angle BEF$), $\angle CEG$, ($\angle GEC$), $\angle GED$, ($\angle DEG$). An angle in parentheses names the same angle as the one preceding it.

   (b) right angles: $\angle AEB$, ($\angle BEA$), $\angle BEC$, ($\angle CEB$), $\angle CED$, ($\angle DEC$), $\angle AED$, ($\angle DEA$)

   (c) obtuse angles: $\angle FEC$, ($\angle CEF$), $\angle FED$, ($\angle DEF$), $\angle FEG$, ($\angle GEF$), $\angle BEG$, ($\angle GEB$), $\angle AEG$, ($\angle GEA$)

3. The measure of $\angle XYZ$ is 55°.

4. (a) acute: ΔHIJ, ΔKLM

   (b) equilateral: ΔKLM

   (c) isosceles: ΔHIJ, ΔABC, ΔKLM

   (d) obtuse: ΔEFG

   (e) right: ΔABC

   (f) scalene: ΔEFG

5.

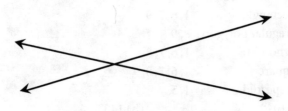

(a) a pair of intersecting lines

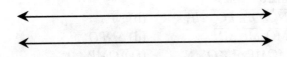

(b) a pair of parallel lines

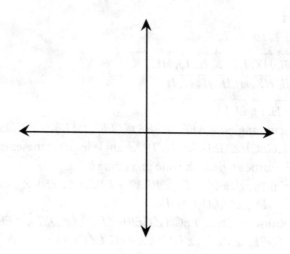

(c) a pair of perpendicular lines

6. A. hexagon   3
   B. octagon   4
   C. parallelogram   1, 6, 7
   D. pentagon   2
   E. quadrilateral   1
   F. rectangle   1, 6, 7, 9
   G. regular polygon   8, 9
   H. rhombus   1, 6, 7, 8
   I. square   1, 6, 7, 8, 9
   J. trapezoid   1, 5

7. (a) 104°   (b) 145°
8. (a) 102°   (b) 12°
9. (a) $m\angle 1 = 32°$ (b) $m\angle 2 = 148°$ (c) $m\angle 3 = 32°$
   (d) $m\angle 4 = 148°$ (e) $m\angle 6 = 148°$ (f) $m\angle 7 = 32°$
   (g) $m\angle 8 = 148°$
10. (a) $\overline{NQ}, \overline{QP}, \overline{PO}, \overline{NP},$ (b) $\overline{NP}$
    (c) $\overline{MO}, \overline{MP}, \overline{MN}$ (d) $\triangle NPQ$
    (e) $\angle OMP,$ or $\angle OMN$ (f) $\triangle OMP$

11. Figure 1 is a reflection.
    Figure 2 is a translation.
    Figure 3 is a rotation.

12.

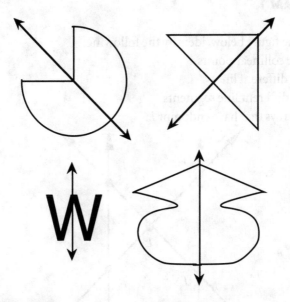

13. (a) $\overline{JK} \cong \overline{HI}$ (b) $\angle F \cong \angle M$
    (c) $m\angle L = m\angle E$ (d) $\overline{HG} \cong \overline{JN}$
    (e) $\overline{LM} \cong \overline{EF}$ (f) $\angle N \cong \angle G$
14. $a = 17.5$ units. $b = 20$ units.

HOW-TO GUIDE

PROBLEM 1

Using the figure below, identify the following:
(a) three collinear points
(b) four different lines
(c) four different line segments
(d) four rays that have endpoint L.

Answer

1. (a) J, L, I or H, L, K
   (b) $\overleftrightarrow{JI}$ or $\overleftrightarrow{IJ}$, $\overleftrightarrow{HK}$ or $\overleftrightarrow{KH}$, $\overleftrightarrow{HJ}$ or $\overleftrightarrow{JH}$, $\overleftrightarrow{IK}$ or $\overleftrightarrow{KI}$
   (c) $\overline{JI}$, $\overline{HK}$, $\overline{HJ}$, $\overline{IK}$, $\overline{JL}$, $\overline{LI}$, $\overline{HL}$, $\overline{LK}$
   (d) $\overrightarrow{LH}$, $\overrightarrow{LJ}$, $\overrightarrow{LI}$, $\overrightarrow{LK}$

The most basic geometric figure is a *point*. A point designates a specific location in space. The symbol for a point is an upper-case letter beside a dot. For example,

• Q is read as "point Q."

Groups of points form other geometric figures. We think of a *line* as a straight set of points that goes in two directions without end. The symbol for a line is two uppercase letters with this symbol, $\leftrightarrow$, above the letters. We read

$$\overset{\longleftrightarrow}{XY}$$

as, "line *XY*." Any two points on a line can be used to name the line. The order of the letters is not important, for example, $\overset{\longleftrightarrow}{XY}$ and $\overset{\longleftrightarrow}{YX}$ are the same line.

When one straight line can be drawn through a set of points, your child learns to call these points *collinear*.

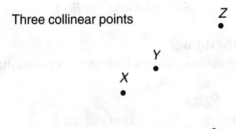

Three collinear points

Three noncollinear points

A *plane* is a flat geometric surface that is continuous in all directions. Three non-collinear points determine a plane. Examples of planes would be a blackboard, a floor, and a desktop.

A part of a line is called a *line segment*. A line segment is composed of the two points at its ends, called *endpoints,* and all the points between. The symbol for line segment is the two endpoints, written in capital letters, with a line segment drawn above them. The order of the letters is not important.

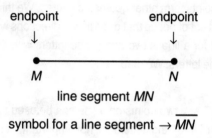

line segment *MN*

symbol for a line segment → $\overline{MN}$

A portion of a line with only one endpoint is called a *ray*. It extends, without end, in only *one* direction. When writing about rays with symbols, the first letter is *always* the endpoint.

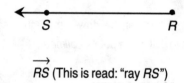

$\overrightarrow{RS}$ (This is read: "ray *RS*")

How to Get the Answer

1. To find the collinear points, look for three points that are in a straight line.

   (a) *J, L, I* or *H, L, K*

   The order of the points does not matter.

2. Because any two points can name a line, and a line segment is part of a line, the answers for parts (b) and (c) are essentially the same, except for the notation. Be certain that your child uses the correct notation. Remind your child that the order of the letters does not matter

   (e.g., $\overleftrightarrow{HJ}$ and $\overleftrightarrow{JH}$ name the same line).

3. The essential thing to remember when locating a ray is that it is named using the endpoint letter first. Therefore, the letter that is furthest away from the arrow of the ray is the first letter written in the notation.

PROBLEM 2

Using the figure below, name all
(a) acute angles
(b) right angles
(c) obtuse angles

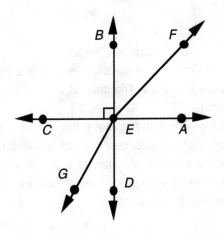

Answer

(a) acute angles: ∠AEF, (∠FEA), ∠FEB, (∠BEF), ∠CEG, (∠GEC),
    ∠GED, (∠DEG)

(b) right angles: ∠AEB, (∠BEA), ∠BEC, (∠CEB), ∠CED,
    (∠DEC), ∠AED, (∠DEA)

(c) obtuse angles: ∠FEC, (∠CEF), ∠FED, (∠DEF), ∠FEG,
    (∠GEF), ∠BEG, (∠GEB), ∠AEG, (∠GEA)

When two rays share a common endpoint, they form an *angle*.
The common endpoint is called the *vertex*.

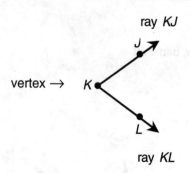

∠JKL (This is read "angle JKL.")

The usual way to name an angle is with three letters. The middle letter is always the vertex. The order of the remaining letters does not matter.

Your child is taught that angles are also named by placing a small number on the inside, near the vertex. When the angle does not share a vertex with another angle, designating the angle by its vertex point is a way to name the angle as well.

Four names for the same angle:

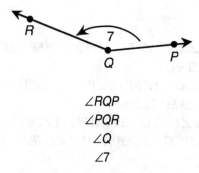

∠RQP
∠PQR
∠Q
∠7

When we measure a geometric figure, we are assigning a number to it. To do this, we use a *protractor,* an instrument designed to measure angles in unit measurements called *degrees.*

Angles can be classified based on the number of degrees. An angle with a measure more than 0°, but less than 90°, is called an *acute angle.* An angle of exactly 90° is a *right angle.* (The sides of right angles form corners and are said to be *perpendicular).* *Obtuse angles* are angles of more than 90°, but less than 180°.

Acute angles

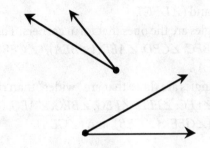

Right angles

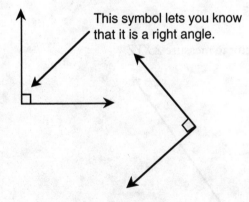

This symbol lets you know that it is a right angle.

Obtuse angles

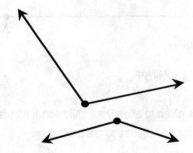

How to Get the Answer
Your child would rarely use a protractor to find the answer to this problem, although it could be used as a check.

1. The acute angles are the ones that seem "more closed." They are ∠AEF, ∠FEB, ∠CEG, ∠GED, (∠FEA), (∠BEF), (∠GEC), and (∠DEG).
2. The right angles are the ones that form corners. They are: ∠AEB, ∠BEC, ∠CED, ∠AED, (∠BEA), (∠CEB), (∠DEC), and (∠DEA).
3. The obtuse angles are those that are "wider" than right angles. They are ∠FEC, ∠FED, ∠FEG, ∠BEG, ∠AEG, (∠CEF), (∠DEF), (∠GEF), (∠GEB), and (∠GEA).

PROBLEM 3

Use a protractor to measure ∠XYZ.

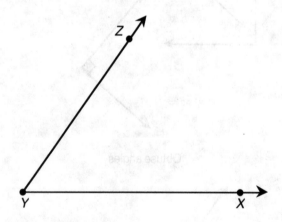

Answers
The measure of ∠XYZ is 55°.

> This problem is given to allow your child some hands-on experience with measuring angles using a *protractor*.

How to Get the Answer

1. Examine your protractor to see if the scale of degrees begins at the outer edge or at the inner edge.
2. Find the center point of this edge and place it on the vertex of the angle to be measured.
3. Carefully line up this edge with one side of the angle.
4. Count the degrees from the zero to the point where the other side of the angle crosses the protractor.

PROBLEM 4

Using the figures below, name all the triangles that are:
(a) acute   (b) equilateral   (c) isosceles
(d) obtuse   (e) right   (f) scalene

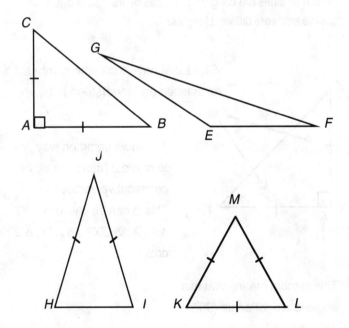

Answers

(a) acute: $\triangle HIJ, \triangle KLM$
(b) equilateral: $\triangle KLM$
(c) isosceles: $\triangle HIJ, \triangle ABC, \triangle KLM$
(d) obtuse: $\triangle EFG$
(e) right: $\triangle ABC$
(f) scalene: $\triangle EFG$

Basically, there are two ways to classify triangles: by the types of angles they contain and by the number of congruent sides they have. *Congruent* means they measure the same.

An *acute triangle* is a triangle with three acute angles. A *right triangle* is a triangle that contains a right angle. An *obtuse triangle* is one that contains an obtuse angle.

When a triangle has two equal (or congruent) sides it is called an *isosceles triangle.* An *equilateral triangle* is one in which all sides are congruent. A *scalene triangle* is one in which all the sides are different lengths.

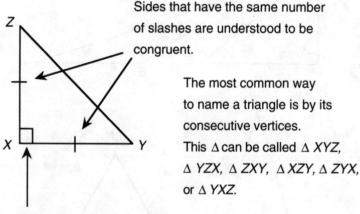

Sides that have the same number of slashes are understood to be congruent.

The most common way to name a triangle is by its consecutive vertices.
This △ can be called △ *XYZ*, △ *YZX,* △ *ZXY,* △ *XZY,* △ *ZYX,* or △ *YXZ.*

This symbol means that this angle is a right angle (90°).

How to Get the Answer

(a) To find the acute triangle, look for one with three acute angles: ΔHIJ, ΔKLM.

(b) To find the equilateral triangle, look for one with three slash marks, indicating three congruent sides: ΔKLM.

(c) An isosceles triangle only needs two congruent sides: ΔABC and ΔHIJ are isosceles triangles. An equilateral triangle is also an isosceles triangle, so ΔKLM is another answer.

(d) An obtuse triangle contains an obtuse angle. ΔEFG is the answer.

(e) A right triangle contains a right angle. ΔABC is the answer.

(f) A scalene triangle, because it has no congruent sides, will have none of its sides marked with slashes. ΔEFG is the answer.

PROBLEM 5

Using a straightedge, draw, label, and identify:
(a) a pair of intersecting lines
(b) a pair of parallel lines
(c) a pair of perpendicular lines

Answer

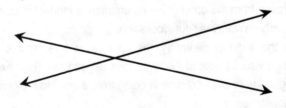

(a) a pair of intersecting lines

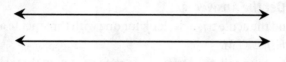

(b) a pair of parallel lines

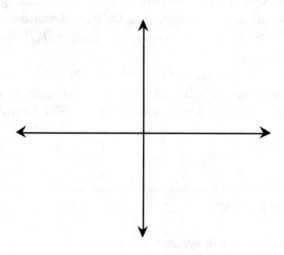

(c) a pair of perpendicular lines

In a formal geometry course, no assumptions can be made with regard to a drawing. Unless a property has been assigned or can be proved from the other given information, a student is taught not to rely on what the figure looks like.

At this level of geometry, the opposite is true. Your child needs a visual sense of the definitions of geometry. This exercise gives your child practice in going from a word to a pictorial representation.

Your child will need a *straightedge* (i.e. a rigid border) to draw straight lines.

How to Get the Answer

1. Intersecting lines are straight lines that meet and cross at a point. Because lines, and not line segments, are asked for throughout this exercise, be certain that your child's lines have arrows at each end.
2. Parallel lines are lines that will never meet or cross, regardless of how far they are extended.
3. Perpendicular lines are lines that meet to form four angles that are all the same size. Each of these angles measures 90°. Perpendicular angles look like corners.

PROBLEM 6

Match the terms for different types of figures below with all of the characteristics that apply from the second list below. (There may be more than one answer.):

A. hexagon _____

B. octagon _____

C. parallelogram _____

D. pentagon _____

E. quadrilateral _____

F. rectangle _____

G. regular polygon _____

H. rhombus _____

I. square _____

J. trapezoid _____

1. has four sides
2. has five sides
3. has six sides
4. has eight sides
5. has only one pair of parallel sides
6. opposite sides parallel

7. opposite sides congruent
8. all sides congruent
9. all angles congruent

Answer

A. hexagon   3
B. octagon   4
C. parallelogram   1, 6, 7
D. pentagon   2
E. quadrilateral   1
F. rectangle   1, 6, 7, 9
G. regular polygon   8, 9
H. rhombus   1, 6, 7, 8
I. square   1, 6, 7, 8, 9
J. trapezoid   1, 5

A polygon is a simple, closed figure whose sides are line segments.

These are polygons: These are *not* polygons:

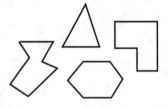
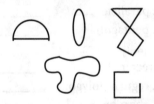

The figures below help explain what the terms *closed* and *open* mean. In a closed figure, the "beginning point" and the "ending point" are the same.

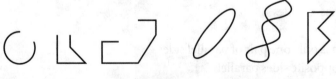

      open figures   closed figures

In a simple figure, the outer boundary does not cross itself.

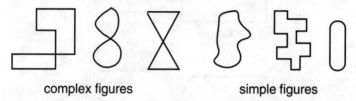

complex figures   simple figures

Of all the polygons, the most important for your child to know at this stage are the three-sided polygons (all of which are called *triangles*) and the subgroup of four-sided polygons called *quadrilaterals*. Your child usually is expected to know only the number of sides of the other polygons. All polygons can be drawn to be *regular* (i.e., all the sides are congruent and all the angles are congruent).

Your child is expected to know two main types of quadrilaterals:

1. A *trapezoid* is a quadrilateral with *just one* pair of parallel sides.

trapezoids

2. A *parallelogram* is a quadrilateral in which the opposite sides are both parallel and congruent. A *rhombus* is a parallelogram with 4 congruent sides. A *rectangle* is a parallelogram with 4 congruent angles. *Squares* are parallelograms with 4 congruent sides and 4 congruent angles.

parallelograms

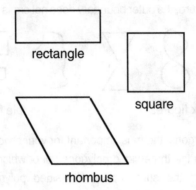

How to Get the Answer

A. A *hexagon* is a polygon with six sides.

B. An *octagon* is a polygon with eight sides.

C. A *parallelogram* is a polygon with four sides in which the opposite sides are parallel and congruent.

D. A *pentagon* is a polygon with five sides.

E. A *quadrilateral* is a polygon with four sides.

F. A *rectangle* is a polygon with four sides in which the opposite sides are parallel and all four angles are congruent.

G. A *regular polygon* is any polygon that is drawn so that all angles are congruent and all sides are congruent.

H. A *rhombus* is a polygon with four sides in which the opposite sides are parallel and all sides are congruent.

I. A *square* is a polygon with four sides in which the opposite sides are parallel, all sides are congruent, and all angles are congruent.

J. A *trapezoid* is a polygon with four sides in which there is only one pair of parallel sides.

PROBLEM 7

Complete the following statements:
(a) The measure of the third angle of a triangle is ____ when the other two angles measure 59° and 17°.
(b) If three angles of a quadrilateral measure 42°, 98° and 75°, the measure of the fourth angle is ____.

Answers
(a) 104°   (b) 145°

Most children love the fact that the sum of the angles of *any* triangle is 180°. One of the ways this is explored in school is to (a) cut out a triangle and tear off the edges, and then (b) fit them together edge to edge:

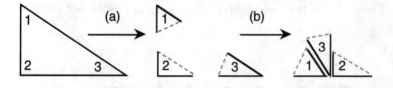

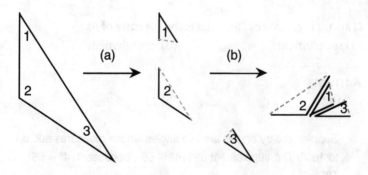

The bottom edge of the fitted pieces always makes a straight line. (Try it. It's fun.)

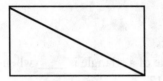 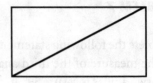

A *diagonal* is a straight line that connects two vertices that are not adjacent. A diagonal of a quadrilateral divides it into two triangles. Your child should already know that the sum of a triangle's angles is 180°. So, the sum of the angles of a quadrilateral (which is equivalent to two triangles) is 360°.

How to Get the Answer

1. For the triangle, add the two given angles (59° + 17° = 76°) and subtract this total from 180° (180° - 76° = 104°).

2. For the quadrilateral, add the three given angles (42° + 98° + 75° = 215°) and subtract this total from 360° (360° - 215° = 145°).

PROBLEM 8

If an angle measures 78°, what is the measure of its
(a) supplement?   (b) complement?

Answer

(a) 102°   (b) 12°

    Supplementary angles are two angles whose measures add up to 180°. The supplement of 114° is 66°, because 114° + 66° = 180°.

    Complementary angles are two angles whose measures add up to 90°. The complement of 13° is 77°, because 13° + 77° = 90°.

Your child knows that 180° angles are straight angles and 90° angles are right angles. In formal geometry, they will encounter a number of proofs that depend on these angles.

How to Get the Answer

1. To find the supplement, subtract the given angle from 180° (180° - 78° = 102°).
2. To find the complement, subtract the given angle from 90° (90° - 78° = 12°).

PROBLEM 9

Transversal *KN* intersects the parallel lines *JL* and *PM*. If m∠5 = 32°, what is the measure of:

(a) ∠1 (b) ∠2 (c) ∠3 (d) ∠4
(e) ∠6 (f) ∠7 (g) ∠8

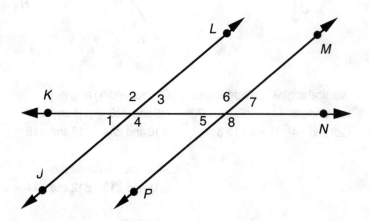

Answer

(a) m∠1 = 32° (b) m∠2 = 148° (c) m∠3 = 32°
(d) m∠4 = 148° (e) m∠6 = 148° (f) m∠7 = 32°
(g) m∠8 = 148°

When straight lines intersect, they form a variety of angles:

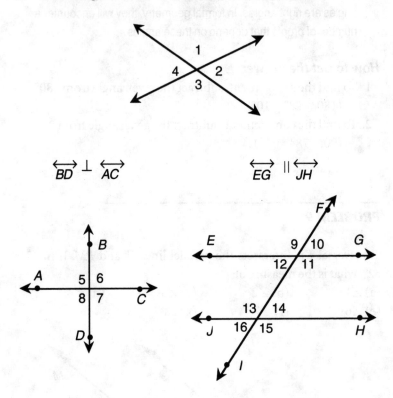

Vertical angles
∠1 and ∠3
∠2 and ∠4

Right angles
∠5, ∠6, ∠7,
and ∠8

Corresponding angles
∠9 and ∠13   ∠11 and ∠15
∠10 and ∠14   ∠12 and ∠16

Alternate interior angles
∠11 and ∠13   ∠12 and ∠14

Adjacent angles are two angles that share a vertex and a side, but their interiors do not overlap. An angle's interior is all the points that are between its two sides.

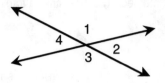

∠1 is adjacent to ∠2.
∠1 is also adjacent to ∠4.
∠2 is adjacent to ∠3.
∠3 is adjacent to ∠4.

When two lines intersect by crossing one another, the two pairs of angles that are across from one another are called *vertical angles.* Vertical angles are congruent.

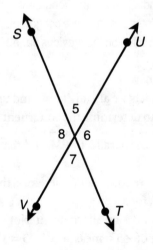

$\overleftrightarrow{ST}$ intersects $\overleftrightarrow{UV}$.
∠5 and ∠7 are vertical angles.
∠6 and ∠8 are vertical angles.

We call a line that intersects two other lines a *transversal*.

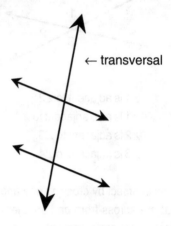

← transversal

The transversal to two parallel lines forms congruent angles:
(a) corresponding angles are congruent.
(b) alternate interior angles are congruent.
(See the illustration on the previous page.)

How to Get the Answer

1. Start with the facts we already know and use the various definitions to determine the congruent angles.
2. We know that $\overleftrightarrow{JL}$ is parallel to $\overleftrightarrow{PM}$, and that the measure of $\angle 5 = 32°$.
3. Vertical angles are congruent; therefore, the measure of $\angle 7$ must be 32°, too.
4. Because $\angle 5$ and $\angle 3$ are alternate interior angles, we know that the measure of $\angle 5$ = measure of $\angle 3 = 32°$.
5. We know that $\angle 5$ and $\angle 1$ are corresponding angles and are congruent. We determine that the measure of $\angle 5$ = measure of $\angle 1 = 32°$.
6. $\angle 5$ and $\angle 6$ are supplementary angles. Therefore, the measure of $\angle 5$ plus the measure of $\angle 6 = 180°$. If $m\angle 5 = 32°$, $m\angle 6 = 148°$.

$m\angle 6 = 148°$

$m\angle 8 = 148°$ (because $\angle 6$ and $\angle 8$ are vertical angles)

$m\angle 4 = 148°$ (because $\angle 6$ and $\angle 4$ are alternate interior angles)

$m\angle 2 = 148°$ (because $\angle 6$ and $\angle 2$ are corresponding angles)

PROBLEM 10

M is the center of the circle below. Identify the following:

(a) the chords
(b) the diameter
(c) the radii (plural of radius)
(d) one inscribed triangle
(e) the central angle
(f) one isosceles triangle

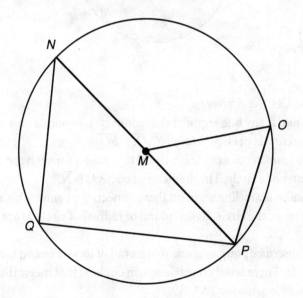

Answers

(a) $\overline{NQ}, \overline{QN}, \overline{QP}, \overline{PQ}, \overline{PO}, \overline{OP}, \overline{NP}, \overline{PN}$ (b) $\overline{NP}$ or $\overline{PN}$

(c) $\overline{MO}, \overline{MP}, \overline{MN}$ or $\overline{OM}, \overline{PM}, \overline{NM}$ (d) $\triangle NPQ$

(e) $\angle OMP$ or $\angle OMN$ (f) $\triangle OMP$

A *circle* is the set of points that are the same distance away from a point designated as the *center of a circle*. Many students make the mistake that the points inside the circle are part of the circle. Your child should come to know this distinction.

A circle divides a space into three regions: (1) the area outside the circle, (2) the points on the circle itself, and (3) the area within the circle.

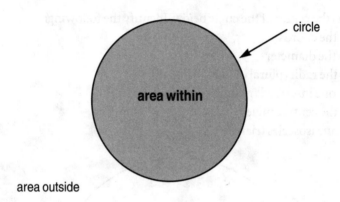

How to Get the Answer

(a) A *chord* is any line segment that connects two points on a circle. The chords of circle M are $\overline{NQ}, \overline{QP},\ \overline{PO},\ \overline{NP}$.

(b) The *diameter* of a circle is a chord that passes through the center of a circle. The diameter of circle M is $\overline{NP}$.

(c) A *radius* is any line segment that connects the center with any point on the circle. Radii (plural of radius) of circle M are $\overline{MO}$, $\overline{MP}, \overline{MN}$.

(d) An *inscribed polygon* is one that has all of its vertices on the circle. There is only one triangle in circle M that meets this condition, namely, $\triangle NPQ$.

(e) A *central angle* is an angle whose vertex is the center of the circle. Central angles of circle M are $\angle OMP, \angle OMN$.

(f) Because all radii of a circle are congruent, $\overline{MP} \cong \overline{MO}$ and $\triangle OMP$ is an isosceles triangle.

PROBLEM 11

Choose the term *rotation, translation* or *reflection* to describe the change from A to B for each figure:

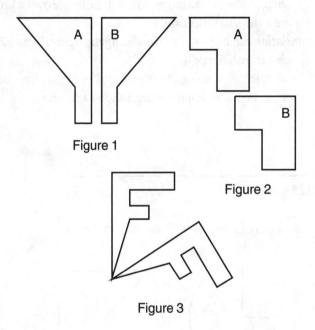

Figure 1

Figure 2

Figure 3

Answers
Figure 1 is a reflection.
Figure 2 is a translation.
Figure 3 is a rotation.

Angles are congruent when they have the same measure. Figures are congruent when they have the same shape and the same size. When you studied geometry in high school, you might remember theorems that you had to memorize concerning the congruency of triangles such as SAS (for side-angle-side), or SSS (for side-side-side).

Your child is introduced to the concept of congruency through visualizing the figure moving through space. Often these concepts are taught with computers so the student can actually see the movement.

How to Get the Answer

1. A *reflection* can be visualized as flipping the figure over a line. Figure 1 shows a reflection.
2. A *translation* can be visualized as sliding the figure. Figure 2 shows a translation.
3. When we think of turning a figure about a point, we have the description of a *rotation*. Figure 3 shows a rotation.

PROBLEM 12

Draw in the lines of symmetry for each figure below:

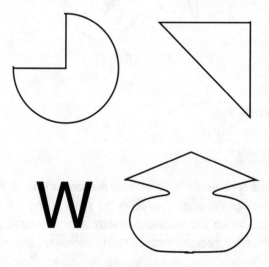

Answer

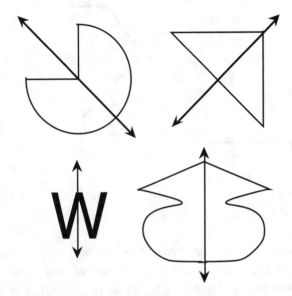

The *line of symmetry* is a line that divides a figure into two congruent parts. Most children have little difficulty with these exercises. Those who do are usually helped by actually folding the figure so that one half of the figure fits exactly over the other half. The fold line is the line of symmetry.

How to Get the Answer
1. Place a straightedge over the figure to divide it in half. When you are certain that one half is a reflection of the other, draw the line. This line is the line of symmetry.

PROBLEM 13

The following two pentagons are congruent. Complete each statement about their corresponding parts:

(a) $\overline{JK} \cong$ (b) $\angle F =$ (c) $m\angle L =$

(d) $\overline{HG} \cong$ (e) $\overline{LM} \cong$ (f) $\angle N \cong$

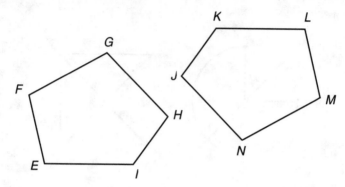

Answer

(a) $\overline{JK} \cong \overline{HI}$ (b) $\angle F \cong \angle M$ (c) $m\angle L = m\angle E$

(d) $\overline{HG} \cong \overline{JN}$ (e) $\overline{LM} \cong \overline{EF}$ (f) $\angle N \cong \angle G$

Your child knows that if one figure can be turned (rotation), flipped (reflection), or slid about (translation), and it fits over another exactly, then the two figures are *congruent*. The symbol for the words "is congruent to" is ≅. *Corresponding parts* are the matching sides and angles of the congruent figures. Corresponding angles have the same measure. Corresponding sides are the same length.

How to Get the Answer

1. Trace the figures on separate pieces of paper. Then turn, flip, and translate them until they look identical when they are placed side by side. Be careful to copy the letters correctly.

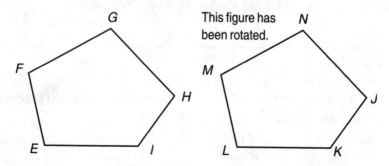

This figure has been rotated.

2. Using the new drawings, name the figures by listing the letters in the order they are arranged in the figures (e.g., If you begin naming one figure from the lower left vertex, moving clockwise, then begin naming the other figure in the same way, from the lower left vertex, moving clockwise.)

pentagon $EFGHI \cong$ pentagon $LMNJK$

Written this way, corresponding parts can be easily seen, because E corresponds to L, F corresponds to M, for example.

Thus, the corresponding parts are:

(a) $\overline{JK} \cong \overline{HI}$ (b) $\angle F \cong \angle M$

(c) $m\angle L = m\angle E$ (d) $\overline{HG} \cong \overline{JN}$

(e) $\overline{LM} \cong \overline{EF}$ (f) $\angle N \cong \angle G$

In designating corresponding parts, the order of naming the segments is important. For example, $\overline{HG} \cong \overline{JN}$, but not to $\overline{NJ}$, because of the corresponding vertices.

PROBLEM 14

$\triangle JKL \sim \triangle MNO$. Use proportions to find the measures of a and b.

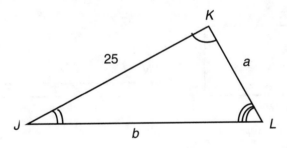

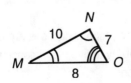

Answer

$a = 17.5$ units $b = 20$ units

Similar figures are ones that are the same shape, but may be a different size. When trying to decide if two figures are similar, your child can be taught to think of shrinking the larger figure and trying to visualize a perfect fit of one over the other.

The symbol for the expression "is similar to" is ~.

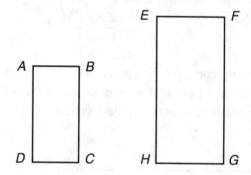

Two rectangles that are similar. *ABCD* ~ *EFGH* (this is read, "*ABCD* is similar to *EFGH*").

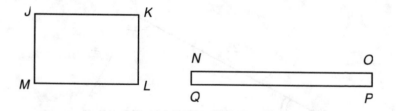

Two rectangles that are *not* similar. Keep in mind that a shrinkage or enlargement implies that all dimensions are changed proportionately.

In similar figures, corresponding sides are proportional. This gives your child the ability to find the dimensions of the missing sides of similar polygons.

How to Get the Answer

The measures of corresponding angles of similar triangles are equal and are marked with the same number of arcs.

1. In $\triangle JKL$, side a is across from an angle marked with two arcs. In $\triangle MNO$, the side with length 7 is across from an angle with two arcs. Therefore, we can set up one of the ratios of the proportion:

$$\frac{a}{7}$$

2. There is only one side in the larger triangle that is known. This side is 25 units. The side corresponding to this in $\triangle MNO$ is 10 units. We use these lengths to complete our proportion:

$$\frac{a}{7} = \frac{25}{10}$$

3. We cross multiply and then solve for a:

$$10a = 25 \cdot 7$$
$$10a = 175$$
$$\frac{10a}{10} = \frac{175}{10}$$
$$a = 17.5$$

4. Side b in $\triangle JKL$ is across from an angle marked with one arc, so its corresponding side in $\triangle MNO$ is 8 units:

$$\frac{b}{8}$$

5. Completing the proportion by using the other known sides as before, we get the following proportion:

$$\frac{b}{8} = \frac{25}{10}$$

6. We cross multiply and then solve for b:

$$10b = 25 \cdot 8$$
$$10b = 200$$
$$\frac{10b}{10} = \frac{200}{10}$$
$$b = 20$$

PART II: CONSTRUCTIONS

SAMPLE PROBLEMS

1. Using a straightedge and a compass, construct a line segment that is congruent to $\overline{JK}$ below.

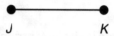

2. Using a straightedge and a compass, bisect $\overline{JK}$.

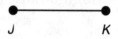

3. Using a straightedge and a compass, copy $\angle QRS$.

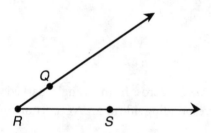

4. Using a straightedge and a compass, bisect $\angle JKL$.

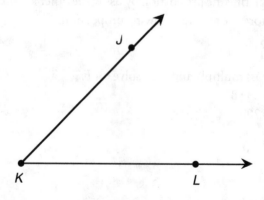

5. Using a straightedge and a compass, construct a line segment perpendicular to $\overline{JK}$ through point L.

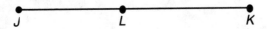

6. Using a straightedge and a compass, construct a line segment perpendicular to $\overline{JK}$ through point L.

7. Construct a line through point J that is parallel to $\overset{\longleftrightarrow}{LM}$.

8. Construct a triangle XYZ with sides congruent to the three line segments below.

Answers

1. $\overline{JK} \cong \overline{LM}$.

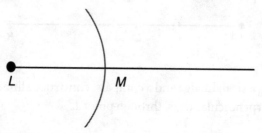

2. $\overline{JP} \cong \overline{PK}$, $\overline{LM}$ bisects $\overline{JK}$, and point P is the midpoint of $\overline{JK}$.

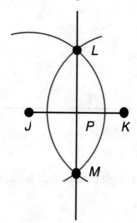

3. $\angle VTU \cong \angle QRS$

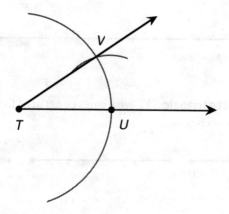

4. $\overrightarrow{KM}$ bisects $\angle JKL$, and $\angle JKM \cong \angle MKL$

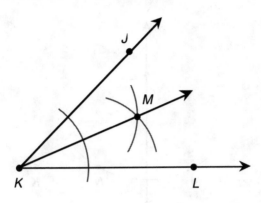

5. $\overline{PL} \perp \overline{JK}$

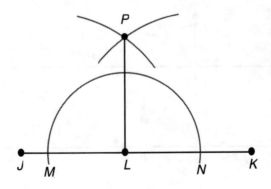

6. $\overline{LP} \perp \overline{JK}$

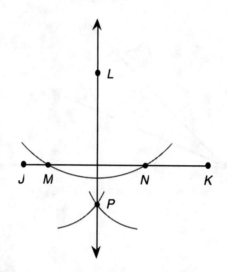

7. $\overleftrightarrow{JR} \parallel \overleftrightarrow{LM}$

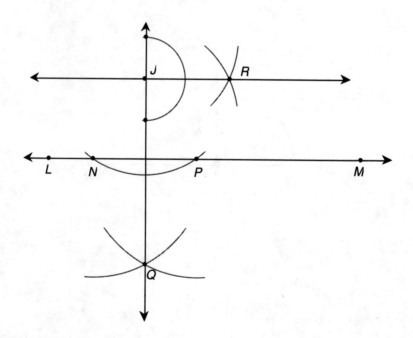

8.

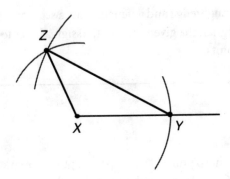

How-To Guide

PROBLEM 1

Using a straightedge and a compass, construct a line segment that is congruent to $\overline{JK}$ below.

A *construction* is a precise drawing that is made using only a compass (a mechanical device for drawing and dividing circles), a straightedge, and a pencil.

The instructions for a construction use a style of language that your child learns to translate from the given formal format. For example, your child reads:

"With center *J* and radius $\overline{JK}$, draw the arc through *K*."

They understand this to mean:

"With the sharp point of the compass at point *J*, mark off an arc through point *K*."

How to Get the Answer

1. With a straightedge and a pencil, draw a segment that appears longer than the given segment. Assign a letter to one of its endpoints.

2. With the sharp point of a compass at point *J*, mark off an arc (a part of a circle) through point *K*. By doing this, you are making a precise measurement of $\overline{JK}$.

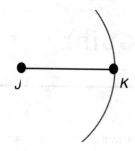

3. Being careful not to squeeze the compass, place the sharp point on the endpoint of the line segment you just drew. Mark off an arc. Assign a letter to that point of intersection.

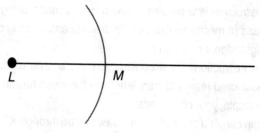

Conclusion: $\overline{JK} \cong \overline{LM}$.

        (Reminder: The symbol $\cong$ means "is congruent to.")

PROBLEM 2

Using a straightedge and a compass, bisect $\overline{JK}$, given below.

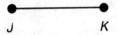

To *bisect* means to divide a line segment or an angle into two congruent parts. When a line segment is bisected, the point that marks the place at which the segment can be divided in half is called the *midpoint*.

How to Get the Answer

1. With the sharp point of the compass at endpoint *J*, open the compass to draw an arc that will be beyond the middle and that will cross above and below $\overline{JK}$.

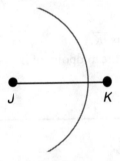

2. Being careful not to squeeze the compass, place the sharp point on the other endpoint *K*. Draw the arc to cross above and below $\overline{JK}$. Assign a letter to each of these points.

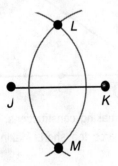

3. Connect the two points where the arcs meet with a line segment. Assign a letter to the point where the original line segment is intersected.

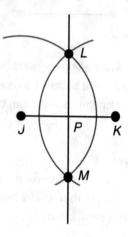

Conclusions: $\overline{JP} \cong \overline{PK}$

$\overline{LM}$ bisects $\overline{JK}$.

Point P is the midpoint of $\overline{JK}$.

PROBLEM 3

Using a straightedge and a compass, copy $\angle QRS$.

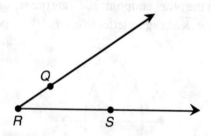

When your child is making constructions, caution him or her against making the arcs too short. Making short arcs could

require him or her to repeat a procedure that might jeopardize
the precision of the construction.

How to Get the Answer

1. With a straightedge and a pencil, draw a line segment that
   appears to be the length of $\overrightarrow{RS}$. Label the endpoint this way.

2. With the sharp point of the compass at point R, mark off an
   arc through point S.

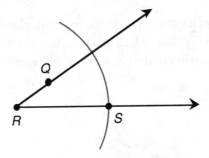

3. Being careful not to squeeze the compass, place the sharp
   point on point T. Mark off a long arc. Assign a letter to the
   point of intersection.

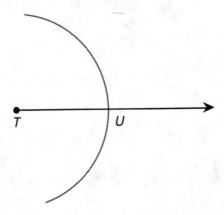

4. With the sharp point of the compass at point S, mark off an arc through the point where the first arc and $\overrightarrow{RQ}$ intersect.

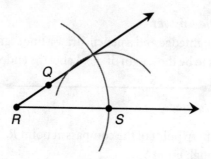

5. Being careful not to squeeze the compass, place the sharp point on point U. Mark off an arc to cross the long arc. Assign a letter to the point at which the arcs cross.

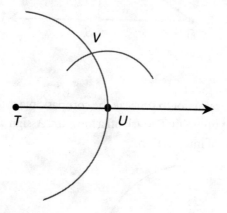

6. Draw a ray from point *T* through this new point of intersection. The angle formed is a copy of ∠*QRS*.

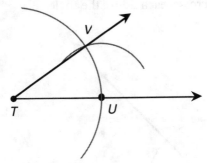

Conclusion: ∠*VTU* ≅ ∠*QRS*

PROBLEM 4

Using a straightedge and a compass, bisect ∠*JKL*.

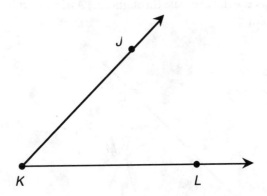

Errors occur most often in these types of constructions when the compass point is not placed directly on the point of the intersection and when the radius of the compass is changed by squeezing the compass between steps. Remind your child that practice and care are needed to produce accurate results.

How to Get the Answer

1. With the sharp point of the compass at point *K*, mark off an arc that crosses each side of the angle.

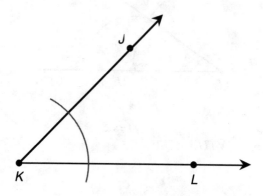

2. With the sharp point of the compass at each intersection point of the arc, in turn, draw two new arcs. (Be careful not to squeeze the compass throughout.) Assign a letter to this point.

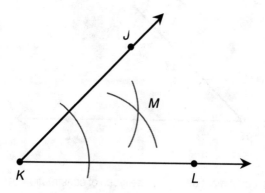

3. From point *K*, draw a ray through the intersection of the two arcs.

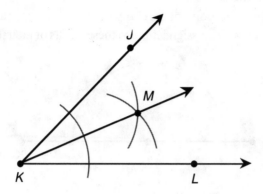

Conclusions: $\overrightarrow{KM}$ bisects $\angle JKL$
$\angle JKM \cong \angle MKL$

PROBLEM 5

Using a straightedge and a compass, construct a line segment perpendicular to $\overline{JK}$ through point *L*.

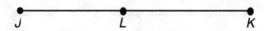

Adjacent angles are angles that share a vertex and a common side between them. *Perpendicular lines* create two adjacent 90° angles.

A line segment can be considered to be a *straight angle* (one containing 180°). A perpendicular is constructed by bisecting this straight angle, since two adjacent 90° angles are the result of this bisection.

How to Get the Answer

1. With the sharp point of the compass at point L, make an arc to cut across $\overline{JK}$. Assign letters to these points of intersection.

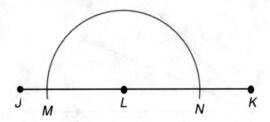

2. With the sharp point at M, widen the compass a bit, and mark off an arc above the semicircle. Being careful not to squeeze the compass, place the sharp point at N, and mark off an arc. Assign a letter to this point of intersection.

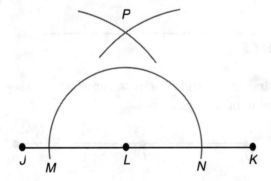

3. Draw $\overline{PL}$.

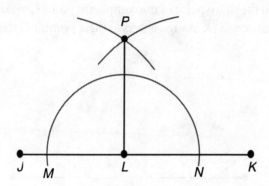

Conclusion: $\overline{PL} \perp \overline{JK}$

PROBLEM 6

Using a straightedge and a compass, construct a line segment perpendicular to $\overline{JK}$ through point L.

When your child is doing this construction, encourage her or him to take care when making the first arc. If this arc is too wide, the original line segment might need to be extended in order to see the point of intersection.

How to Get the Answer

1. With the sharp point of the compass at point *L*, make an arc to cut across $\overline{JK}$. Assign letters to these points of intersection.

2. With the sharp point of the compass at *M*, mark off an arc below the one just drawn. Being careful not to squeeze the compass, place the sharp point at *N*, and mark off an arc. Assign a letter to this point of intersection.

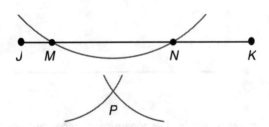

3. Draw $\overline{PL}$.

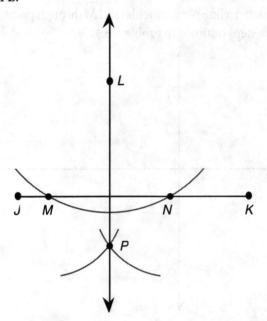

Conclusion: $\overline{LP} \perp \overline{JK}$

PROBLEM 7

Construct a line through point *J* that is parallel to $\overleftrightarrow{LM}$.

• *J*

There is a formal proof in geometry that shows that two lines perpendicular to the same line are parallel to each other. This construction is based on that proof.

How to Get the Answer

1. Construct a line perpendicular to $\overleftrightarrow{LM}$ through point *J*. (Follow the steps outlined in problem 6.)

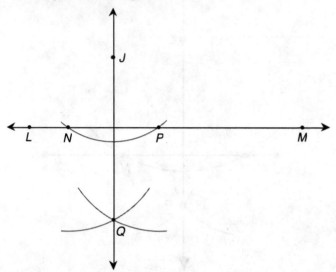

2. Construct a line segment perpendicular to $\overline{JQ}$ through point *J*. (Follow the steps outlined in problem 5.) You can turn the paper 90° when doing this to make it easier to draw.

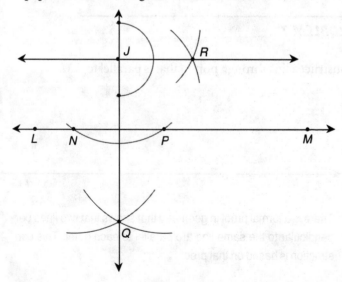

Conclusion: $\overleftrightarrow{JR} \parallel \overleftrightarrow{LM}$

PROBLEM 8

Construct a triangle *XYZ* with sides congruent to the three line segments below.

The success of this construction depends on the accuracy of three different measurements. Each time your child changes the compass to a new position, remind him or her to take care to place the compass directly on the endpoint.

How to Get the Answer

1. Construct a line segment $\overline{XY}$ congruent to $\overline{AB}$. (Follow the steps outlined in problem 1.)

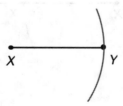

2. With the sharp point of the compass at point *C*, mark off an arc through point *D*. Being careful not to squeeze the compass, place the sharp point at point *Y* and draw an arc above $\overline{XY}$.

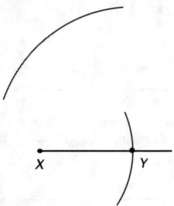

3. With the sharp point of the compass at point *E*, mark off an arc through point *F*. Being careful not to squeeze the compass, place the sharp point at point *X* and draw an arc to cross the one above $\overline{XY}$. This is point *Z*.

   You might need to lengthen the arc in the previous step to make the point of intersection at *Z*.

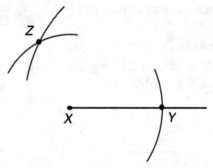

4. Draw triangle *XYZ*.

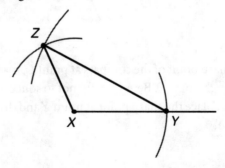

PART III: MEASUREMENT

SAMPLE PROBLEMS

1. Complete.
   (a) 72 km = _____ hm = _____ dam = _____ cm
   (b) 24,000 mm = _____ cm = _____ m = _____ km = _____ dam
2. Complete.
   (a) .250 kg = _____ g = _____ mg
   (b) _____ kg = .06 g = _____ mg
3. Complete
   (a) 600 ml = _____ l
   (b) 30 l = _____ ml
   (c) .001 l = _____ ml
   (d) .38 ml = _____ l
4. Add or subtract.
   (a)   4 yd   1 ft   5 in
       + 3 yd   2 ft   8 in
       _____

   (b)   12 yd   2 ft   5 in
        - 5 yd   7 in
        _____

5. Complete.
   (a) 7 c = ___ pt ___ c
   (b) 137 oz = ___ gal ___ qt ___ oz
   (c) 24 oz = ___ lb ___ oz
   (d) 13 T 33,018 oz = ___ T ___ lb ___ oz
6. Choose the best temperature.
   (a) a bedroom: 70° C or 20° C?
   (b) building a snowman: -5° C or 19° C?
   (c) a picnic in the park: 75° C or 25° C?

Answers
1. (a) 72 km = 720 hm = 7,200 dam = 7,200,000 cm
   (b) 24,000 mm = 2,400 cm = 24 m = .024 km = 2.4 dam
2. (a) .250 kg = 250 g = 250,000 mg
   (b) .00006 kg = .06 g = 60 mg
3. (a) 600 ml = 0.6 l
   (b) 30 l = 30,000 ml
   (c) .001 l = 1 ml
   (d) .38 ml = .00038 l
4. (a) 8 yd 1 ft 1 in
   (b) 7 yd 1 ft 10 in
5. (a) 7 c = 3 pt 1 c
   (b) 137 oz = 1 gal 0 qt 9 oz
   (c) 24 oz = 1 lb 8 oz
   (d) 13 T 33,018 oz = 14 T 63 lb 10 oz
6. (a) 20° C
   (b) -5° C
   (c) 25° C

HOW-TO GUIDE

PROBLEM 1

Complete
(a) 72 km = _____ hm = _____ dam = _____ cm
(b) 24,000 mm = _____ cm = _____ m = _____ km = _____ dam

Answers
(a) 72 km = 720 hm = 7,200 dam = 7,200,000 cm
(b) 24,000 mm = 2,400 cm = 24 m = .024 km = 2.4 dam

When we use the term *conversion,* we are referring to the process of changing from one unit of measurement to another.

There are three basic standards of measurement in the metric system. The meter (the symbol is m) is the standard unit of length, the gram (the symbol is g) is the standard unit of weight, and the liter (the symbol is l) is the standard unit of volume.

When a student understands the meanings of the metric prefixes, conversions are easier to make. Below are the metric prefixes and their meanings:

Prefix	Meaning	Abbreviation
kilo	thousand	k
hecto	hundred	h
deka	ten	da
deci	tenth	d
centi	hundredth	c
milli	thousandth	m

Some children memorize the order of the prefixes by using the statement, *k*etchup *h*as *d*ropped *s*tone *d*ead *c*ried *m*ustard. The *s* in stone is a reminder for the standard unit. In this example, the standard measure is a meter. So, if they were working in meters, they would write this heading across the top of their paper to help them remember the conversions.

km   hm   dam   m   dm   cm   mm

Each unit in the heading is ten times larger than the unit to its right. Changing units in the metric system, therefore, is a matter of moving the decimal to the left or right to indicate a change by a power of 10.

How to Get the Answer

1. Be sure that the decimal point is "showing" in the problem.
   72 km becomes 72. km
   24,000 mm becomes 24,000. mm

2. Write the progression of the prefixes, from the greatest to the
   least, for the units of length.

   km   hm   dam   m   dm   cm   mm

3. Count the number of moves it would take (in the progression
   of the prefixes listed above) to get from one prefix in the
   problem to the next. Note the direction of the move.

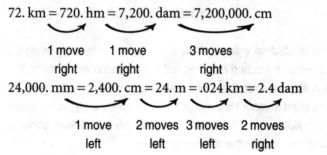

4. Move the decimal point the same number of places and in the
   same direction for the conversion.

   72. km = 720. hm = 7,200. dam = 7,200,000. cm

   | 1 move | 1 move | 3 moves |
   | right | right | right |

   24,000. mm = 2,400. cm = 24. m = .024 km = 2.4 dam

   | 1 move | 2 moves | 3 moves | 2 moves |
   | left | left | left | right |

PROBLEM 2

Complete.

(a) .250 kg = _____ g = _____ mg

(b) _____ kg = .06 g = _____ mg

Answers

(a) .250 kg = 250 g = 250,000 mg

(b) .00006 kg = .06 g = 60 mg

A *gram* is said to be the standard unit of *weight* in the metric system. However, the gram actually measures *mass,* the amount of matter an object has. Weight can change with the gravitational pull (so one's body weight would be less on the moon than it is on earth). But mass never changes. For our purposes, weight and mass are used interchangeably.

There are some metric units of mass that are seldom used in this country (one example is the hectogram). The exercises in this problem involve conversions between the commonly used units including kilograms (kg), grams (g) and milligrams (mg).

How to Get the Answer

1. Be sure that the decimal point is "showing" in the problem.
   (a) .250 kg
   (b) .06 g
2. Write the progression of the prefixes from the greatest to the least, for the units of weight:
kg	hg	dag	g	dg	cg	mg
3. Count the number of moves it would take (in the progression of the prefixes above) to get from one prefix to the next. Note the direction of the move.
   (a) .250 kg = ___ g = ___ mg

          3 moves 3 moves
            right   right

   (b) ___ kg = .06 g = ___ mg

          3 moves 3 moves
            left   right
4. Move the decimal point the same number of places and in the same direction for the conversion.
   (a) .250 kg = 250. g = 250,000. mg
   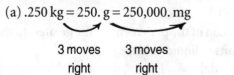

          3 moves   3 moves
           right   right

(b) .00006 kg = .06 g = 60. mg

3 moves 3 moves
left   right

PROBLEM 3

Complete.
(a) 600 ml = _____ l
(b) 30 l = _____ ml
(c) .001 l = _____ ml
(d) .38 ml = _____ l

Answer
(a) 600 ml = 0.6 l
(b) 30 l = 30,000 ml
(c) .001 l = 1 ml
(d) .38 ml = .00038 l

The standard unit of liquid volume in the metric system is the *liter*. Your child has probably had the greatest exposure to this unit than to any other, because most soft drinks are available in 1- or 2-liter bottles. The exercises in this problem involve conversions between the commonly used units of *milliliters* (ml) and *liters* (l).

How to Get the Answer
1. Be certain that the decimal point is "showing" in the problem.
   (a) 600 ml becomes 600. ml
   (b) 30 l becomes 30. l
2. Write the progression of the prefixes from the greatest to the least for the units of liquid volume:

   kl   hl   dal   l   dl   cl   ml

3. Count the number of moves it would take (in the progression
of the prefixes above) to get from one prefix to the next.
Note the direction of the move.

  (a) 600 ml = ___ l

    3 moves left

  (b) 30 l = ___ ml

    3 moves right

  (c) .001 l = ___ ml

    3 moves right

  (d) .38 ml = ___ l

    3 moves left

4. Move the decimal point the same number of places and in the
same direction for the conversion.

  (a) 600 ml = .6 l

    3 moves left

  (b) 30 l = 30,000. ml

    3 moves right

  (c) .001 l = 1. ml

    3 moves right

  (d) .38 ml = .00038 l

    3 moves left

PROBLEM 4

Add or subtract.

(a)   4 yd   1 ft   5 in
       + 3 yd   2 ft   8 in
     _____

(b)   12 yd   2 ft   5 in
       - 5 yd   7 in
     _____

Answers
(a) 8 yd 1 ft 1 in
(b) 7 yd 1 ft 10 in

What you might have called the British system of measurements is now known to your child as *customary units of measurement.* This exercise is typical. Your child is expected to know the conversion equivalencies within the customary units of measurement so that substitutions can be made appropriately.

How to Get the Answer
(a) *Adding*
  1. Add each column of units.

       4 yd   1 ft   5 in
       3 yd   2 ft   8 in
     _____ _____   _____
       7 yd   3 ft   13 in

  2. Know the conversion equivalencies for measures of length.
     1 foot = 12 inches
     1 yard = 3 ft = 36 inches
     1 mile = 5,280 ft = 1,760 yd

  3. Make the appropriate conversions. Add these to the existing units.
     Think: I have 3 ft. I know that 3 ft = 1 yd. I'll substitute and add this to the 7 yd to make 8 yd.
     7 yd 3 ft 13 in = 8 yd 0 ft 13 in

Think: I have 13 in. This is the same as 1 ft. 1 in. I'll make this
substitution.

8 yd 0 ft 13 in = 8 yd 1 ft 1 in

(b) *Subtracting*

1. Inspect the example column by column for situations in which
   "borrowing" units will be necessary. *Borrowing* is the old
   term for *renaming* (meaning to replace with an equivalent
   value). We do this when the number being subtracted
   (subtrahend) is larger than the number being subtracted
   from *(minuend)*.

no	no	yes
↓	↓	↓
12 yd	2 ft	5 in
- 5 yd		7 in

2. Know the conversion equivalencies. In this case, 1 foot = 12
   inches.

3. Make the appropriate conversion.
   Because 2 ft is the same as 1 ft, 12 in, we can "borrow" to make
   the 5 inches display a larger quantity.

   "borrow" from here   display a larger quantity here

	↓	↓
12 yd	2 ft	5 in
- 5 yd		7 in
	↓	
12 yd	1 ft	17 in
- 5 yd		7 in

4. Subtract each column of units.

12 yd	1 ft	17 in
- 5 yd		7 in
7 yd	1 ft	10 in

PROBLEM 5

Complete.
(a) 7 c = ___ pt ___ c
(b) 137 oz = ___ gal ___ qt ___ oz
(c) 24 oz = ___ lb ___ oz
(d) 13 T 33,018 oz = ___ T ___ lb ___ oz

Answer
(a) 7 c = 3 pt 1 c
(b) 137 oz = 1 gal 0 qt 9 oz
(c) 24 oz = 1 lb 8 oz
(d) 13 T 33,018 oz = 14 T 63 lb 10 oz

Some math educators believe that long division will become extinct like the slide rule; however, long division can still be useful for doing some conversions. Included in these exercises are such examples.

How to Get the Answer

1. Know the conversion equivalencies for liquid volume and weight.

   Liquid Capacity
   1 cup (c) = 8 fluid ounces (fl oz)
   1 pint (pt) = 2 cups = 16 fl oz
   1 quart (qt) = 2 pt = 32 fl oz
   1 gallon (gal) = 4 qt = 128 fl oz

   Weight
   1 pound (lb) = 16 ounces (oz)
   1 ton (T) = 2,000 lb

2. (a) To find the number of pints in 7 cups, divide 7 cups by 2 cups (1 pint). The remainder is in cups.

$$\begin{array}{r} 3 \text{ pints} \\ 2 \text{ cups} \overline{\smash{\big)}\ 7 \text{ cups}} \\ -6 \\ \hline 1 \text{ cup} \end{array}$$

Therefore, 7c = 3 pt 1 c

(b) To find the number of gallons in 137 ounces, divide 137 ounces by 128 ounces because 128 fl ounces equal 1 gallon.

$$\begin{array}{r} 1 \\ 128 \text{ oz} \overline{\smash{\big)}\ 137 \text{ oz}} \\ 128 \\ \hline 9 \text{ oz} \end{array}$$

(c) To find the number of pounds in 24 ounces, divide 24 ounces by 16 ounces.

$$\begin{array}{r} 1 \\ 16 \overline{\smash{\big)}\ 24 \text{ oz}} \\ 16 \\ \hline 8 \text{ oz} \end{array}$$

Therefore, 24 oz = 1 lb 8 oz

(d) To find the number of pounds in 33,018 ounces, divide 33,018 ounces by 16 ounces.

$$\begin{array}{r} 2{,}063 \text{ lb} \\ 16 \text{ oz} \overline{\smash{\big)}\ 33{,}018 \text{ oz}} \\ 32 \\ \hline 1\ 0 \\ 0 \\ \hline 1\ 01 \\ 96 \\ \hline 58 \\ 48 \\ \hline 10 \text{ oz} \end{array}$$

Therefore, 33,018 oz = 2,063 lb 10 oz. However, because 2,000 pounds equal 1 ton, this should be converted. To find the number of tons in 2,063 pounds, 10 ounces, divide by 2,000 pounds because 2,000 pounds equal 1 ton.

$$\begin{array}{r} 1 \text{ ton} \\ 2{,}000 \text{ lb} \overline{\smash{)}\, 2{,}063 \text{ lb } 10 \text{ oz}} \\ \underline{2{,}000} \\ 63 \text{ lb } 10 \text{ oz} \end{array}$$

Therefore, 13T 33,018 oz = 14T 63 lb 10 oz.

PROBLEM 6

Choose the best temperature.
(a) a bedroom: 70° C or 20° C?
(b) building a snowman: -5° C or 19° C?
(c) a picnic in the park: 75° C or 25° C?

Answer
(a) 20° C
(b) -5° C
(c) 25° C

Celsius is the scale that measures temperature, with 0° being the freezing point of pure water and 100° being the boiling temperature of water.

How to Get the Answer
1. Keep in mind some common Celsius temperatures.

Water boils	100° C	Jacket weather	10° C
Body temperature	37° C	Water freezes	0° C
Shorts weather	25° C	Coat weather	-5° C
Room temperature	20° C		

2. Use these as guides for reasonable choices for your answers.

PART *IV*: PERIMETERS, AREAS, AND VOLUME

SAMPLE PROBLEMS

1. Find the perimeter of each of the following polygons:

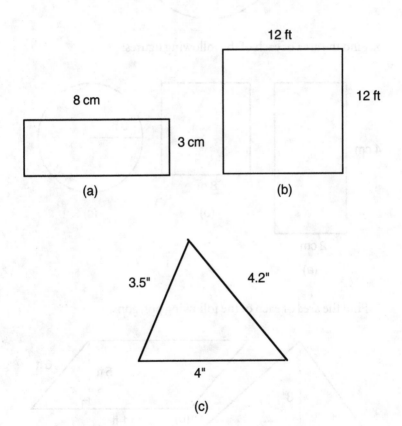

2. Find the circumference of a circle when its radius is 5 cm.

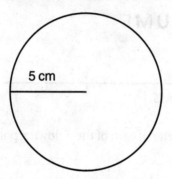

3. Find the area of each of the following figures:

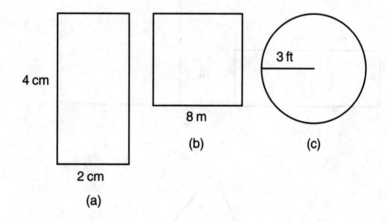

4. Find the area of each of the following polygons:

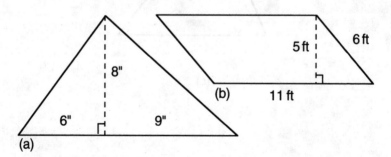

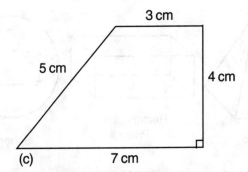

3 cm

5 cm

4 cm

(c)   7 cm

5. From the list of properties below, choose the number of each property that applies to each of the following three-dimensional solids and write it underneath the figure.

List of Properties

1 All the faces are polygons.

2 The bases are parallel and congruent.

3 The lateral faces are parallelograms.

4 The base(s) are circle(s).

5 Has only one base.

6 Made with a curved surface.

7 Has no base.

Three-Dimensional Solids

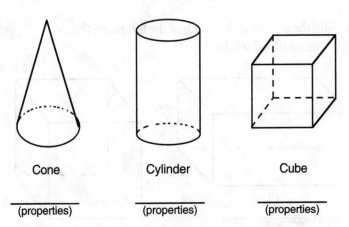

Cone   Cylinder   Cube

(properties)   (properties)   (properties)

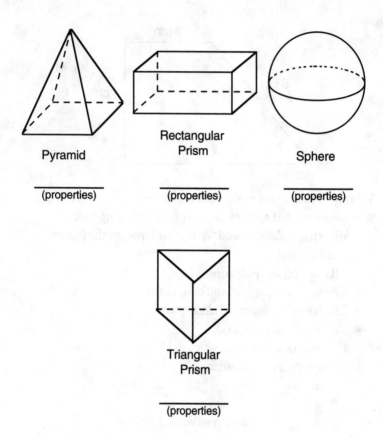

Pyramid

(properties)

Rectangular Prism

(properties)

Sphere

(properties)

Triangular Prism

(properties)

6. Find the surface area of each of the following three-dimensional solids:

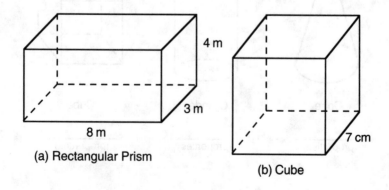

4 m

3 m

8 m

(a) Rectangular Prism

7 cm

(b) Cube

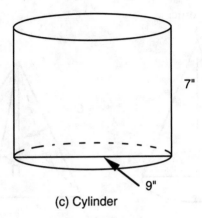

(c) Cylinder

7. Find the volume of each of the following three-dimensional solids:

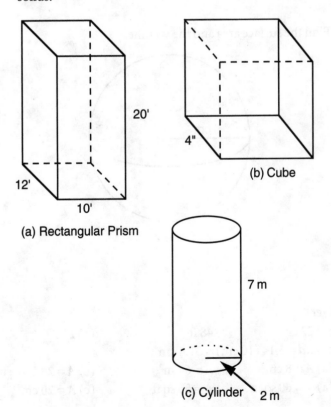

20'

12'

10'

(a) Rectangular Prism

4"

(b) Cube

7 m

(c) Cylinder   2 m

8. Find the volume:

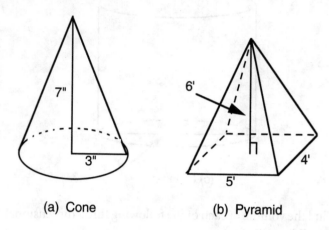

(a) Cone   (b) Pyramid

9. Find the surface area and the volume:

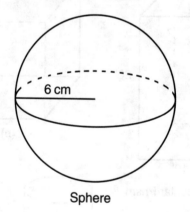

Sphere

Answers

1. (a) 22 cm   (b) 48 ft   (c) 11.7"
2. $c = \pi d = 3.14 \,(10 \text{ cm}) = 31.4 \text{ cm}$
3. (a) $A = 8 \text{ cm}^2$ (b) $A = 64 \text{ m}^2$ (c) $A = 28.26 \text{ sq ft}$
4. (a) $A = 60 \text{ sq in}$ (b) $A = 55 \text{ sq ft}$ (c) $A = 20 \text{ cm}^2$

5.   Cone: 4, 5, 6
          Cylinder: 2, 4, 6
              Cube: 1, 2, 3
           Pyramid: 1, 5
Rectangular Prism: 1, 2, 3
            Sphere: 6, 7
 Triangular Prism: 1, 2, 3

6. (a) 136 m²   (b) 294 cm²   (c) 325 sq in
7 (a) $V = 2400$ cu ft   (b) $V = 64$ cu in   (c) $V = 87.92$ cu m
8 (a) $V = 65.94$ cu in   (b) $V = 40$ cu ft
9. Surface area = 452.16 cm²
   Volume = 904.32 cm³

HOW-TO GUIDE

PROBLEM 1

Find the perimeter of each of the following polygons:

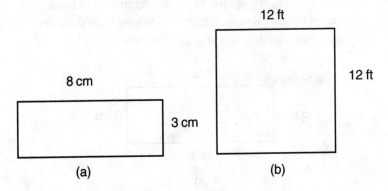

(a)   (b)

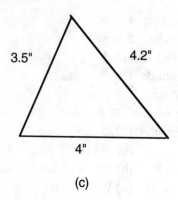

(c)

Answers
(a) 22 cm
(b) 48 ft
(c) 11.7"

The *perimeter* of a figure is the distance around its outer border. Your child finds the perimeter of a polygon by adding the lengths of all the sides that form it.

How to Get the Answer
1. The shapes of the polygons suggest that figure (a) is a rectangle and figure (b) is a square. From the definitions of squares and rectangles, we can determine the lengths of the sides that were not labeled. These are shown below.

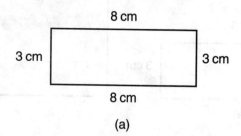

(a)

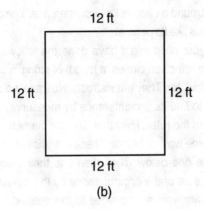

(b)

2. We find the perimeter of all three figures by finding the sum of the lengths of the sides.
   (a) 8 cm + 3 cm + 8 cm + 3 cm = 22 cm
   (b) 12 ft + 12 ft + 12 ft + 12 ft = 48 ft
   (c) 4.2" + 4" + 3.5" = 11.7"

PROBLEM 2

Find the circumference of a circle when its radius is 5 cm.

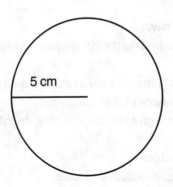

Answer

$c = \pi d = 3.14 \,(10 \text{ cm}) = 31.4 \text{ cm}$

The distance around a circle is its *circumference*. The circumference of a circle is like its perimeter.

In school, your child might have done the following experiment: Students are given circles, a length of string, a centimeter ruler, and a calculator. They are instructed to trace the circle with the string and to find its circumference by measuring the length of the string with the ruler. They then find the diameter using the string in the same way as before. These lengths are recorded in a chart like the one below. They then use their calculators to divide the measure of the circumference by the measure of the diameter. The answers are rounded to the nearest hundredth. Some typical measurements appear below:

Circle	Circumference	Diameter	Circumference/Diameter
A	30 cm	10 cm	3.00
B	2.9 cm	0.9 cm	3.22
C	10.1 cm	3 cm	3.37
D	1.0 cm	0.32 cm	3.13

What they discover is that this ratio (the circumference divided by the diameter) is approximately the same for all circles, regardless of their size. This number (approximately 3.14) is called *pi,* and is symbolized by the Greek letter, π.

How to Get the Answer

1. The formula for finding the circumference of a circle is
   $C = \pi d$
   (Read as: the circumference of a circle is equal to pi (3.14) times the measure of the diameter.)
2. Since the radius is given in this example, double it to find the diameter.
   $d = 2 \times 5 \text{ cm} = 10 \text{ cm}$
3. Substitute the given values and solve.
   $C = \pi d$
   $ = 3.14 \, (10 \text{ cm})$
   $ = 31.4 \text{ cm}$

PROBLEM 3

Find the area of each of the following figures:

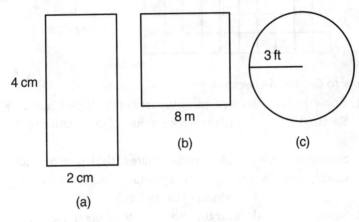

3 ft

4 cm

8 m

(b)

(c)

2 cm

(a)

Answers

(a) $A = 8 \text{ cm}^2$
(b) $A = 64 \text{ m}^2$
(c) $A = 28.26 \text{ sq ft}$

Area is the measurement of the inside space of a figure. Area is measured in square units.

Students are often taught about area with a hands-on exercise in which they are given tiny squares of the same size and several figures of various sizes. Each tiny square is designated as a "unit square." The purpose of the exercise is to see how many unit squares it will take to fill in the inside space of the figure.

In time, students begin to see the origin of some of the formulas for area. For example, multiplying the length times the width (the formula for the area of a rectangle) is a quick way to calculate the number of unit squares needed to cover the inner space of a rectangle.

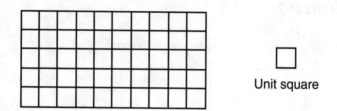

Unit square

How to Get the Answer

1. Know the formulas for finding the area of the given figures.

   Rectangle: $A = lw$ (Area is the product of the length and width.)

   Square: $A = s^2$ (Area is the square of the length of a side.)

   Circle: $A = \pi r^2$ (Area is the product of 3.14 and the square of the radius.)

2. Substitute the values for the known dimensions and solve.

Rectangle	Square	Circle
$A = lw$	$A = s^2$	$A = \pi r^2$
$= 4\,\text{cm} \cdot 2\,\text{cm}$	$= (8\,\text{m})^2$	$= 3.14(3\,\text{ft})^2$
$= 8\,\text{cm}^2$	$= 8\,\text{m} \cdot 8\,\text{m}$	$= 3.14(9\,\text{ft}^2)$
	$= 64\,\text{m}^2$	$= 28.26\,\text{ft}^2$
		or 28.26 sq ft

PROBLEM 4

Find the area of each of the following polygons:

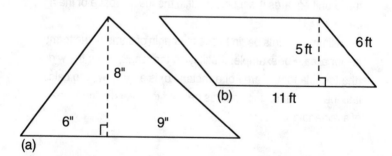

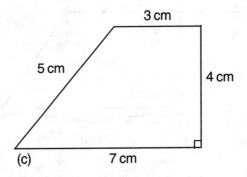

Answers

(a) $A = 60$ sq in
(b) $A = 55$ ft^2 or 55 sq ft
(c) $A = 20$ cm^2

Understanding the formula for finding the area of a rectangle is fairly easy for most children (see problem 3). However, understanding the derivation of the area formulas for triangles, parallelograms, and trapezoids might be a little harder.

Labeled drawings of these figures, including the formulas for their areas, are shown below:

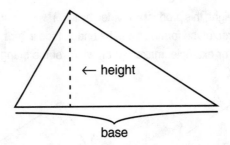

Triangle: $A = \frac{bh}{2}$ (Area is the product of the base and height divided by 2.)

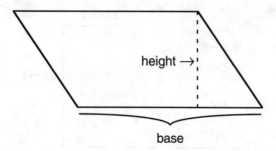

Parallelogram: $A = bh$ (Area is the product of the base and height.)

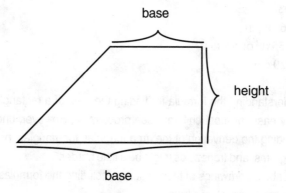

Trapezoid: $A = \dfrac{(b_1 + b_2)h}{2}$ (Area is the sum of the bases multiplied by the height; this product is divided by two.)

All three of the formulas can be understood in terms of a rectangle. For example, make two drawings of the triangle and cut them out.

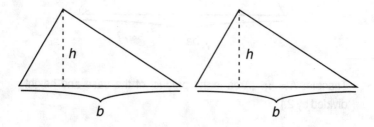

Cut one of the triangles into two pieces by cutting along the dotted line. Place this split triangle around the other one, so that a rectangle is formed.

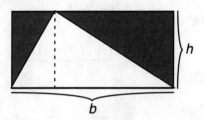

The formula for the area of the rectangle that is formed is $A = bh$.

The formula for the area of the unshaded triangle is half of this: $A = \dfrac{bh}{2}$.

By cutting and reshaping the parallelogram and the trapezoid, your child begins to see how the formulas for the areas of these figures also have their roots in the formula for area of a rectangle.

How to Get the Answer

1. Know the formulas for finding the areas of the given figures.

   Triangle: $\qquad A = \dfrac{bh}{2}$

   Parallelogram: $\quad A = bh$

   Trapezoid: $\qquad A = \dfrac{(b_1 + b_2)h}{2}$

2. Substitute the values for the given dimensions and solve.

   (a) Triangle: $\quad A = \dfrac{bh}{2}$

   $$= \dfrac{15 \text{ in} \cdot 8 \text{ in}}{2}$$

   $$= \dfrac{120 \text{ sq in}}{2}$$

   $$= 60 \text{ sq in}$$

(b) Parallelogram: $A = bh$
$$= 5 \text{ ft} \cdot 11 \text{ ft}$$
$$= 55 \text{ sq ft}$$

(c) Trapezoid: $A = \dfrac{(b_1 + b_2)h}{2}$

$$= \dfrac{(3 \text{ cm} + 7 \text{ cm})4 \text{ cm}}{2}$$

$$= \dfrac{(10 \text{ cm})4 \text{ cm}}{2}$$

$$= \dfrac{40 \text{ sq cm}}{2}$$

$$= 20 \text{ cm}^2$$

PROBLEM 5

From the list of properties below, choose the number of each property that applies to each of the following three-dimensional solids and write it underneath the figure.

List of Properties

1 All the faces are polygons.
2 The bases are parallel and congruent.
3 The lateral faces are parallelograms.
4 The base(s) are circle(s).
5 Has only one base.
6 Made with a curved surface.
7 Has no base.

Three-Dimensional Solids

Cone

(properties)

Cylinder

(properties)

Cube

(properties)

Pyramid

(properties)

Rectangular
Prism

(properties)

Sphere

(properties)

Triangular
Prism

(properties)

Answers

Cone: 4, 5, 6

Cylinder: 2, 4, 6

Cube: 1, 2, 3

Pyramid: 1, 5

Rectangular Prism: 1, 2, 3

Sphere: 6, 7

Triangular Prism: 1, 2, 3

Figures like circles, squares, and triangles have all of their points on one flat surface, called a plane.

Examples of plane figures:

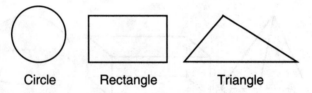

Circle   Rectangle   Triangle

When a figure has points in more than one plane, it is called a solid, a space, or a three-dimensional figure.

Examples of space figures:

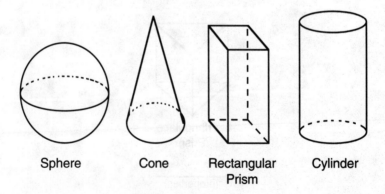

Sphere   Cone   Rectangular   Cylinder
                                   Prism

In a plane figure, two sides (i.e., lines) meet at a common point called a *vertex*. In a space figure, the sides are called *faces* (which are flat surfaces that enclose the inner space). When two faces meet, a line segment, called an *edge,* is formed.

A cube has six faces and twelve edges.

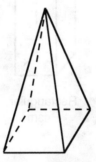

This pyramid has five faces and eight edges.

The face upon which the solid seems to rest is called the *base.* (A figure can have more than one designated base.)

The bases of this cylinder are shaded.

Some space figures (such as cones, cylinders, or spheres) have curved surfaces. On the other hand, some have all their faces made from polygons. The members of this latter group are called *polyhedrons*. *Prisms* are special polyhedrons that meet two criteria (see the examples below):

    1. Two of the faces must be parallel and congruent. (These are the designated bases.)

    2. The remaining faces (called *lateral faces*) are parallelograms.

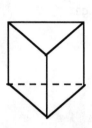 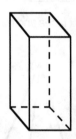 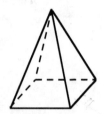

| Triangular Prism | Rectangular Prism | Pyramid—This is not a prism, but it is a polyhedron. |

How to Get the Answer

1. A cone looks like a dunce cap. It has a curved surface and its one base is a circle. (Answer: 4, 5, 6).

2. An example of a cylinder is an oatmeal container. It has a curved surface and two circular bases that are parallel and congruent. (Answer: 2, 4, 6).

3. Dice are good examples of cubes. All the faces are squares, which means they are polygons as well as parallelograms. The bases are parallel and congruent. (Answer: 1, 2, 3).

4. A pyramid has one base. The lateral faces of a pyramid are triangles, which means they are polygons.(Answer: 1, 5).

5. A cereal box is an example of a rectangular prism. All of the faces are rectangles, which means they are polygons, by

definition, as well as parallelograms. The bases are parallel and congruent. (Answer: 1, 2, 3).

6. A sphere is the solid counterpart of a circle. All the points on the surface of a sphere are equally distant from its center. A sphere has only a curved surface. It has no base. (Answer: 6, 7).

7. A wedge illustrates the shape of a triangular prism. The lateral faces of a triangular prism are parallelograms, and, therefore, by definition polygons. The two parallel bases are congruent triangles. (Answer: 1, 2, 3).

PROBLEM 6

Find the surface areas of each of the following solids:

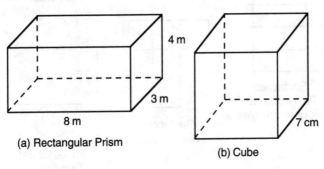

4 m

3 m

8 m

(a) Rectangular Prism

7 cm

(b) Cube

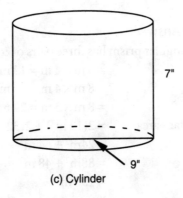

7"

9"

(c) Cylinder

Answers
(a) 136 m²
(b) 294 cm²
(c) 325 sq in

> The *surface area* is the measure of the total outer surface of a solid. Your child finds this area by first finding the areas of the faces of the solid, then adding these areas together. Sometimes, it is easier to see the faces of a space figure when it is flattened out.

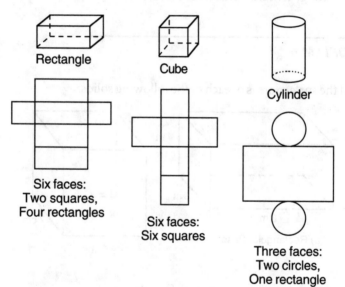

Rectangle

Cube

Cylinder

Six faces:
Two squares,
Four rectangles

Six faces:
Six squares

Three faces:
Two circles,
One rectangle

How to Get the Answer

1. (a) The rectangular prism has three pairs of congruent bases:

Area (1)	$= 3\,\text{m} \times 4\,\text{m} = 12\,\text{m}^2$
Area (2)	$= 8\,\text{m} \times 4\,\text{m} = 32\,\text{m}^2$
Area (3)	$= 8\,\text{m} \times 3\,\text{m} = 24\,\text{m}^2$
Total surface area	$= 2(12\,\text{m}^2) + 2(32\,\text{m}^2) + 2(24\,\text{m}^2)$
	$= 24\text{m}^2 + 64\,\text{m}^2 + 48\,\text{m}^2$
	$= 88\text{m}^2 + 48\,\text{m}^2$
	$= 136\,\text{m}^2$

(b) The cube has six congruent faces:

Area of square	$= 7 \text{ cm} \times 7 \text{ cm} = (7 \text{ cm})^2 = 49 \text{ cm}^2$
Total surface area	$= 6 (49 \text{ cm}^2)$
	$= 294 \text{ cm}^2$

(c) The cylinder has two congruent circular bases and one rectangle:

Area of circle	$= \pi (4.5 \text{ in})^2$ (The radius is half the diameter.)
	$= \pi (20.25 \text{ sq in})$
	$= 63.59 \text{ sq in}$
Area of rectangle	$= \text{width} \times \text{circumference of circle}$
	$= 7 \text{ in} \times 2 \pi r$
	$= 7 \text{ in} \times 2 (3.14)(4.5 \text{ in})$
	$= 7 \text{ in} \times 28.26 \text{ in}$
	$= 197.82 \text{ sq in}$
Total surface area	$= 2 (63.59 \text{ sq in}) + 197.82 \text{ sq in}$
	$= 325 \text{ sq in}$

PROBLEM 7

Find the volume:

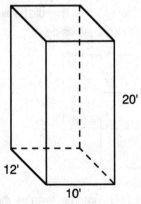

20'

12'

10'

(a) Rectangular Prism

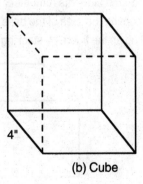

4"

(b) Cube

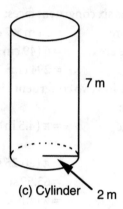

7 m

(c) Cylinder   2 m

Answer

(a) $V = 2400$ cu ft
(b) $V = 64$ cu in
(c) $V = 87.92$ cu m

The *volume* is the measure of the space contained inside a solid. The formula for finding the volume of a rectangular prism and a cube is

$v = l\,w\,h$ (Volume is the product of the length, the width, and the height.)

Some students remember this formula by thinking in terms of summing the area of the base *h* number of times. It would be like filling up the figure by stacking base-size planes inside.

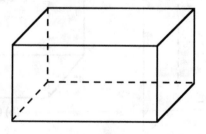

The formula for a cylinder, $V = (\pi\,r^2)h$, can be seen as the area of the base $(\pi\,r^2)$ taken *h* number of times. (This would be

like filling up the cylinder by stacking circles that are the same size as the base.)

How to Get the Answer

1. Know the formulas for finding the volume of the given figures:
   For a rectangular prism (a) and a cube (b): $V = lwh$
   For a cylinder (c): $V = (\pi r^2)h$

2. (a) V $= (12\,ft)\,(10\,ft)\,(20\,ft)$
   $= (120\,sq\,ft)\,(20\,ft)$
   $= 2400\,ft^3$ or 2400 cu ft

   (b) V $= (4\,in)\,(4\,in)\,(4\,in)$
   $= (16\,in^2)\,(4\,in)$
   $= 64\,in^3$ or 64 cu in

   (c) V $= 3.14\,(2\,m)^2\,(7\,m)$
   $= 3.14\,(4\,m^2)\,(7\,m)$
   $= (12.56\,m^2)\,(7\,m)$
   $= 87.92m^3$ or 87.92 cu m

PROBLEM 8

Find the volume:

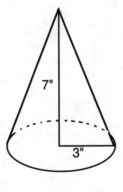 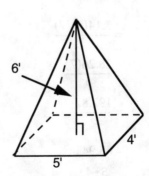

(a) Cone   (b) Pyramid

Answers

(a) $V = 65.94$ cu in

(b) $V = 40$ cu ft

The volume of a cone is found by finding the area of the circular base (πr^2), multiplying this by the height (h), and taking ⅓ of this product:

$$V = \frac{\pi r^2 h}{3}$$

The volume of a pyramid is found by finding the area of the base ($l \cdot w$), multiplying this by the height (h), and taking ⅓ of this product:

$$V = \frac{lwh}{3}$$

How to Get the Answer

1. Know the formulas for finding the volumes of the given figures.

    For a cone (a): $V = \frac{\pi r^2 h}{3}$

    For a pyramid (b): $V = \frac{lwh}{3}$

2. Substitute the given values and solve.

    (a) $v = \dfrac{3.14(3)^2(7)}{3}$

    $= \dfrac{3.14(9)(7)}{3}$

    $= \dfrac{28.26(7)}{3}$

    $= \dfrac{197.82}{3}$

    $= 65.94 \text{ in}^3$

    (b) $v = \dfrac{5 \cdot 4 \cdot 6}{3}$

$$= \frac{20 \cdot 6}{3}$$

$$= \frac{120}{3}$$

$$= 40 \text{ ft}^3$$

PROBLEM 9

Find the surface area and the volume:

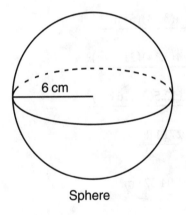

6 cm

Sphere

Answer

Surface area = 452.16 cm²

Volume = 904.32 cm³

> As the formulas get more complicated, much care must be taken when substituting the given values. Most students run into difficulties by trying to do too many calculations in a single step. The best strategy is to record each product. Then it is possible to trace the source of an error if one occurs.

How to Get the Answer

1. Know the formulas for finding the surface area and volume of a sphere.

   Surface area: $A = 4\pi r^2$

   Volume: $V = \dfrac{4\pi r^3}{3}$

2. Substitute in the values and solve.

   Surface area: $A = 4\,(3.14)\,(6\text{ cm})^2$
   $$= 4\,(3.14)\,(36\text{ cm}^2)$$
   $$= (12.56)\,(36\text{ cm}^2)$$
   $$= 452.16\text{ cm}^2$$

   Volume: $V = \dfrac{4\pi r^3}{3}$

   $$= \frac{4(3.14)(6\text{ cm})^3}{3}$$

   $$= \frac{4(3.14)(216\text{ cm})^3}{3}$$

   $$= \frac{(12.56)(216\text{ cm})^3}{3}$$

   $$= \frac{2712.96\text{ cm}^3}{3}$$

   $$= 904.32\text{ cm}^3$$

6 PREALGEBRA

Problem

Nancy needs to score a 90 on her French quiz to maintain her average. She is certain that she got the twelve-point bonus question correct; how many other questions must she answer correctly if they are worth six points each?

By the end of a one-year prealgebra course, most middle schoolers would know (a) how to write an equation to solve this problem, (b) how to graph the written equation, and (c) how to use this graph to solve additional related questions.

In math, we have letters and symbols (called variables) that take the place of unknown quantities. We can find the value of these unknown quantities by using the basic principles of algebra. Prealgebra introduces students to some of the basic principles before they take a formal one-year algebra course.

The Language of Algebra
When we communicate with others, we use phrases and sentences. Phrases are partial statements and sentences are complete thoughts. In math, we use phrases and sentences, too. Phrases are

called mathematical expressions and complete thoughts are called equations—both are part of the language of algebra.

Perhaps when you were a student, only a small, selected group of 7th- and 8th-grade students were considered able enough to handle algebra. This was true because algebra was seen not so much as a mathematical language as it was a set of rules and procedures that needed to be drilled and memorized. Luckily, this is changing today. With the emphasis on problem solving starting in even the earliest elementary grades, children are encouraged to think of solutions in ways that make sense to them. As they work to devise, to test, and to revise strategies, they are involved in peer discussions that call for a need for a common language. Algebra provides both the vocabulary and a storehouse of methods that can be applied to a variety of problems—including the one your child might be trying to solve. In this light, a procedure or formula is a tool and not a meaningless headache.

The vocabulary of prealgebra includes terms such as *graph, number line, absolute value, opposite numbers, evaluate, substitute, solve, inverse operation, two-step equation, open sentence, like terms, numerical coefficient, constant, power, algebraic fraction, solutions, table of values, ordered pair, coordinate plane* and *function.*

Take time now to skim through and preview the sample problems. When you are ready, work through them. Compare your responses with the given answers. Afterward, turn to the "How-To Guide" for an outline of not only how to get the answer, but also additional information about prealgebra for your middle schooler. The more you know, the more equipped you will be to help your child become a better math student.

Topics in This Chapter

Graphing points on a number line

Comparing positive and negative numbers using the symbols >
    (greater than) and < (less than)

Finding the absolute value of positive and negative numbers

Adding and subtracting positive and negative numbers

Multiplying and dividing positive and negative numbers
Writing mathematical phrases and equations
Evaluating equations
Solving open equations
Simplifying powers using the law of exponents
Factoring powers
Finding the GCF (greatest common factor) and LCM (least
    common multiple) for terms with variables
Finding equivalent algebraic fractions (fractions with variables)
Simplifying an algebraic fraction
Adding and subtracting algebraic fractions
Finding the LCD (least common denominator)
Multiplying and dividing algebraic fractions
Finding coordinates and points on a graph
Creating a table of values for an equation
Graphing an equation

SAMPLE PROBLEMS

1. Graph these points on a number line and label them with the
   given letters:

   $A: 1\frac{1}{2}$ $B: -1$ $C: -2.6$ $D: 0$ $E: 2$

2. Use the correct symbol ($<$ or $>$) between each pair of numbers:
   (a) -7 ___ -8   (b) 18 ___ 35
   (c) 0 ___ -10   (d) -4 ___ 3

3. Simplify:

   (a) $|-10|$ (b) $|3.2|$

   (c) $\left|-\frac{1}{2}\right|$ (d) $|-10-(-6)|$

4. Add:
   (a) -42 + -31   (b) +42 + -31
   (c) -42 + +31   (d) +42 + +31

5. Subtract:
   (a) 31 - 37
   (b) -8 - (-21)
   (c) 0 - 41
   (d) -5 - 17

6. Multiply or divide as indicated:
   (a) $-13 \cdot 2$
   (b) $-21 \cdot -3$
   (c) $+69 \div +3$
   (d) $+54 \div -3$

7. Translate these word phrases into mathematical equations or phrases:
   (a) the sum of a number x and 7
   (b) the sum of x and 6 is 34
   (c) 7 less than the number x
   (d) 34 decreased by a number x
   (e) 34 increased by 6 is x
   (f) 34 decreased by 7 is x
   (g) 7 times the number x
   (h) six more than a number 34
   (i) 34 decreased by a number x is 7

8. Evaluate: $z^3 + 9$, when $z = 2$.

9. Solve:
   (a) $w + 19 = 51$
   (b) $p - 38 = 55$
   (c) $13N = 91$
   (d) $\frac{M}{34} = 22$

10. Solve: $\frac{z}{-9} + 8 = 0$

11. Solve: $63 = 8 + 8z + 10 + z$

12. Simplify by using the laws of exponents:
    (a) $z^5 \cdot z^3$
    (b) $\frac{m^7}{m^4}$

13. Give the algebraic factorization of
    (a) $30m^3$
    (b) $63a^4b^3$

14. Find the GCF and LCM of $36m^4n^3$ and $12mn$.

15. Solve: $\frac{12w}{5q} = \frac{?}{15qw}$

16. Simplify: $\frac{18c}{24c^2n}$

17. Add or subtract as indicated:

    (a) $\dfrac{m}{n} - \dfrac{2z}{n}$

    (b) $\dfrac{3q}{4p} + \dfrac{7q}{4p}$

18. Find the LCD:

    (a) $\dfrac{3y}{2x}, \dfrac{1}{6xy^2}$

    (b) $\dfrac{4}{d^2c}, \dfrac{3d}{7m}$

19. Add or subtract as indicated:

    (a) $\dfrac{7n}{8} + \dfrac{m}{12}$

    (b) $\dfrac{4}{ab} - \dfrac{1}{b^2}$

20. Multiply:

    (a) $\dfrac{9}{b} \cdot \dfrac{2b}{f}$

    (b) $\dfrac{6}{m} \cdot \dfrac{n}{12}$

21. Divide:

    (a) $\dfrac{6z}{m} \div \dfrac{3}{m}$

    (b) $\dfrac{7x}{y} \div \dfrac{35x^2}{y}$

22. Use the coordinate plane pictured below.

    (a) Give the coordinates of the points: A___ C___.

    (b) Name the point for each of the ordered pairs: (0, -2)___

       (-3,4)___

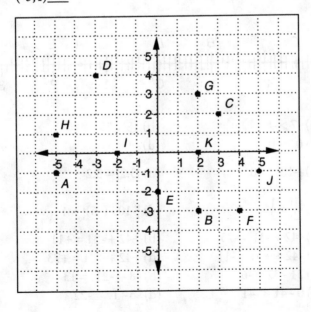

23. Maureen can order CDs from her record club for $6.00 each.
There is a $3.00 shipping and handling charge per order—
not per CD.

(a) If you let c = cost and n = the number of CDs to be ordered,
write an equation that Maureen could use each time to
calculate her cost for a given order.

(b) Using your equation, complete the following table of
values for the given number of CDs ordered:

n	c
1	
2	
3	
4	

(c) Graph the equation.

(d) If Maureen wanted to keep her cost under $40.00, what is
the maximum number of CDs she can order? (Use the
graph to help you.)

Answers

1.

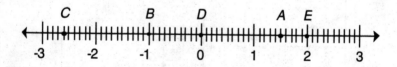

2. (a) -7 > -8   (b) 18 < 35
   (c) 0 > -10   (d) -4 < 3

3. (a) $|-10| = 10$ (b) $|3.2| = 3.2$

   (c) $\left|\frac{1}{2}\right| = \frac{1}{2}$ (d) $|-10 - (-6)| = 4$

4. (a) -42 + -31 = -73   (b) +42 + -31 = +11
   (c) -42 + +31 = -11   (d) +42 + +31 = +73

5. (a) 31 - 37 = -6   (b) -8 - (-21) = 13
   (c) 0 - 41 = -41   (d) -5 - 17 = -22

6 (a) $-13 \cdot 2 = -26$ (b) $-21 \cdot -3 = 63$
   (c) $+69 \div +3 = 23$ (d) $+54 \div -3 = -18$

7. (a) $x + 7$ (b) $x + 6 = 34$ (c) $x - 7$
   (d) $34 - x$ (e) $34 + 6 = x$ (f) $34 - 7 = x$
   (g) $7x$ (h) $34 + 6$ (i) $34 - x = 7$

8. $z^3 + 9 = 17$, when $z = 2$

9. (a) $w = 32$ (b) $p = 93$
   (c) $N = 7$ (d) $M = 748$

10. $z = 72$

11. $z = 5$

12. (a) $z^5 \cdot z^3 = z^8$ (b) $\dfrac{m^7}{m^4} = m^3$

13. (a) $30m^3 = 2 \cdot 3 \cdot 5 \cdot m \cdot m \cdot m$
   (b) $63a^4b^3 = 3 \cdot 3 \cdot 7 \cdot a \cdot a \cdot a \cdot a \cdot b \cdot b \cdot b$

14. The GCF is $12mn$. The LCM is $36m^4n^3$.

15. (a) $\dfrac{12w}{5q} = \dfrac{36w^2}{15qw}$

16. $\dfrac{18c}{24c^2n} = \dfrac{3}{4cn}$

17. (a) $\dfrac{m}{n} - \dfrac{2z}{n} = \dfrac{m - 2z}{n}$

   (b) $\dfrac{3q}{4p} + \dfrac{7q}{4p} = \dfrac{10q}{4p} = \dfrac{5q}{2p}$

18. (a) $6xy^2$ (b) $7cd^2m$

19. (a) $\dfrac{7n}{8} + \dfrac{m}{12} = \dfrac{21n + 2m}{24}$

   (b) $\dfrac{4}{ab} - \dfrac{1}{b^2} = \dfrac{4b - a}{ab^2}$

20. (a) $\dfrac{9}{b} \cdot \dfrac{2b}{f} = \dfrac{18}{f}$ (b) $\dfrac{6}{m} \cdot \dfrac{n}{12} = \dfrac{n}{2m}$

21. (a) $\dfrac{6z}{m} \div \dfrac{3}{m} = 2z$ (b) $\dfrac{7x}{y} \div \dfrac{35x^2}{y} = \dfrac{1}{5x}$

22. (a) $A(-5,-1)$ $C(3,2)$
   (b) $(0,-2)$ E $(-3,4)$ D

23. (a) $c = 6n + 3$

(b)

n	c
1	9
2	15
3	21
4	27

(c)

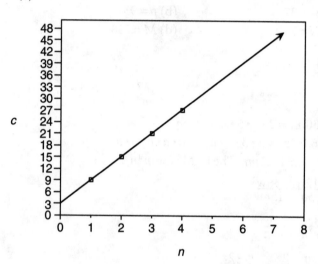

(d) 6 CDs

HOW-TO GUIDE

PROBLEM 1

Graph these points on a number line and label them with the given letters:

$A: 1\frac{1}{2}$ $B: -1$ $C: -2.6$ $D: 0$ $E: 2$

Answer

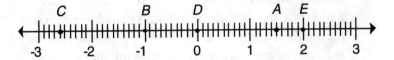

Negative numbers are more commonplace in your child's world than they were for you at a similar age. Children today hear about wind-chill factors that are expressed as negative numbers; they are familiar with space shuttle countdowns expressed as, "minus 10 minutes and counting." Nevertheless, they may not fully grasp the concept. For example, they may have trouble understanding that the value of -5 is less than the value of -3.

A number line is a good tool for visualizing where negative numbers fall in the ordering scheme. This problem is designed to evaluate your child's ability to draw a number line and to graph positive and negative numbers on this line.

Once children learn that positive numbers are the numbers that they have been using all along, they are given the option of showing the positive sign or leaving it understood.

How to Get the Answer

Steps for drawing a number line accurately:

1. Draw a horizontal line.

2. Place short perpendicular marking lines at equally spaced intervals.

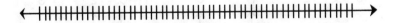

3. When both positive and negative numbers (such as those in this problem) are involved, it is important to place a zero on

the number line (this is called the *origin*). Negative numbers are placed to the left of the origin and positive numbers to the right. Zero is typically placed somewhere in the middle, but it is not an absolute requirement. For this example, we are going to place it in the middle.

4. Label the marking lines with correctly ordered numbers that are appropriate for the problem. What is appropriate numbering for this problem? If we let each marking be an *integer* (i.e., a whole number), we will run into trouble when we graph the points for (*A*), a fraction, and (*C*), a decimal. Instead, let each marking line be a tenth. Since 1/2 is the same as 0.5, all the numbers listed in the problem can be graphed easily. So they are easily recognized, make the marking lines for the origin and the whole numbers longer than the others.

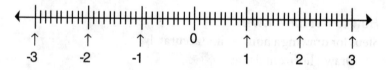

5. Locate where the given number would fall and graph the spot by placing a dot.

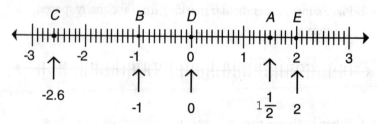

PROBLEM 2

Use the correct symbol (< or >) between each pair of numbers:
(a) -7 ___ -8   (b) 18 ___ 35
(c) 0 ___ -10   (d) -4 ___ 3

Answers
(a) -7 > -8   (b) 18 < 35
(c) 0 > -10   (d) -4 < 3

Algebra is a language. This type of problem is usually given as an oral exercise to test how well your child has mastered reading mathematical expressions. At this stage, your child must begin seeing mathematical symbols as a way of replacing words and phrases. Two of the symbols that your child should know are <, which replaces the words "is less than," and >, which replaces the words "is greater than."

Unfortunately, your child might have learned to remember these symbols this way: "The 'alligator' (i.e. <) always eats the largest number," meaning that the child is to place the symbol with its wide end next to the larger number. Although this is a way to show how to make a true statement, it does not teach how to read the expression. Learning to read mathematic expressions from left to right is essential.

How to Get the Answer
1. If necessary, draw a number line that displays most of the numbers in the problem. Keep in mind that the number farther to the left on a number line is the lesser of two numbers.

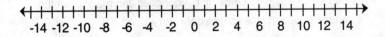

2. Ask yourself the following question:
   Q. How would I make a true statement reading the two given
   numbers from left to right?
   A. Negative seven is greater than negative eight.
3. Substitute the proper symbols for the words:
   (a) $-7 > -8$
4. Extend the number line to 35 for (b) and repeat steps 2 and 3
   for (b), (c), and (d).

PROBLEM 3

Simplify:

(a) $|-10|$ (b) $|3.2|$

(c) $\left|-\frac{1}{2}\right|$ (d) $|-10-(-6)|$

Answers

(a) $|-10| = 10$ (b) $|3.2| = 3.2$

(c) $\left|-\frac{1}{2}\right| = \frac{1}{2}$ (d) $|-10 - (-6)| = 4$

There are times when your child will be asked to work with negative and positive numbers and to disregard the negative sign as
part of the answers. In these types of problems, the amount of
change is more important than the direction of the change (i.e.,
we are not concerned if it was a gain or a loss). For example,
suppose the temperature at noon was +2° F, but at 6:30 PM was
-12° F, and we want to know how many degrees the temperature
changed. By using a number line, your child can readily see the
change by counting the spaces between +2 and -12.

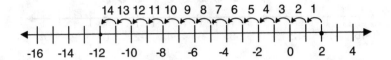

There is a 14° difference. In fact, if the situation had been reversed and the temperature had been -12° at noon and +2° at 6:30 PM, the difference still would have been 14 degrees.

Situations in which we are concerned with distance, but not direction, are designated by placing the number or numerical phrase inside two vertical parallel lines and is known as finding the *absolute value.*

When there is only a single number inside the parallel lines, such as

|-8| (which is read as "the absolute value of negative 8"),

we are asking "How far is the given number from zero on the number line?"

When there is a subtraction phrase within the parallel lines, such as:

|-12-2| = 14 (which is read as "the absolute value of negative 12 minus 2 is 14"),

we are asking for the distance between the two given numbers on the number line.

The absolute value is always a positive number.

How to Get the Answer

1. If necessary, draw a number line that displays most of the numbers in the problem.

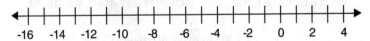

2. If there is a single number inside the absolute value sign, find that number and zero on the number line. Then count the spaces between the two numbers.

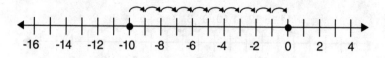

$$|-10| = 10$$

3. If there is a subtraction problem inside the absolute value sign, find the two numbers on the number line, then count the spaces between them.

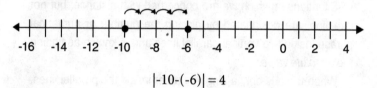

$$|-10-(-6)| = 4$$

___

PROBLEM 4

Add:
(a) -42 + -31   (b) +42 + -31
(c) -42 + +31   (d) +42 + +31

Answers

(a) -42 + -31 = -73   (b) +42 + -31 = +11
(c) -42 + +31 = -11   (d) +42 + +31 = +73

This problem is designed to assess how well students have mastered the rules for adding negative and positive numbers.

Addition of negative and positive numbers begins with the use of a concrete model. For example, to add -11+ 7, they might write:

- - - - - - - - - - - to represent negative 11.

Directly underneath this they would place seven plus signs for the positive 7:

- - - - - - - - - - -

+ + + + + + +

In science, students have been exposed to the concept of opposite charges neutralizing one another. With this idea in mind, they "loop" pairs of plus and minus signs to show that these will be eliminated.

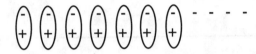

What will remain are 4 negative signs, representing the answer of negative four:

-11 + +7 = -4

As children work with very large and very small numbers, however, concrete models can become tedious. Rules are given to codify the patterns that they have already begun to notice through repeated use of these models.

How to Get the Answer

1. Find all the examples in which both the addends have the same sign. Apply one of these two rules to determine the sign of the answer:

   positive + positive = positive
   negative + negative = negative

   Now add the numerals (meaning, add the two numbers as if the negative or positive signs were not there).

   (a) -42 + -31 = -73   (d) +42 + +31 = +73

2. Find the examples in which the addends have different signs and apply the following steps:

   STEP 1: Remember that absolute value can be thought of as the number without the sign. With this is mind, determine the sign of the answer. It will be the same sign as the addend(s) with the larger absolute value.

   (b) +42 + -31 = positive   (c) -42 + +31 = negative

   STEP 2: Find the "number part" of each answer by subtracting the absolute value of each addend.

(b) +42 + -31 = 11   (c) -42 + +31 = -11
(NOTE: The number portion of both of these answers is 11
    because 31, the absolute value of both -31 and 31, when it is
    subtracted from 42, which is the absolute value of both 42
    and -42, is 11.)

PROBLEM 5

Subtract:
(a) 31 - 37   (b) -8 - (-21)
(c) 0 - 41   (d) -5 - 17

Answers
(a) 31 - 37 = -6   (b) -8 - (-21) = 13
(c) 0 - 41 = -41   (d) -5 - 17 = -22

Mastering the rules for adding negative and positive numbers is
one of the toughest tasks in prealgebra. It makes it easier on
everyone to wait until these rules have been mastered with addition before moving on to subtraction. The advantage in allowing
the time to do this is that children are more likely to discover for
themselves that the same rules for addition can be used in subtraction. This discovery is the result of an understanding of the
concept of opposite numbers and how these opposites connect
the operations of addition and subtraction.

On a number line, a number and its opposite are the same
distance away from zero, but in opposite directions. (5 and -5 are
opposites. They are both 5 units away from zero).

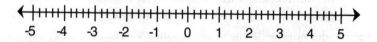

Eventually your child will figure out that when a number is
added to a quantity, the answer is the same as the answer

obtained when subtracting its opposite. Note the example below:

Adding -37 to 100 gives the same answer as subtracting 37 from 100

$100 + -37 = 63$

$100 - 37 = 63$

With this knowledge, a student can write every subtraction problem as an addition problem. The advantage of this rewriting is that the same rules can be used to do both addition and subtraction.

How to Get the Answer

1. Remember that subtracting a number is the same as adding its opposite. Use this information to rewrite the problem by (a) leaving the first number of the given problem the same, (b) changing the minus sign following this first number to a plus sign, and (c) replacing the final number with its opposite.

   In the following examples, the original subtraction problem is on the left of the equal sign, and the equivalent addition problem is on its right.

   (a) $\quad 31 - 37 = 31 + -37$

   (b) $-8 - (-21) = -8 + 21$

   (c) $\quad 0 - 41 = 0 + -41$

   (d) $\quad -5 - 17 = -5 + -17$

2. Remember that adding two numbers that have the same sign is like adding numbers without regard to the signs (positive + positive = positive, and negative + negative = negative). Adding two numbers that have different signs is like subtracting the numbers without regard to the signs. The sign of the answer is determined by the addend with the larger absolute value.

   (a) $\quad 31 + -37 = -6$

   (b) $\quad -8 + 21 = 13$

   (c) $\quad 0 + -41 = -41$

   (d) $\quad -5 + -17 = -22$

PROBLEM 6

Multiply or divide as indicated:
(a) -13 • 2   (b) -21 • -3
(c) +69 ÷ +3   (d) +54 ÷ -3

Answers
(a) -13 • 2 = -26   (b) -21 • -3 = 63
(c) +69 ÷ +3 = 23   (d) +54 ÷ -3 = -18

The question teachers hear very often when teaching multiplication and division of negative and positive numbers is, How can two negatives give a positive? Some children gain an understanding of this through language and the concept of a double negative. (For example, the statement, "It's not not raining," implies that it is raining.)

Some students can follow a step-by-step mathematical explanation such as the following:

$$-7(0) = 0 \quad \text{(Any number times zero is zero.)}$$

$$-7(2 + -2) = 0 \quad \text{(Because a number added to its opposite is zero, we can substitute } 2 + -2 \text{ for zero.)}$$

$$-7(2) + (-7)(-2) = 0 \quad \text{(We applied the distributive property as described in Chapter 2.)}$$

$$-14 + (-7)(-2) = 0 \quad (-7 \bullet 2 = -14, \text{ because a negative times a positive equals a negative.)}$$

$$(-7)(-2) = 14 \quad \text{(To get a true equation, our answer must be a positive 14. Thus, a negative times a negative equals a positive.)}$$

Be aware that regardless of how many models are devised to show why two negatives are positive, your child might still say he or she doesn't understand why. If that happens, encourage your child to concentrate on the *how* and not the *why*. Some rules need to be used before they are completely understood; this might be one example.

How to Get the Answer

1. Know the rules for multiplying and dividing negative and positive numbers to determine the sign of the answer:

   positive × positive = positive   positive ÷ positive = positive
   negative × negative = positive   negative ÷ negative = positive
   positive × negative = negative   positive ÷ negative = negative
   negative × positive = negative   negative ÷ positive = negative

2. Use the rules to determine the sign of the answer.

   (a) -13 • 2 = negative   (b) -21 • -3 = positive
   (c) +69 ÷ +3 = positive   (d) +54 ÷ -3 = negative

3. Multiply (or divide) the numbers as usual (as if the signs were not present).

   (a) -13 • 2 = -26   (b) -21 • -3 = 63
   (c) +69 ÷ +3 = 23   (d) +54 ÷ -3 = -18

PROBLEM 7

Translate these word phrases into mathematical equations or phrases:

(a) the sum of a number x and 7
(b) the sum of x and 6 is 34
(c) 7 less than the number x
(d) 34 decreased by a number x
(e) 34 increased by 6 is x
(f) 34 decreased by 7 is x
(g) 7 times the number x
(h) six more than a number 34
(i) 34 decreased by a number x is 7

Answers

(a) $x + 7$ (b) $x + 6 = 34$ (c) $x - 7$
(d) $34 - x$ (e) $34 + 6 = x$ (f) $34 - 7 = x$
(g) $7x$ (h) $34 + 6$ (i) $34 - x = 7$

One of the purposes of algebra is to make problem solving easier by helping us to see the problem more clearly. With algebra, we can represent information we are given as mathematical expressions and equations. These expressions and equations allow us to move through the problem with greater ease, and we gain faster access to the solution.

When studying prealgebra, children start to develop the skill of translating language phrases and sentences into mathematical expressions and equations. To do this effectively, they must be able to identify the operation (or operations) that are implied by the language phrasing. In addition, they must learn how to construct an equation that correctly represents the problem. Obviously, the solution to an incorrectly written equation will be meaningless.

Below is an alphabetized list of some commonly used words and phrases, as well as the operation that is implied by them:

Word	The Implied Operation
add, add to	+
decreased by	-
difference (the difference when)	-
divided by	÷
from now	+
increased by	+
less than	-
minus	-
more than	+
multiply, multiply by	×
plus	+
product, the product of	×
quotient, the quotient of	÷
subtract	-
sum, the sum of	+
times	×
total, the total of	+

Once the operation is known, the next task is finding the components of the operation and representing them in symbols. For example, consider the phrase, Mary's age ten years from now. The words "from now" imply that we are going to have to add. We now need to find the addends (the numbers to be added). If we represent the words "Mary's age" as a variable (*a*), our translation would be "*a* + 10."

One of the challenges of determining a symbolic representation of a situation is that a mathematical expression or equation can be used for several different statements. "A box of candy with a 10 cent tax," "John works 10 hours more than Tom," and "The temperature increasing by 10 degrees," all can be reasonably represented by the mathematical expression, "*a* + 10."

How to Get the Answer

1. Decide which operation is implied by the words used in the given phrase or sentence:
   (a) and (b) "the sum" implies addition
   (c) "less than" implies subtraction
   (d), (f), (i) "decreased by" implies subtraction
   (e) "increased by" implies addition
   (g) "times" implies multiplication
   (h) "more than" implies addition

2. Use a variable (*x* and *y* are commonly used) for any unknown quantity and substitute numerals for number words. Read the sentence correctly to help you place the symbols properly. Keep in mind that equations usually represent sentences, and expressions usually represent phrases.
   (a) $x + 7$
   (b) $x + 6 = 34$
   (c) $x - 7$
   (d) $34 - x$
   (e) $34 + 6 = x$
   (f) $34 - 7 = x$
   (g) $7x$ (Remember that a number placed right next to a variable implies multiplication.)

(h) $34 + 6$

(i) $34 - x = 7$

PROBLEM 8

Evaluate: $z^3 + 9$, when $z = 2$.

Answer

$z^3 + 9 = 17$, when $z = 2$

In mathematics, the directions to a problem often can mean more than what initially meets the eye. One word can signal students to apply a certain sequence of procedures. The word *evaluate* is such a word. To your children, this word tells them to (a) put in the given value for the variable and (b) carry out the operation (mathematical procedure) indicated by the equation or expression.

How to Get the Answer

1. Replace the variables with the given values.

   $2^3 + 9$ (z was replaced by 2.)

2. Perform the operations (multiplication followed by addition).

   $2 \cdot 2 \cdot 2 + 9$ (Remember that 2^3 means that 2 is used as a factor three times.)

   $8 + 9$

   17

PROBLEM 9

Solve:

(a) $w + 19 = 51$ (b) $p - 38 = 55$

(c) $13N = 91$ (d) $\dfrac{M}{34} = 22$

Answers
(a) $w = 32$ (b) $p = 93$
(c) $N = 7$ (d) $M = 748$

An *open equation* is one that has a variable. For example $x + 7 = 13$ is an open equation, but $32 - 18 = 14$ is not.

When the word "solve" is used with an open equation, it means that your child needs to find the value of the variable that will make the equation true.

Some solutions can be readily seen. For example, for $x - 9 = 3$, your child might answer that the solution is $x = 12$. In other equations, such as $-x - 21 = -9$, the solutions are not that obvious. Algebra gives your child a procedure for solving equations that involve changing the form of an equation while maintaining its equality. We call this *transformation*.

As your child solves an equation using transformation, it looks as if quantities are disappearing on one side and reappearing on another. Your child might even speak of "isolating" the variable or "moving" everything away from it.

Students are taught that an equation is like a balance scale. On these scales, if the same amount of weight is added (or subtracted) to both sides simultaneously, the needle stays in the center indicating equality. In equations, if the same operation (addition, subtraction, multiplication, or division) is performed on both sides, using the same quantity, the two sides remain equal. An example would be multiplying both sides of the equation, $14 = 24 - 10$, by two. The result, $28 = 48 - 20$, is still true.

There are two basic rules for doing a transformation:

1. Whichever operation is applied to one side of the equation must also be applied to the other.

2. A transformation is complete when the equation is in the form "$x = \underline{\quad}$."

An example of what an equation would look like before and after a transformation is shown below:

$5x + 7 = 52$ (the unsolved equation)

$x = 9$ (the equation after transformation)

Students seem to be impressed by the fact that, regardless of how the transformation starts, if the same operation is done on both sides, the solution will be the same. What follows are two transformations for the equation $-x - 21 = -9$:

Solution 1:

$-x - 21 + x = -9 + x$ (add x to both sides)

$-21 = -9 + x$ (on the left, $-x + x = 0$)

$-21 + 9 = -9 + x + 9$ (add 9 to both sides)

$-12 = x$ (on the right, $-9 + 9 = 0$; on the left, $-21 + 9 = -12$)

$x = -12$ (law of symmetry of equations, p. 255)

Solution 2:

$-x - 21 + 21 = -9 + 21$ (add 21 to both sides)

$-x = 12$ (on the left, $-21 + 21 = 0$; on the right, $-9 + 21 = 12$)

$x = -12$ (multiply both sides by -1)

Obviously, knowing which operation to apply to both sides saves time. Your child is taught to use an *inverse operation* because an inverse operation will undo the effect of the operation that is present in the original problem. Addition and subtraction are inverse operations, and multiplication and division are inverse operations.

How to Get the Answer

1. Examine the given equation. Make a mental note of both the operation and the number used in the operation:

   (a) $w + 19 = 51$

   Think: "19 is added to the variable. I must subtract a 19 in order to isolate *w* and solve the equation."

   (d) $\frac{M}{34} = 22$

   Think: "The variable is divided by 34. I must multiply by 34 to isolate *M* and solve the equation."

2. Now apply the inverse operation to both sides of the equation:

(a) $w + 19 = 51$

$w + 19 - 19 = 51 - 19$

$w = 32$

(b) $p - 38 = 55$

$p - 38 + 38 = 55 + 38$

$p = 93$

(c) $13N = 91$

$13N \div 13 = 91 \div 13$

$N = 7$

(d) $\dfrac{M}{34} = 22$

$34 \times \dfrac{M}{34} = 22 \times 34$

$M = 748$

PROBLEM 10

Solve: $\dfrac{z}{-9} + 8 = 0$

Answer

$z = 72$

An equation such as $q - 31 = -9$ involves only one operation (the operation of subtraction). The equation $2q - 31 = -9$ involves two operations—the operations of multiplication (2 times q) and subtraction ($2q - 31$).

Equations like $2q - 31 = -9$, are sometimes called *two step equations* because finding the solution requires the application of two inverse operations.

When solving two-step equations and applying the inverse operations, apply addition or subtraction first, followed by multiplication or division.

How to Get the Answer

1. Make a mental note of which two operations are involved in the original equation.

$$\frac{z}{-9} + 8 = 0$$

Think: "The equation contains division and addition."

2. Decide which inverse operations are needed to solve the equation and which one to use first.

Remember: Addition or subtraction should be done first. Multiplication or division should be done last.

Think: "I'll use subtraction, then multiplication."

3. Solve for the variable. Keep in mind that whatever you do on one side, you must do on the other side.

$$\frac{z}{-9} + 8 = 0$$

$\frac{z}{-9} + 8 - 8 = 0 - 8$ (Subtract 8 on both sides.)

$\frac{z}{-9} = -8$ (On the left, $8 - 8 = 0$; on the right, $0 - 8 = -8$.)

$-9 \cdot \frac{z}{-9} = -8 \cdot -9$ (Multiply both sides by a -9.)

$z = 72$ (On the left, -9 cancels the -9 in the denominator; on the right, $-8 \cdot -9 = 72$.)

PROBLEM 11

Solve: $63 = 8 + 8z + 10 + z$

Answer

$z = 5$

The equation, $7 = -4m^2 + 3m + 2 + 5m + 9$ has six terms: 7, $-4m^2$, $3m$, 2, $5m$, and 9. *Terms* are quantities separated by plus or minus signs.

The terms, $2m$, $-4m^2$, and $3m$ all have a variable m, but only $2m$ and $3m$ are considered *like terms* to one another because their variables are exactly alike.

Notice that three of the terms in $7 = -4m^2 + 3m + 2 + 5m + 9$ are numbers without a variable (7, 2, and 9). These are called constant terms. *Constant terms* are considered to be like terms to one another.

Whenever like terms are on the same side of the equation, they should be combined (expressed as one term) before starting the transformation. We add constants $(2 + 9 = 11)$ when combining like terms. To combine like terms that are not constant terms, we add their leading numbers, which are called *numerical coefficients*, as shown in the following example: $3m + 5m = 8m$.

How to Get the Answer

1. Because of the commutative property (p. 57), we are able to rewrite the problem $63 = 8 + 8z + 10 + z$ so that like terms are next to one another. (This helps to reduce errors.)

$$63 = 8z + z + 8 + 10$$

2. Combine like terms to express them as a single term. Keep in mind that z in the equation means $1z$.

$$63 = 9z + 18$$

3. Use transformations to solve for the variable.

$$63 = 9z + 18$$
$$63 - 18 = 9z + 18 - 18$$
$$45 = 9z$$
$$\frac{45}{9} = \frac{9z}{9}$$
$$5 = z$$

PROBLEM 12

Simplify by using the laws of exponents:

(a) $z^5 \cdot z^3$ (b) $\dfrac{m^7}{m^4}$

Answers

(a) $z^5 \cdot z^3 = z^8$ (b) $\dfrac{m^7}{m^4} = m^3$

Expressions such as w^7 are called powers. The small raised number, the 7 in this example, is called the *exponent*. The w, in this example, is the *base*.

Your child can do multiplication and division with two powers that have the same base, for example, m^5 and m^4, if the child knows the factored form of each. See the explanation below.

Power	Factored form
m^5	$m \cdot m \cdot m \cdot m \cdot m$
m^4	$m \cdot m \cdot m \cdot m$

Then $m^5 \cdot m^4 = m \cdot m \cdot m \cdot m \cdot m \cdot m \cdot m \cdot m \cdot m = m^9$

$$\frac{m^5}{m^4} = \frac{m \cdot m \cdot m \cdot m \cdot m}{m \cdot m \cdot m \cdot m}$$

The law of exponents gives your child permission to use the shortcuts that he or she has probably already discovered. They are as follows:

1. To multiply powers that have the same base, add their exponents.

2. To divide powers that have the same base, subtract their exponents.

How to Get the Answer

1. For multiplication: If the bases are the same, keep the base for the answer, then add the exponents of the factors:
   (a) $z^5 \cdot z^3 = z^{5+3} = z^8$

2. For division: If the bases are the same, keep the base for the

answer, then subtract the exponent of the divisor (the power in the denominator) from the exponent of the dividend (the power in the numerator).

(b) $\frac{m^7}{m^4} = m^{7-4} = m^3$

PROBLEM 13

Give the algebraic factorization of
(a) $30m^3$ (b) $63a^4b^3$

Answers
(a) $30m^3 = 2 \cdot 3 \cdot 5 \cdot m \cdot m \cdot m$
(b) $63a^4b^3 = 3 \cdot 3 \cdot 7 \cdot a \cdot a \cdot a \cdot a \cdot b \cdot b \cdot b$

Factors, as stated before, are quantities that are multiplied together. When students are asked to give an *algebraic factorization,* they are being asked to show all the factors that make up the term:

Term	Algebraic factorization
$6t^2$	$2 \cdot 3 \cdot t \cdot t$

Multiplying all the numbers in the algebraic factorization should always produce the original term. This is an excellent way to check if the problem was done correctly.

How to Get the Answer
1. Use a factor tree (p. 48) to help your child express the numerical coefficient (the leading number) as a product of prime numbers.

(a)   30   (b)   63
           / \   / \
         5 · 6   9 · 7
         / / \   / \   \
      5 · 2 · 3 = 2 · 3 · 5   3 · 3 · 7

2. Express each power in factored form.
   (a) $m^3 = m \cdot m \cdot m$
   (b) $a^4 b^3 = a \cdot a \cdot a \cdot a \cdot b \cdot b \cdot b$
3. Write the two parts of the answer as one product.
   (a) $2 \cdot 3 \cdot 5 \cdot m \cdot m \cdot m$
   (b) $3 \cdot 3 \cdot 7 \cdot a \cdot a \cdot a \cdot a \cdot b \cdot b \cdot b$
4. Check the algebraic factorization by multiplying the factors in the answers to see if you get the original term.
   (a) $2 \cdot 3 \cdot 5 \cdot m \cdot m \cdot m = 30m^3$
   $$30m^3 = 30m^3$$
   (b) $3 \cdot 3 \cdot 7 \cdot a \cdot a \cdot a \cdot a \cdot b \cdot b \cdot b = 63a^4 b^3$
   $$63a^4 b^3 = 63a^4 b^3$$

PROBLEM 14

Find the GCF and LCM of $36m^4 n^3$ and $12mn$.

Answer
The GCF is $12mn$. The LCM is $36m^4 n^3$.

The GCF (greatest common factor) and the LCM (least common multiple) are useful when working with fractions. The GCF helps us to reduce the fraction to the lowest terms. For example, if we wanted to reduce $\frac{18}{42}$ to lowest terms and we are told that the GCF for 18 and 42 is 6, we could reduce the fraction in one step (see p. 43), as shown below:

$$\frac{18}{42} = \frac{18 \div 6}{42 \div 6} = \frac{3}{7}$$

The LCM helps when we have to add or subtract fractions that have unlike denominators. For example, consider the problem of adding $\frac{1}{12}$ and $\frac{5}{18}$. The LCM of 12 and 18 is 36, which means that the denominators of the two fractions must be adjusted to 36 before they can be added (see p. 44):

$$\frac{1}{12} = \frac{3}{36}$$
$$+\frac{5}{18} = \frac{10}{36}$$
$$\overline{\hspace{2cm}}$$
$$\frac{13}{36}$$

For terms with variables, the LCM and the GCF are found in the same way as terms without variables.

How to Get the Answer

1. Write out the algebraic factorization of the two given terms.
   $36m^4n^3 = 2 \cdot 2 \cdot 3 \cdot 3 \cdot m \cdot m \cdot m \cdot m \cdot n \cdot n \cdot n$
   $12mn = 2 \cdot 2 \cdot 3 \cdot m \cdot n$

2. Find the common factor pairs by drawing a loop around those factors that are present in both factorizations. (Note: This is not always possible, because there may be no common factors.)

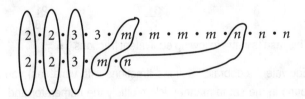

3. From each loop, take out one factor and write a product of those factors.
   $2 \cdot 2 \cdot 3 \cdot m \cdot n$

4. Multiply these factors to get the GCF.
   $12mn = \text{GCF}$

5. To find the LCM:
   (a) Follow steps 1-3 above for finding the GCF.
   $2 \cdot 2 \cdot 3 \cdot m \cdot n$

(b) Beside these factors, write all the factors that were not
looped in step 2.

$$2 \cdot 2 \cdot 3 \cdot m \cdot n \cdot 3 \cdot m \cdot m \cdot m \cdot n \cdot n$$

6. Multiply these factors to get the LCM.

$$36m^4n^3$$

PROBLEM 15

Solve: $\dfrac{12w}{5q} = \dfrac{?}{15qw}$

Answer

(a) $\dfrac{12w}{5q} = \dfrac{36w^2}{15qw}$

One of the ways by which your child has been taught to make an equivalent fraction is by multiplying the numerator and the denominator of the given fraction by the same number:

Given Fraction	Making a New Fraction	New Fraction
$\dfrac{3}{4}$	$\dfrac{3 \times 7}{4 \times 7}$	$\dfrac{21}{28}$

This results in the following equivalent fractions $\dfrac{3}{4} = \dfrac{21}{28}$.

Equivalent algebraic fractions (fractions with variables) can be found in the same manner. We multiply the numerator and the denominator of the given algebraic fraction by the same number or variable:

Given Fraction	Making a New Fraction	New Fraction
$\dfrac{3m}{q}$	$\dfrac{3m \times 2}{q \times 2}$	$\dfrac{6m}{2q}$

This gives us the following equivalent fractions $\dfrac{3m}{q} = \dfrac{6m}{2q}$.

In problem 15, a pair of equivalent algebraic fractions is given with a numerator missing. To find the missing part, your child must find the factor that was used on one fraction to make the other. This factor, used with the known numerator, will produce the missing numerator.

How to Get the Answer

1. Write out the algebraic factorization (see problem 13) of each denominator. (When the two denominators are written out in this way, we can determine the factor that makes one different from the other.)

Denominator	Algebraic Factorization
$5q$	$5 \cdot q$
$15qw$	$3 \cdot 5 \cdot q \cdot w$

2. Cross out the factors common to both.

$$\cancel{5} \cdot \cancel{q}$$
$$3 \cdot \cancel{5} \cdot \cancel{q} \cdot w$$

Multiplying the leftover factors (those not common to both, will give the factor we seek: factor $= 3 \cdot w = 3w$

3. The known numerator times this factor gives the unknown numerator:

$$12w \cdot 3w = 12 \cdot 3 \cdot w \cdot w = 36w^2$$

PROBLEM 16

Simplify: $\dfrac{18c}{24c^2n}$

Answer

$$\frac{18c}{24c^2n} = \frac{3}{4cn}$$

We saw in problem 15 that multiplying both the numerator and the denominator by the same number produces a fraction that is equal to the one we began with. Similarly, dividing both the numerator and the denominator by the same number (what we do when we "simplify") produces an equivalent fraction as well.

When you were in school, simplifying fractions might have been called "reducing a fraction to its lowest terms." As you reduced, you crossed out numbers to indicate division. As students simplify algebraic fractions, they, too, cross through common factors as an indication of division. This process is called *canceling*.

How to Get the Answer

1. Write the algebraic factorization of the numerator and the denominator of the given fraction. (This form shows the factors clearly.)

$$\frac{2 \cdot 3 \cdot 3 \cdot c}{2 \cdot 2 \cdot 2 \cdot 3 \cdot c \cdot c \cdot n}$$

2. Cross out common factor pairs.

$$\frac{\cancel{2} \cdot \cancel{3} \cdot 3 \cdot \cancel{c}}{\cancel{2} \cdot 2 \cdot 2 \cdot \cancel{3} \cdot \cancel{c} \cdot c \cdot n}$$

3. Multiply the remaining factors across the top and across the bottom. The result is the simplified fraction.

$$\frac{3}{4cn}$$

PROBLEM 17

Add or subtract as indicated:

(a) $\dfrac{m}{n} - \dfrac{2z}{n}$

(b) $\dfrac{3q}{4p} + \dfrac{7q}{4p}$

Answers

(a) $\dfrac{m}{n} - \dfrac{2z}{n} = \dfrac{m - 2z}{n}$

(b) $\dfrac{3q}{4p} + \dfrac{7q}{4p} = \dfrac{10q}{4p} = \dfrac{5q}{2p}$

Adding (or subtracting) numerical fractions that have the same denominators is easy. The procedure is to add (or subtract) the numerators and to keep the denominator for the answer.

$$\frac{1}{5} + \frac{3}{5} = \frac{1+3}{5} = \frac{4}{5} \text{ and } \frac{7}{9} - \frac{2}{9} = \frac{7-2}{9} = \frac{5}{9}$$

Follow the same procedure with algebraic fractions with the same denominators.

How to Get the Answer

1. Since the answer will have the same denominator as the fractions being added or subtracted, write your partial answer.

   (a) $\dfrac{m}{n} - \dfrac{2z}{n} = \dfrac{\ }{n}$ partial answer

   (b) $\dfrac{3q}{4p} + \dfrac{7q}{4p} = \dfrac{\ }{4p}$ partial answer

2. Write both numerators on the top of the partial answer. Place a plus sign between the pair to indicate addition and a minus sign to indicate subtraction where applicable.

   (a) $\dfrac{m - 2z}{n}$

   (b) $\dfrac{3q + 7q}{4p}$

3. If the terms in the numerator are not like terms, the problem is complete.

   (a) $\dfrac{m - 2z}{n}$

   If the terms are like terms, they should be combined and written as a single term.

   (b) $\dfrac{3q + 7q}{4p} = \dfrac{10q}{4p}$

4. Simplify the answer, if necessary. In these examples, only (b) needs to be simplified:

(b) $\dfrac{10q}{4p} = \dfrac{\cancel{2} \cdot 5 \cdot q}{\cancel{2} \cdot 2 \cdot p} = \dfrac{5q}{2p}$

PROBLEM 18

Find the LCD:

(a) $\dfrac{3y}{2x}, \dfrac{1}{6xy^2}$

(b) $\dfrac{4}{d^2c}, \dfrac{3d}{7m}$

Answers
(a) $6xy^2$

(b) $7cd^2m$

Adding and subtracting unlike fractions involve changing the denominators of the given fractions to ones that have the same denominator. This is called finding the LCD (least common denominator) of the two fractions.

The least common denominator is found using the same technique as finding the least common multiple.

How to Get the Answer
1. Write out the algebraic factorization (p. 261) of the denominators of the given fraction pair.
   (a) $2x = 2 \cdot x$
   $6xy^2 = 2 \cdot 3 \cdot x \cdot y \cdot y$
   (b) $d^2c = d \cdot d \cdot c$
   $7m = 7 \cdot m$
2. Find the common factor pairs by drawing a loop around those factors that are present in both factorizations. (Remember, this is not always possible. There may be no common factors.)
   (a) $2x = 2 \cdot x$
   $6xy^2 = 2 \cdot 3 \cdot x \cdot y \cdot y$

(b) $d^2c = d \cdot d \cdot c$ No common factors

$7m = 7 \cdot m$

3. From each loop, take out one factor and write a product of the factors.

   (a) $2 \cdot x$

   (b) no common factors (i.e., no loops)

4. Beside these factors, write all the factors that were not looped in step 2.

   (a) $2 \cdot x \cdot 3 \cdot y \cdot y$

   (b) $d \cdot d \cdot c \cdot 7 \cdot m$

5. Multiply these factors to get the LCD. It is customary to write the number first and then the variables in alphabetical order.

   (a) LCD $= 2 \cdot 3 \cdot x \cdot y \cdot y$

      $= 6xy^2$

   (b) LCD $= 7 \cdot c \cdot d \cdot d \cdot m$

      $= 7cd^2m$

PROBLEM 19

Add or subtract as indicated:

(a) $\dfrac{7n}{8} + \dfrac{m}{12}$ (b) $\dfrac{4}{ab} - \dfrac{1}{b^2}$

Answers

(a) $\dfrac{7n}{8} + \dfrac{m}{12} = \dfrac{21n + 2m}{24}$

(b) $\dfrac{4}{ab} - \dfrac{1}{b^2} = \dfrac{4b - a}{ab^2}$

This problem deals with adding and subtracting algebraic fractions with unlike denominators. To understand the steps your child takes to solve these problems, it might help to think of how you were taught to subtract a problem such as the following:

$$\frac{2}{3}$$
$$-\frac{1}{8}$$
___

First, you were told to find a number that both denominators would divide into without a remainder. (You were finding the LCD, the least common denominator.)

$$\frac{2}{3} = \frac{}{24} \qquad\qquad \frac{1}{8} = \frac{}{24}$$

Next, you found the top of the new fraction. You might have said to yourself as you worked, "3 goes into 24 eight times. So 8 times 2 gives 16." And you placed 16 across from the 2. You repeated the process for the bottom fraction. (You were finding equivalent fractions.)

$$\frac{2}{3} = \frac{16}{24}$$
$$-\frac{1}{8} = \frac{3}{24}$$
___

Your final step was to keep the denominator for the answer and to subtract the numerators.

$$\frac{2}{3} = \frac{16}{24}$$
$$-\frac{1}{8} = \frac{3}{24}$$
___
$$\frac{13}{24}$$

How to Get the Answer

1. Some children find fractions easier to work with when they are written vertically. Find the LCD and use it for the new denominator.

    (a) **Finding the LCD of 8 and 12.**

    $$8 = 2 \cdot 2 \cdot 2$$
    $$12 = 2 \cdot 2 \cdot 3$$

$$\text{LCD} = 2 \cdot 2 \cdot 2 \cdot 3 = 24$$

$$\frac{7n}{8} = \frac{}{24}$$

$$+\frac{m}{12} = \frac{}{24}$$

(b) **Finding the LCD of ab and b^2.**

$$ab = a \cdot \widehat{b}$$
$$b^2 = b \cdot \widehat{b}$$
$$\text{LCD} = b \cdot a \cdot b = ab^2$$

$$\frac{4}{ab} = \frac{}{ab^2}$$

$$-\frac{1}{b^2} = \frac{}{ab^2}$$

2. To find the tops (numerators) of the fractions, you might turn back to problem 15, which gives a procedure for finding equivalent fractions. Or you might apply the same procedure you used for numerical fractions:

$$\frac{7n}{8} = \frac{21n}{24}$$

Think: 8 goes into 24 three times.
So three times $7n$ is $21n$.

(a) $\quad \dfrac{7n}{8} = \dfrac{21n}{24}$

$$+\frac{m}{12} = \frac{2m}{24}$$

(b) $\quad \dfrac{4}{ab} = \dfrac{4b}{ab^2}$

$$-\frac{1}{b^2} = \frac{a}{ab^2}$$

3. For each problem, keep the denominator for the answer and add the numerators in (a) and subtract the numerators in (b).

(a) $\dfrac{7n}{8} = \dfrac{21n}{24}$

$+\dfrac{m}{12} = \dfrac{2m}{24}$

_____

$\dfrac{21n + 2m}{24}$

(b) $\dfrac{4}{ab} = \dfrac{4b}{ab^2}$

$-\dfrac{1}{b^2} = \dfrac{a}{ab^2}$

_____

$\dfrac{4b - a}{ab^2}$

PROBLEM 20

Multiply:

(a) $\dfrac{9}{b} \cdot \dfrac{2b}{f}$

(b) $\dfrac{6}{m} \cdot \dfrac{n}{12}$

Answers

(a) $\dfrac{9}{b} \cdot \dfrac{2b}{f} = \dfrac{18}{f}$

(b) $\dfrac{6}{m} \cdot \dfrac{n}{12} = \dfrac{n}{2m}$

When multiplying numerical fractions, students are given the option of canceling (dividing out common factors) before the actual multiplication. This makes it easier to express the answer in lowest terms. For example,

$\dfrac{7}{12} \cdot \dfrac{12}{21}$ would give $\dfrac{84}{254}$

by direct multiplication. Simplifying this answer would take some
time. But, canceling (see p. 266) before multiplying makes the
problem an easier one to solve, as shown below:

$$\overset{1}{\cancel{7}} \cdot \overset{1}{\cancel{12}} = \frac{1}{3}$$
$$\underset{1}{\cancel{12}} \cdot \underset{3}{\cancel{21}}$$

Algebraic fractions, too, are much easier to solve if work is done
to divide out common factors (i.e., cancel) before beginning the
multiplication.

How to Get the Answer

1. To prepare for canceling, write the algebraic factorization of
   each numerator and denominator. (This helps to see the
   factors more clearly.)

   (a) $\dfrac{9}{b} \cdot \dfrac{2b}{f} = \dfrac{3 \cdot 3}{b} \cdot \dfrac{2 \cdot b}{f}$

   (b) $\dfrac{6}{m} \cdot \dfrac{n}{12} = \dfrac{2 \cdot 3}{m} \cdot \dfrac{n}{2 \cdot 2 \cdot 3}$

2. Cancel factors by marking through common factor pairs
   (those factors that are found both in the numerator and in the
   denominator.)

   (a) $\dfrac{3 \cdot 3}{\cancel{b}} \cdot \dfrac{2 \cdot \cancel{b}}{f}$

   (b) $\dfrac{\cancel{2} \cdot \cancel{3}}{m} \cdot \dfrac{n}{\cancel{2} \cdot 2 \cdot \cancel{3}}$

3. Multiply the remaining factors across the top to get the final
   numerator. Multiply across the bottom for the final
   denominator.

   (a) $\dfrac{3 \cdot 3 \cdot 2}{f} = \dfrac{18}{f}$

   (b) $\dfrac{n}{m \cdot 2} = \dfrac{n}{2m}$

PROBLEM 21

Divide:

(a) $\dfrac{6z}{m} \div \dfrac{3}{m}$

(b) $\dfrac{7x}{y} \div \dfrac{35x^2}{y}$

Answers

(a) $\dfrac{6z}{m} \div \dfrac{3}{m} = 2z$

(b) $\dfrac{7x}{y} \div \dfrac{35x^2}{y} = \dfrac{1}{5x}$

The division of algebraic fractions is like the division of numerical fractions. The second fraction (the divisor) is flipped (replaced by its reciprocal). After this is done, the same procedure is followed that was used in multiplication: cancel like factors and multiply those that remain.

How to Get the Answer

1. Rewrite the division problem as a multiplication problem by replacing the divisor with its reciprocal (i.e., flip the second fraction).

	Original Problem	Rewritten Problem
(a)	$\dfrac{6z}{m} \div \dfrac{3}{m}$	$\dfrac{6z}{m} \cdot \dfrac{m}{3}$
(b)	$\dfrac{7x}{y} \div \dfrac{35x^2}{y}$	$\dfrac{7x}{y} \cdot \dfrac{y}{35x^2}$

2. To prepare for canceling, write the algebraic factorization of each numerator and denominator. (This helps us to see the factors more clearly).

(a) $\dfrac{2 \cdot 3 \cdot z}{m} \cdot \dfrac{m}{3}$

(b) $\dfrac{7 \cdot x}{y} \cdot \dfrac{y}{5 \cdot 7 \cdot x \cdot x}$

3. Cancel factors by marking through common factor pairs (those factors that are found both in the numerator and the denominator).

(a) $\dfrac{2 \cdot \cancel{3} \cdot z}{\cancel{m}} \cdot \dfrac{\cancel{m}}{\cancel{3}}$

(b) $\dfrac{7 \cdot \cancel{x}}{\cancel{y}} \cdot \dfrac{\cancel{y}}{5 \cdot \cancel{7} \cdot \cancel{x} \cdot x}$

When all the factors have been crossed out in either the numerator or denominator, 1 still remains as a factor.

4. Multiply the remaining factors across the top for the final numerator. Multiply across the bottom for the final denominator.

(a) $\dfrac{2 \cdot z}{1} = \dfrac{2z}{1} = 2z$

(b) $\dfrac{1}{5 \cdot x} = \dfrac{1}{5x}$

PROBLEM 22

Use the coordinate plane pictured below.
(a) Give the coordinates of the points:

     *A*____   *C*____.

(b) Name the point for each of the ordered pairs:

     (0, -2)____   (-3,4)____

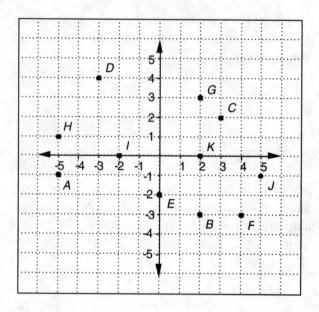

Answers

(a) $A(-5,-1)$ $C(3,2)$

(b) $(0,-2) E$ $(-3,4) D$

Two perpendicular number lines are used to locate a point in space. The two number lines are called *axes.* The horizontal number line is the *x-axis,* and the vertical number line is the *y-axis.* The place where they meet is called the *origin.*

To name a point in space, we use two numbers. The first number is determined by dropping straight down (or up) from the point to the x-axis and reading the number we land on.

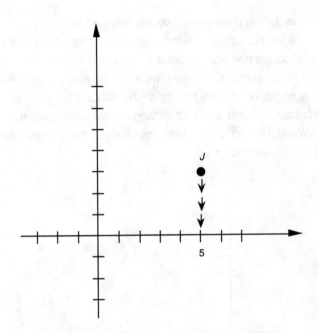

The first number is called the *x-coordinate* or *abscissa*.

The second number is determined by drawing a straight line from the given point over to the *y-axis*.

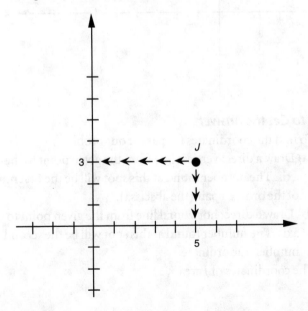

This number is called the *y-coordinate* or *ordinate*.

The two numbers are placed together in parentheses and are called an *ordered pair of numbers*. Whenever we are asked to give the *coordinates* of a point, we are being asked to give the ordered pair of numbers that define the point's place in the provided space, which is called a *rectangular coordinate system*.

When labeling points with coordinates, the *x*-coordinate always comes first, (*x, y*).

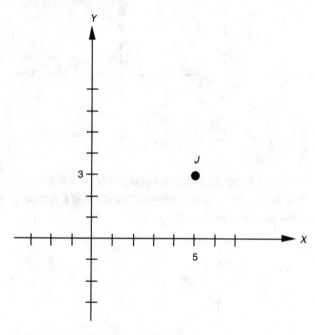

How to Get the Answer

1. To find the coordinates for part of our problem:
   (a) Draw a direct vertical line from the given point to the *x*-axis. The number found at this spot will be the first number of the ordered pair (the abscissa).
   (b) Draw a direct horizontal line from the given point to the *y*-axis. The number found at this spot will be the second number, the ordinate.

The coordinates of *J* are (5, 3).

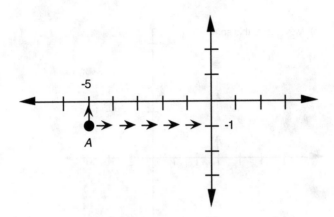

2. When the coordinates are given and the point is being asked
for, do the following:
(a) Find the location of the abscissa (the first number of the
ordered pair) on the x-axis.
(b) From this spot, move your finger in a vertical line until it is
directly across from the location of the second number (the
ordinate) on the y-axis.
To find (-3, 4)

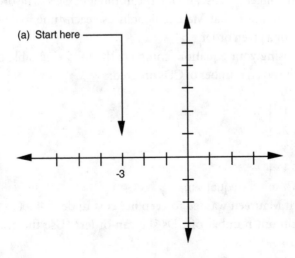

(b) Move up to this spot.

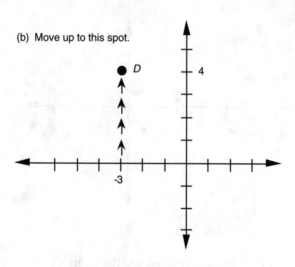

PROBLEM 23

Maureen can order CDs from her record club for $6.00 each. There is a $3.00 shipping and handling charge, but this is per order and not per CD.

(a) If you let c = cost and n = the number of CDs to be ordered, write an equation that Maureen could use each time to calculate her cost for a given order.

(b) Using your equation, complete the following table of values for the given number of CDs ordered:

n	c
1	
2	
3	
4	

(c) Graph the equation.

(d) If Maureen wanted to keep her cost under $40.00, what is the maximum number of CDs she can order? (Use the graph to help you.)

Answer

(a) $c = 6n + 3$

(b)

n	c
1	9
2	15
3	21
4	27

(c)

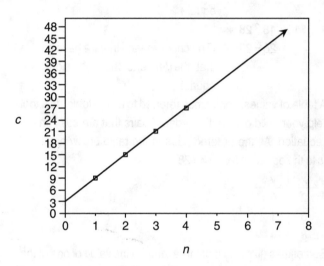

(d) 6 CDs

Earlier in this prealgebra chapter, your child practiced changing words into symbols. These translations involved equations with only one variable. Now your child will be given opportunities to write equations with two variables and will learn to find solutions for these equations.

This problem is an example of a situation that would translate into a two variable equation. It is designed to give your child experience in applying graphing to a real-life situation.

A solution to an equation with one variable, you may recall, is a value of the variable that will make the equation true. When an equation has two variables, each solution will consist of two values that are written as an ordered pair.

For example, one solution of $5x + 3y = 28$ is $(2, 6)$. This means that the equation will work if we replaced x with 2 and y with 6:

$5(2) + 3(6) \overset{?}{=} 28$ (The question mark above the equal sign means that we are testing to see if the left and the right sides are indeed equal.)

$10 + 18 \overset{?}{=} 28$

$28 = 28$ √   (The check means that we have shown that the left and the right sides are equal.)

A table of values, sometimes referred to as a T table, is a tool to help your child display the ordered pairs that are solutions to the equation. All the ordered pairs in the table below are solutions to the equation $5x + 3y = 28$:

x	y
2	6
5	1
8	-4

Sometimes (like part b of this example) the value of one of the variables is given and the others must be found. With a set of ordered pairs from a table of values, we are able to graph the equation. By extending this graph, your child learns to draw conclusions and make predictions.

How to Get the Answer

1. Summarize the problem in a sentence. Translate the sentence into an equation using the given variables.

   Summary: "The cost of an order will be the number of CDs times 6; added to this will be a $3 charge for shipping and handling." (Let c = cost and n = number of CDs).

   Equation: $c = 6n + 3$

2. Using the equation $c = 6n + 3$, we replace n with one of the

values on the left side of the table. Doing the arithmetic, we are able to get a value for *c*. We place this number beside the value of *n* in the table. We then start the process again with another value of *n*:

n	*c*
1	9
2	
3	
4	

Using $n = 1$
from the table of values
$c = 6(1) + 3$
$c = 6 + 3$
$c = 9$

Using $n = 2$
from the table of values
$c = 6(2) + 3$
$c = 12 + 3$
$c = 15$

Continue in this manner until all the given values of *n* have been used to find *c*. Fill in the chart as you go along.

3. On a piece of graph paper, draw two perpendicular number lines (the axes). Since all the values in the table are positive, we can draw our axes meeting, but not crossing.

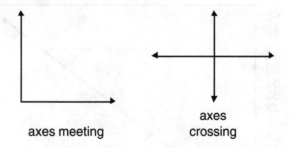

axes meeting   axes crossing

Label the horizontal axis (the *x*-axis), counting by ones. Label the vertical axis (the *y*-axis), counting by threes. Graph the points by taking ordered pairs from the table of values and plotting the points (see p. 281).

You would plot $(1, 9)$, $(2, 15)$, $(3, 21)$ and $(4, 27)$. Draw the line to connect the points.

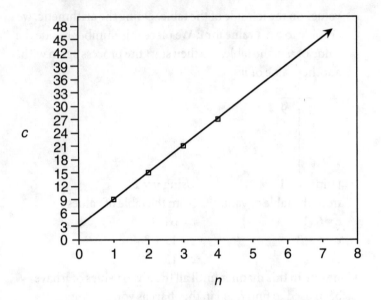

4. Extend the line beyond the points. Then (a) Find where 40 would be on the *y*-axis (an approximation). Draw a horizontal line from this point to the graph of the line.

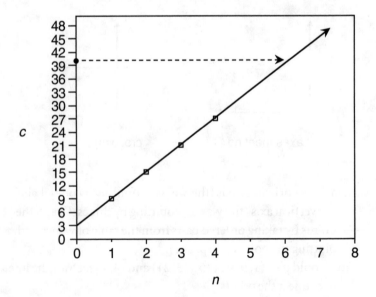

(b) From this point, draw a vertical line to meet the *x*-axis.

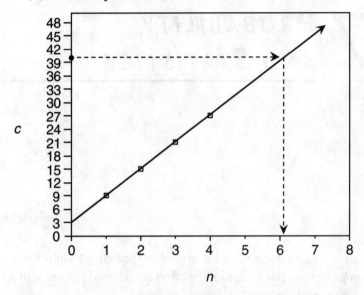

This point is between 6 and 7 on the *x*-axis which means that the greatest number of CDs that Maureen can buy is six.

7 PROBABILITY AND STATISTICS

We live in an information society. With the help of sophisticated computers, we can gather information quickly and present it in an understandable way.

Statistics is the branch of mathematics that deals with gathering, recording, observing, and explaining information. The charts, graphs, tables, and displays that your child sees on television and in newspapers and magazines represent statistical information.

Besides wanting to know about what is happening now, people have always been fascinated with thinking ahead to what might happen in the future. This desire is at the core of probability. Probability uses past observations of data patterns to predict the outcome of some future event.

With advances in technology, gathering data is now easier than ever before, making probability and statistics one of the most widely used mathematical disciplines in today's world. It has also become a vital part of your child's math curriculum

Since kindergarten, your child has gathered, recorded, and displayed information from class surveys. At the middle-school level these surveying skills are reinforced and broadened to include analysis and evaluation.

In this chapter, we will see how children have learned to analyze and evaluate information. We will also introduce you to the models they have learned to develop—models that make probability and statistics a useful problem-solving tool.

Topics in This Chapter

Finding the mean, median, mode, and range (measures of central tendency)

Making a frequency distribution table

Making a histogram

Reading a bar graph

Making a tree diagram

Using the basic counting principle

Determining permutations and factorials

Finding probabilities, including the concepts of sample space, independent events, odds

---

SAMPLE PROBLEMS

1 Use the data (21, 24, 25, 27, 26, 29, 23, 25, 27, 24, 28, 27, 26, 25 and 22) to compute the following:

   (a) the mean   (b) the median

   (c) the mode   (d) the range

2. Make a frequency distribution table by using the ages of the students in a prealgebra class:

13, 13, 12, 12, 12, 13, 13, 13, 14, 14, 13, 13, 14, 14, 12, 12, 11, 11, 12, 11, 12, 12, 13, 14, 14, 14, 13, 13, 13, 12

3. Make a histogram of these math test scores. (Arrange them in intervals of 60-69, 70-79, 80-89, and 90-100.)

   70   61   64   90   81

   80   92   71   63   74

   82   90   66   68   100

   87   99   85   75   60

4. Use the bar graph below to answer the following questions:

   (a) About how many boxes of cookies did the sixth grade sell?

(b) Which class sold the most boxes of cookies?

(c) Which class sold about twenty boxes of cookies?

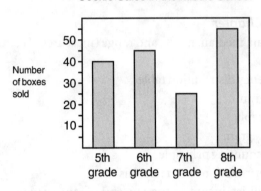

Cookie Sales in the Middle School

5. To get home from work, Jane has to take the train. She has three possible ways of getting to the train station. She can walk, go by bus, or go by taxi. Once in the train station, Jane can take either the express or the local train. After she gets off the train, Jane has two more choices: she can walk home or go by taxi. Make a tree diagram to show all the possible routes Jane can take from work to her home.

6. A cafeteria offers six flavors of ice cream and four different toppings. How many sundaes of one flavor and one topping can be ordered?

7. Determine the number of different ways that five students can be lined up.

8. A certain game requires tossing a coin and rolling a die.

   Find the probability of:

   (a) getting tails and a four,

   (b) getting heads and a three, and

   (c) getting heads and a number less than four.

Answers:

1. (a) mean = 25.27   (b) median = 25

   (c) modes are 25 and 27   (d) range = 8

2.

Age	Tally	Frequency
11	III	3
12	⊬⊬⊬ IIII	9
13	⊬⊬⊬ ⊬⊬⊬ I	11
14	⊬⊬⊬ II	7

3.

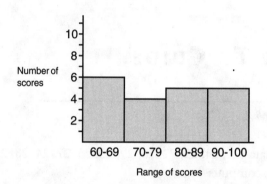

4. (a) 45 boxes   (b) eighth grade   (c) seventh grade
5. There are twelve possible routes from work to home.
   Possible routes from work to home
   walk, express train, walk
   walk, express train, taxi
   walk, local train, walk
   walk, local train, taxi
   bus, express train, walk
   bus, express train, taxi
   bus, local train, walk
   bus, local train, taxi
   taxi, express train, walk
   taxi, express train, taxi

      taxi, local train, walk

      taxi, local train, taxi

6. There are twenty-four different one-flavor/one-topping combinations.

7. $5 \times 4 \times 3 \times 2 \times 1 = 120$

8. (a) $P(T \text{ and } 4) = \frac{1}{12}$

    (b) $P(H \text{ and } 3) = \frac{1}{12}$

    (c) $P(H \text{ and } <4) = \frac{1}{2} \cdot \frac{1}{2} \cdot = \frac{1}{4}$

How-To Guide

PROBLEM 1

Use the data (21, 24, 25, 27, 26, 29, 23, 25, 27, 24, 28, 27, 26, 25 and 22) to compute:

(a) the mean   (b) the median

(c) the mode   (d) the range

Answer

(a) mean = 25.27   (b) median = 25

(c) modes are 25 and 27   (d) range = 8

    A collection of *data* is a collection of numerical facts. In the study of statistics, your child learns techniques for collecting, organizing, and analyzing data.

    The mean, the mode, and the median are called the three *measures of central tendency.* Each one is a technique to analyze data.

    The *mean* is the average of the data numbers. It is found by adding the data numbers together and dividing this sum by the number of entries.

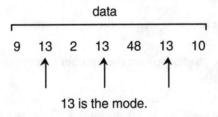

The *mode* is the number (or numbers) that appears most often in the data. It is possible for a set of data to have more than one mode.

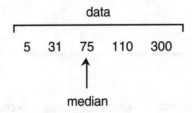

The *median* is the middle number from a list of numbers that are arranged by size. When there is an even count of numbers, the median is the mean of the two middle numbers.

data
```
5    31    75    110    300
           ↑
         median
```

The *range* gives information concerning the spread of the data. It is the difference between the highest and the lowest data entries.

$$\overbrace{75 \quad 66 \quad 88 \quad 73 \quad 99}^{\text{data}}$$

$$\text{range} = 99 - 66 = 33$$

How to Get the Answer

1. Order the data from least to greatest.
   21, 22, 23, 24, 24, 25, 25, 25, 26, 26, 27, 27, 27, 28, 29
2. To find the mean, add the numbers together and divide by 15 (because there are 15 numbers).
   sum = 379
   $$\text{mean} = \frac{379}{15} = 25.27$$
3. To find the median, look for the middle number.
   25 is the median.
4. To find the mode, look for the number that appears most frequently.
   In this set of data, there are two modes: 25 and 27.
5. To find the range, subtract the lowest data entry from the highest data entry.
   29-21 = 8
   Your child might use a calculator on these types of problems.

PROBLEM 2

These are the ages of the students in a prealgebra class:
13, 13, 12, 12, 12, 13, 13, 13, 14, 14, 13, 13, 14, 14, 12, 12, 11, 11, 12, 11, 12, 12, 13, 14, 14, 14, 13, 13, 13, 12
Make a frequency distribution table.

Answer

Age	Tally	Frequency
11					3
12	⊬⊬⊬ ||||	9
13	⊬⊬⊬ ⊬⊬⊬		11
14	⊬⊬⊬ ||	7

A *frequency distribution table* is a diagram that arranges data to show the number of times each particular item appears or occurs. Your child makes this table by categorizing the data, tallying the data as each number is assigned to a category, and counting the tally marks.

How to Get the Answer

1. A frequency distribution table consists of three columns. The first column is for the category of data. For this problem, it will be "Age." In the second column, we will keep the tally. In the third column, we will place the count of the tally marks.

Age	Tally	Frequency

2. Since the ages in our problem are between 11 and 14, list the numbers 11-14 in the first column.

Age	Tally	Frequency
11		
12		
13		
14		

3. Place a single tally mark in the second column of the table for each number in the data.

Age	Tally	Frequency
11	III	
12	⊬⊬⊬ IIII	
13	⊬⊬⊬ ⊬⊬⊬ I	
14	⊬⊬⊬ II	

4. Count the number of tallies for each category and write this number in the frequency column. Total the numbers in the frequency column as a check. This number should be the same as the number of data entries.

Age	Tally	Frequency
11	III	3
12	⊬⊬⊬ IIII	9
13	⊬⊬⊬ ⊬⊬⊬ I	11
14	⊬⊬⊬ II	7
		30 (total)

PROBLEM 3

Make a histogram of these math test scores. (Arrange them in intervals of 60-69, 70-79, 80-89, and 90-100.)

70	61	64	90	81
80	92	71	63	74
82	90	66	68	100
87	99	85	75	60

Answer

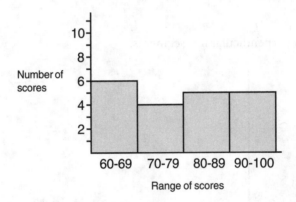

A *histogram* is a bar graph without spaces between the bars. It is a pictorial frequency table.

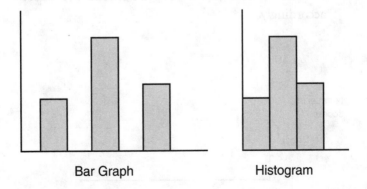

Bar Graph   Histogram

How to Get the Answer

1. Make a frequency distribution table. The heading in the first column will be "scores". Use the ranges listed in the problem.

Scores	Tally	Frequency
60-69	꧁꧂	6
70-79	IIII	4
80-89	꧁꧂	5
99-100	꧁꧂	5

2. Draw perpendicular line segments.

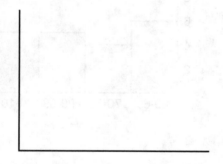

3. On the vertical segment, record the "number of times" or frequency of a range of scores. Number and label this scale accordingly.

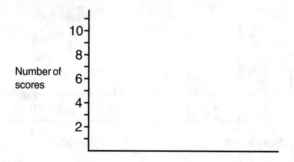

4. Place spacing marks an equal distance apart to accommodate each range of scores in the first column of the frequency distribution table.

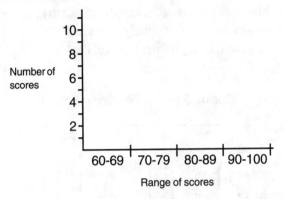

5. Use a straightedge to draw the bars. Remember that the height of each bar will be determined by the number of times this range of scores has occurred in the data.

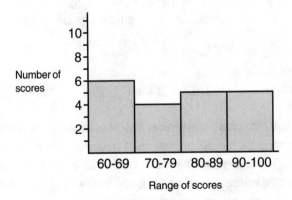

PROBLEM 4

Use the bar graph below to answer the following questions:
(a) About how many boxes of cookies did the sixth grade sell?
(b) Which class sold the most boxes of cookies?
(c) Which class sold about twenty boxes of cookies?

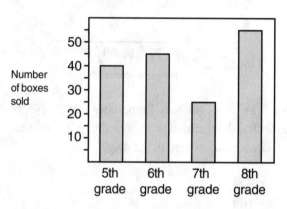

Cookie Sales in the Middle School

Answers

(a) 45 boxes   (b) 8th grade   (c) 7th grade

As in a histogram, the vertical axis of a bar graph is used to determine the number of times an item occurs in a specific category. The categories are designated on the horizontal axis. Since the vertical axis of this bar graph is scaled in increments of five, the bar graph shows approximate amounts.

How to Get the Answer

1. For (a), we need to find the bar that corresponds to the sales for the sixth grade (the second bar).

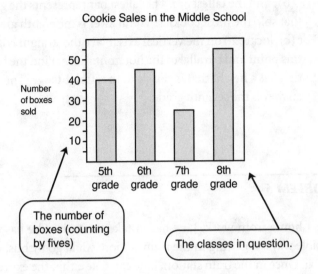

Cookie Sales in the Middle School

Placing a straightedge across the top of the sixth grade bar, read the number on the vertical axis to find the number of boxes sold. The answer is 45.

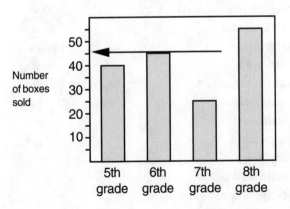

Cookie Sales in the Middle School

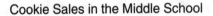

2. For (b), find the tallest bar. The tallest bar represents the grade that sold the most cookies. The answer is the eighth grade.
3. For (c), locate 20 on the vertical axis. Place the straight edge at this point and parallel to the horizontal axis. Find the bar that has a height that is closest to the straightedge. The answer is the seventh grade.

___

PROBLEM 5

To get home from work, Jane has to take the train. She has three possible ways of getting to the train station: walk, go by bus, or go by taxi. Once in the train station, Jane can take either the express or the local train. After she gets off the train, Jane has two more choices: she can walk home, or go by taxi.

Make a tree diagram to show all the possible routes Jane can take from work to her home.

Answer
There are 12 possible routes from work to home.
Possible routes from work to home
walk, express train, walk
walk, express train, taxi
walk, local train, walk
walk, local train, taxi
bus, express train, walk
bus, express train, taxi
bus, local train, walk
bus, local train, taxi
taxi, express train walk
taxi, express train, taxi
taxi, local train, walk
taxi, local train, taxi

A *tree diagram* is a drawing that shows all the possible pairings, using one item from each of the given groups. For example, suppose you had two pairs of pants (a pair of jeans and pair of slacks) and three shirts (one blue, one yellow, one green). In this example, you have two groups: pants and shirts. A tree diagram shows all the possible matches you can make.

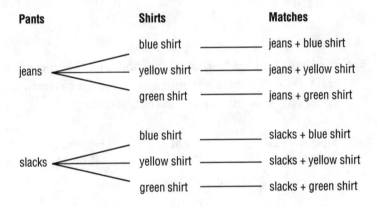

Pants	Shirts	Matches
	blue shirt	jeans + blue shirt
jeans	yellow shirt	jeans + yellow shirt
	green shirt	jeans + green shirt
	blue shirt	slacks + blue shirt
slacks	yellow shirt	slacks + yellow shirt
	green shirt	slacks + green shirt

When problems involve matching more or larger groups, it might be difficult to arrange the categories. A helpful organization scheme is outlined below.

How to Get the Answer

1. Across the top of the working space, write the names of the groups that will be generating choices. Use these as column headings.

From work to train station	Type of train	From train to home

2. Under the first heading, list all the ways for going from work to the train station.

From work to train station	Type of train	From train to home
walk		
bus		
taxi		

3. Under the second heading, list all the choices for the types of
   train. Do *not* list them just once, but list them for as many
   times as choices are indicated in the first column.

From work to train station	Type of train	From train to home
	express	
walk		
	local	
	express	
bus		
	local	
	express	
taxi		
	local	

4. Under the third heading, list all of the ways for going from the
   train station to home. Again, list these for as many times as
   choices are listed in the second column.

From work to train station	Type of train	From train to home
	express	walk taxi
walk		
	local	walk taxi
	express	walk taxi
bus		
	local	walk taxi
	express	walk taxi
taxi		
	local	walk taxi

5. Draw in the "branches" between the columns.

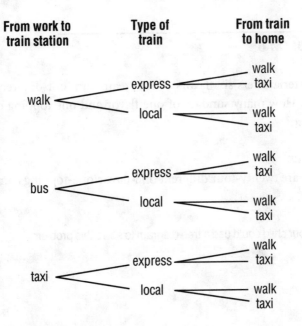

From work to train station	Type of train	From train to home
	express	walk taxi
walk		
	local	walk taxi
	express	walk taxi
bus		
	local	walk taxi
	express	walk taxi
taxi		
	local	walk taxi

6. Starting from the left column, follow each branch and write out the possible matches.

From work to train station	Type of train	From train to home	Possible routes from work to home
walk	express	walk	walk, express train, walk
		taxi	walk, express train, taxi
	local	walk	walk, local train, walk
		taxi	walk, local train, taxi
bus	express	walk	bus, express train, walk
		taxi	bus, express train, taxi
	local	walk	bus, local train, walk
		taxi	bus, local train, taxi
taxi	express	walk	taxi, express train, walk
		taxi	taxi, express train, taxi
	local	walk	taxi, local train, walk
		taxi	taxi, local train, taxi

PROBLEM 6

A cafeteria offers six flavors of ice cream and four different toppings. How many sundaes of one flavor and one topping can be ordered?

Answer

There are twenty-four different one-flavor/one-topping combinations.

Your child could use a tree diagram to solve this problem.

Flavors	Toppings	Matches
1	A B C D	1 A 1 B 1 C 1 D
2	A B C D	2 A 2 B 2 C 2 D
3	A B C D	3 A 3 B 3 C 3 D
4	A B C D	4 A 4 B 4 C 4 D
5	A B C D	5 A 5 B 5 C 5 D
6	A B C D	6 A 6 B 6 C 6 D

But there is also a formula, called the *basic counting principle,* that does the same thing:

The number of choices in group A	×	The number of choices in group B	=	The total number of possible matches

How to Get the Answer

1. Count the number of choices in the first group.
   Number of ice cream flavors = 6
2. Count the number of choices in the second group.
   Number of toppings = 4
3. Multiply.
   6 ice cream flavors × 4 toppings = 24 matches

PROBLEM 7

Determine the number of different ways that five students can be lined up.

Answer

$5 \times 4 \times 3 \times 2 \times 1 = 120$

When your child is given a set of objects and must count the number of different ways that set can be arranged, your child is determining the number of *permutations* for the set.

Your child's introduction to permutations probably began by experimenting with a group of two objects, then a group of three objects. Your child discovered that the number of permutations could be found by counting down from the number of objects in the group and then finding the product of these numbers.

For example, if there are three items to be arranged, the number of permutations can be found by counting down, then multiplying:

$$3 \quad 2 \quad 1 \longrightarrow 3 \times 2 \times 1 = 6$$

In time, students are given a name for these "countdown products." They are called *factorials*. The symbol for factorial is a number followed by an exclamation point.

four factorial = $4! = 4 \times 3 \times 2 \times 1 = 24$

eight factorial = $8! = 8 \times 7 \times 6 \times 5 \times 4 \times 3 \times 2 \times 1 = 40{,}320$

How to Get the Answer

1. Count the number of objects in the given group.
   5 students
2. Determine 5! (This will be the number of arrangements that is possible.)
   (a) Write a countdown from 5 to 1.
   5 4 3 2 1

(b) Multiply these numbers.

$5 \times 4 \times 3 \times 2 \times 1 = 120$

PROBLEM 8

A certain game requires tossing a coin and rolling a die. Find the probability of
(a) getting tails and a four,
(b) getting heads and a three, and
(c) getting heads and a number less than four.

Answers

(a) $P(T \text{ and } 4) = \frac{1}{12}$

(b) $P(H \text{ and } 3) = \frac{1}{12}$

(c) $P(H \text{ and } < 4) = \frac{1}{2} \cdot \frac{1}{2} = \frac{1}{4}$

Probability is the measure of likelihood. It is a fraction made by placing the number of desirable outcomes over the total number of possible outcomes. For example, the probability of drawing a queen from a standard deck of 52 playing cards is $\frac{1}{13}$:

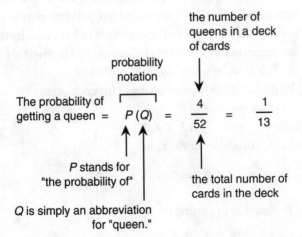

the number of
queens in a deck
of cards

probability
notation

The probability of
getting a queen = $P(Q)$ = $\frac{4}{52}$ = $\frac{1}{13}$

P stands for
"the probability of"

the total number of
cards in the deck

Q is simply an abbreviation
for "queen."

How to Get the Answer

1. One approach for solving part (a) of this problem would be to use a tree diagram to show all the possible outcomes (This is known as producing a *sample space.*) Then count the number of outcomes in the sample space to get the answer.

coin	**die**	**sample space**
	1	H 1
	2	H 2
H	3	H 3
	4	H 4
	5	H 5
	6	H 6
	1	T 1
	2	T 2
T	3	T 3
	4	T 4
	5	T 5
	6	T 6

2. Another way to solve this problem is to use a formula. Tossing a coin and rolling a die are called *independent events,* because the outcomes of doing one is not affected by the outcomes of doing the other. Because this is true, this problem can be solved by multiplication.

(a) Write out the possible outcomes for each event.

coin   →   H, T

die   →   1, 2, 3, 4, 5, 6

Find the probability of each part.

Probability of getting tails = $P(T) = \frac{1}{2}$

Probability of getting four = $P(4) = \frac{1}{6}$

Multiply the probability of the parts together.

$$P(T \text{ and } 4) = \frac{1}{2} \cdot \frac{1}{6} = \frac{1}{12}$$

(b) $P(H \text{ and } 3) = \frac{1}{2} \cdot \frac{1}{6} = \frac{1}{12}$

(c) $P(H \text{ and } < 4) = \frac{1}{2} \cdot \frac{3}{6} = \frac{3}{12} = \frac{1}{4}$

Glossary

absolute value—The distance a number is from zero on the number line. Because distance is not dependent on direction, the absolute value is always a positive number. The symbol | | stands for the words "the absolute value of."

acute angle—An angle that measures more than 0°, but less than 90°. Acute angles appear more pointy.

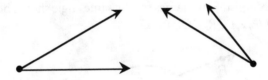

acute triangle—A triangle that contains three acute angles.

addends—The numbers being added together (for example, in $471 + 91 + 4 = 566$, the addends are 471, 91, and 4).

adjacent angles—Two angles that share a side and a common vertex, but whose interiors do not overlap.

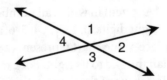

∠1 is adjacent to ∠2. ∠1 is also adjacent to ∠4.

altitude of a polygon—The perpendicular line drawn from the highest point in the polygon to the base. The length of the altitude is also known as the height.

angle—Two rays with a common endpoint. This common endpoint is known as the vertex.

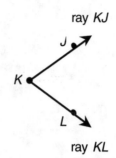

ray *KJ*

ray *KL*

∠*JKL* (read as "angle *JKL*")

The usual way to name an angle is with three letters. The middle letter is always the vertex. It does not matter which of the other two letters comes first. Angles are also named by placing a small number on the inside, near the vertex, and calling the angle by this number. When an angle does not share a vertex with another angle, it is okay to designate the angle by its vertex point. Four names for the same angle shown below are ∠*RQP*, ∠*PQR*, ∠*Q*, and ∠*7*.

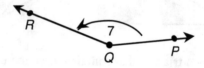

area—The measurement of the inside space of a plane figure.

base—The number that is multiplied by itself. For example, in 7^3, the base is 7. In 5^4, the base is 5.

base eight system—A system in which all numbers are made from a choice of eight digits: 0, 1, 2, 3, 4, 5, 6, and 7. Each heading in the place-value chart represents a value that is eight times greater than the one to its right. For example, 24 is a base eight number. The value of the digits in this number are 4 (4×1) and 16 (2×8).

four thousand ninety-six	five hundred twelve	sixty-four	eight	one

base of a polygon—A designated side of a polygon. In a triangle or parallelogram, any of the sides can be named as the base. In a trapezoid, both of the parallel sides are bases.

base of a solid—The designated face(s) of a space figure. In a plane figure, the base is a line. In a space figure, the base is a plane figure. The bases are shaded in the cylinder below.

base ten system—A number system in which all numbers are made from a choice of ten digits: 0, 1, 2, 3, 4, 5, 6, 7, 8, and 9. Numbers are expressed in terms of powers of ten; hence the term "base ten." For example, 24 has the digits 2 and 4. The value of the digits in this number are 20 and 4.

hundred billions	ten billions	billions	hundred millions	ten millions	millions	hundred thousands	ten thousands	thousands	hundreds	tens	ones
										2	4

base two system— A number system in which all numbers are made from a choice of two digits: 0 and 1. Each heading in the place-value chart represents a value that is two times greater than the one to its right. For example: 10110 is a base two number. That is the same as 22 in base ten.

thirty-two	sixteen	eight	four	two	one
1	0	1	1	0

center of a circle—The point inside the circle that is equidistant from every point on the circle.

chord—Any line segment that connects two points on a circle.

circumference—The distance around the outside of a circle. The perimeter of a circle.

collinear points—Points that lie on or pass through the same straight line.

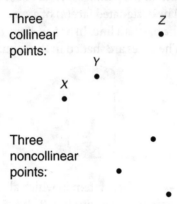

Three collinear points:

Three noncollinear points:

combinations—Groups made from a larger group. The order of the objects in these groups does not matter.

common fraction—A fraction in which the numerator and the denominator are whole numbers. For example, $\frac{13}{8}$ and $\frac{7}{23}$ are common fractions.

complementary angles—Two angles whose measures add up to 90°. For example m$\angle C$ = 13° and m$\angle D$ = 77°; $\angle C$ and $\angle D$ are complementary because 13° + 77° = 90°.

complex fraction—A fraction in which the numerator and/or the denominator is a mixed number or a fraction. Two examples of complex fractions are $\frac{1\frac{1}{2}}{14}$ and $\frac{\frac{3}{2}}{11}$.

composite number—A number that has three or more factors. A number that is not prime. For example, 14 is a composite number. Its factors are 1, 2, 7, and 14.

constant—A term that has a fixed value; a term without a variable attached. For example, in the expression $4m^4 + 13m^2 - 7$, the constant is 7.

counting principle—A way of determining the number of possible combinations when selecting one item from Group A, for example, and one item from Group B that is obtained by multiplying the number of items in Group A times the number of items in Group B.

cross product—The product that is obtained by multiplying the means and the extremes in a proportion. For example, in $\frac{9}{15} = \frac{15}{25}$, the cross product is 225, because multiplying 15×15 (the means) = 225, and multiplying 9×25 (the extremes) = 225.

decimal number—A base ten number that is written in standard form. For example, 45 is a decimal number; 55_{seven} is not.

degree—One unit of measure for angles. A protractor is used to measure angles in degrees.

denominator—The part of a fraction that is below the line. For example, in $\frac{9}{11}$ the denominator is 11.

dependent events—A probability event whose results are influenced by the outcome of another probability event. For example, it is a dependent event if one draws a second card from a deck after a first card has been drawn and not replaced.

diameter—A chord that passes through the center of a circle.

difference—The result, or the answer, obtained by subtracting. For example, in 75.2 -13.1, the difference is 62.1.

dividend—The number that is being divided. In each of the following equations the dividend is 100.

(a) $100/25 = 4$ (b) $2\overline{)100}^{\,50}$ (c) $100 \div 20 = 5$

divisibility—The characteristic of a number that allows it to be divided by another number without a remainder. For example, 26 is divisible by 13, but it is not divisible by 5.

divisor—The number by which another number is divided. For example, in each of the following equations the divisor is 25.

(a) $1000/25 = 40$ (b) $25\overline{)400}^{\,16}$ (c) $175 \div 25 = 7$

edge—The line segment formed by the intersection of two faces.

For example, this figure has 8 edges:

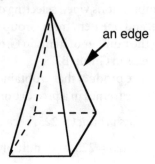

an edge

equally likely events—Events that have the same chance of occurring.

equilateral triangle—A triangle whose sides are the same length (that is, congruent).

equivalent decimals—Decimals that have the same value. Equivalent decimals can be made by adding one or more zeros to the right of the final digit of a given decimal. For example, 0.75, 0.750, and 0.7500 are all equivalent.

equivalent fractions—Fractions that have the same value. For example, $\frac{4}{5}$ and $\frac{12}{15}$ are equivalent fractions.

equivalent ratios—Ratios that have the same value. For example, 12:48, 5 to 20, and 3:12 are equivalent ratios.

estimation—The process of rounding numbers and then adding, subtracting, multiplying, or dividing to obtain an approximate answer quickly. For example, an estimate of 475×12 would be $480 \times 10 = 4,800$.

evaluate—Means to substitute numbers for the variables in an expression and then simplify. Example: $a^2 + b^2$ evaluated when $a = 2$ and $b = 3$ is $2^2 + 3^2 = 13$.

expanded form—The written expression of a number such that each digit shows its value. For example, 571 in expanded form is $500 + 70 + 1$; the expanded form of 3,291 is $3,000 + 200 + 90 + 1$.

exponent—The small raised number written to the right of another number. The exponent tells the number of times to multiply a number by itself. For example, in 7^2 the exponent is 2; in 5^7 the exponent is 7.

extremes—The two outside numbers of a proportion. For example, in the proportion, 1:2 = 8:16, the extremes are 1 and 16.

faces—The flat surfaces that enclose the interior of space figures. For example, a cube has six faces:

factor tree—A method of showing the prime factorization of a given number by showing each step of the factorization process until the prime factors are obtained. Example: the factor tree of 335 is shown below.

$$335$$
$$/\ \backslash$$
$$5\quad 67$$

factored form—An expression that shows a number as a product of its factors. For example, a factored form of 12 is 2×6. A factored form of 64 is $4 \times 4 \times 4$.

factorial—The product obtained by multiplying a given number by all the positive numbers between one and itself. For example, 5! (five factorial) = $5 \times 4 \times 3 \times 2 \times 1 = 120$; 8! = $8 \times 7 \times 6 \times 5 \times 4 \times 3 \times 2 \times 1 = 40{,}320$.

factors—All the numbers that divide a given number evenly—with a zero remainder. For example, all the factors of 8 are 1, 2, 4, and 8.

frequency table—A diagram that arranges data so that it is easier to read. It shows the frequency of each data entry.

graph—To show the location of a point on a line or in a plane. For example, the line below shows the graph of -2.

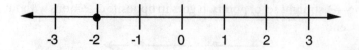

greatest place value—The place value of a number's leading digit. For example, the greatest place value of 32,017 is ten thousand.

height of polygon—The measure of the distance from the highest point in a polygon to its base.

histogram—A bar graph without spaces between the bars. It is a "pictorial" frequency table.

improper fraction—A fraction in which the numerator is a larger number than the denominator. For example,

$\frac{5}{3}$, $\frac{17}{2}$, and $\frac{14}{9}$ all are improper fractions.

independent events—A probability event whose results are not influenced by the outcome of another probability event. For example, it is an independent event if one draws a second card from a deck after a first card has been drawn and replaced.

inscribed polygon—A polygon that has all of its vertices on the circle.

intersecting lines—Lines that meet and cross at a point.

intersection—The set made from the common elements of two or more sets. The symbol ∩ denotes intersection.

inverse operation—An operation that reverses another. For example, addition is the inverse operation of subtraction.

isosceles triangle—A triangle with two congruent sides.

least common denominator (LCD)—The smallest number that the denominators of given fractions will divide into without a remainder. For example,

the LCD of $\frac{3}{5}$ and $\frac{2}{9}$ is 45. The LCD of $\frac{11}{15}$ and $\frac{7}{30}$ is 30.

least common multiple (LCM)—The smallest number that is divisible by each of the given numbers. One way to compute the LCM is to work the acronym backward. Find the multiples (M), find the common multiples (CM), then find the least common multiples (LCM).

like terms—Quantities whose variable parts are exactly the same. For example, $7z$ and $-13z$ are like terms. $4m^2$ and $3m$ are not.

line—A straight set of points. It goes in opposite directions without end.

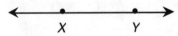

$X \qquad Y$

Use two uppercase letters to represent a line. (These two letters can be any two points on the line.) Above the letters, place this symbol $\longleftrightarrow$. For example, $\overleftrightarrow{XY}$ is read "line *XY*."

line segment—A portion of a line. The two extreme points on a line segment are called endpoints. For example, endpoint *M* and endpoint *N* appear in the line segment below:

$$M \qquad\qquad\qquad N$$

The symbol for line segment MN is $\overline{MN}$.

mean—The average; the mean is found by adding the data entries and dividing the sum by the number of entries. For example, if the data entries are 10, 15, and 26, the sum is 51. The mean is obtained by dividing the sum by 3, which is the number of data entries: $51 \div 3 = 17$.

means—The two inside numbers when the ratios of a proportion are written with a colon. For example, in the proportion $36:18 = 6:3$, the means are 18 and 6.

median—The middle number in a list of numbers that is arranged by size. For example, if the data entries are 5, 31, 75, 110, and 300, the median is 75.

mixed number—A number that is part whole number and part fraction. For example,

$13\frac{1}{2}$ and $21\frac{9}{14}$ are mixed numbers.

mode—The data entry that appears most often. For example, if the data are 9, 13, 2, 13, 48, 13, and 100, the mode is 13.

multiple—The product that results when a given number is multiplied by one of the whole numbers $\{0,1,2,3,...\}$. For example, the first ten multiples of 7 are 0, 7, 14, 21, 28, 35, 42, 49, 56, and 63.

mutually exclusive events—Events that cannot be happening at the same time.

non-terminating decimal—A decimal that is obtained when a fraction is changed into a decimal and the quotient does not come out exactly. For example,

$\frac{1}{22}$ changed into a decimal results in $22\overline{)1.000000000}^{.045454545}$, with

a remainder that keeps recurring.

number line—A visual model of ordered numbers.

numerator—The part of a fraction that is above the line. For

example, the numerator in $\frac{7}{8}$ is 7.

numerical coefficient—The number portion of a variable term. For example, in $17y^3$, the numerical coefficient is 17.

obtuse angle—An angle that has a measure of more than 90°, but less than 180°. Obtuse angles appear wide. See the examples below:

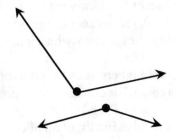

obtuse triangle—A triangle that contains an obtuse angle.

odds—A comparison between the probability of an event not happening with the probability of an event happening.

open sentence—An equation that contains a variable. For example, 14 - 9 = 5 is not an open sentence, but w - 9 = 5 is.

operation—The process of carrying out a set rule on a pair of numbers. For example, the four basic operations in arithmetic are + (addition), - (subtraction), × (multiplication), and ÷ (division).

opposite of a number—Same number, different sign. Examples of opposite numbers are:

7 and -7; -3.2 and 3.2; $-\frac{1}{2}$ and $\frac{1}{2}$.

This is also called the additive inverse.

order—To list numbers by their value. For example, 154, 72, and 3 are ordered from greatest to least.

order of operations—The standard sequence when working out a problem, (a) performing operations within parentheses first, (b) evaluating exponents next, (c) performing multiplication and division from left to right, and (d) performing addition and subtraction from left to right.

outcome—A specified result of an experiment. For example, if a spinner has three different colors (red, yellow, blue) on it, there are three possible outcomes from a spin (red, yellow, blue).

parallel lines—Lines in the same plane that will never meet or cross, regardless of how far they are extended.

parallelogram—A four-sided polygon whose opposite sides are parallel and congruent. See the examples below.

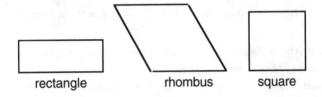

rectangle   rhombus   square

percent—The numerator of a fraction whose denominator is 100. For example, $\frac{71}{100}$ is the same as 71%.

perimeter—The distance around the outside of a polygon.

period—The portion of a number between two consecutive commas. For example, 579,874,321 has three periods. The digits 321 are in the ones' period, 874 is in the thousands' period, and 579 is in the millions' period.

permutation—an arrangement of elements which is characterized by the objects in it and their order. For example, the letters *A* and *B* have two permutations: *AB* and *BA*.

perpendicular lines—Lines that meet to form 90° angles.

pi—The ratio of the circumference of a circle to its diameter. This ratio is approximately 3.14. The symbol for pi is π.

place value—The value of a digit in a numeral. Changing a digit's place in a number, changes its value. For example, the 2 has a value of 20 in 123, but has a value of 200 in 213.

plane figure—A flat figure (as opposed to a space, or a three-dimensional figure). For example, rectangles, squares, circles, and triangles are plane figures, whereas cubes, spheres, and cylinders are space figures.

point—The most basic geometric figure. A point designates a specific location. Use a dot and an uppercase letter to represent a point. For example, • Q is read "point Q."

polygon—A simple, closed figure whose sides are line segments.

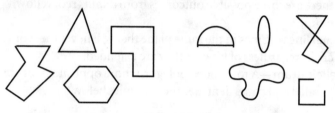

These are polygons.   These are *not* polygons.

polyhedron—A space figure whose faces are all polygonal regions. There are two major groups of space figures: those with curved surfaces (e.g., a cone, a cylinder, or a sphere)and those designated as polyhedrons. Examples:

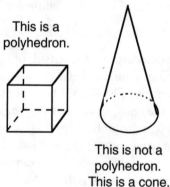

This is a
polyhedron.

This is not a
polyhedron.
This is a cone.

power—The number of times that a number is multiplied by itself. For example, 4^3 is read as "four to the third power" and equals 64.

powers of 10—The number 10 and the result of multiplying 10 by itself any number of times. For example, $100 = 10 \times 10$ and

$1,000 = 10 \times 10 \times 10$. The numbers 100; 1,000; 10,000; all are powers of 10.

prime factorization—The factored form of a number such that all the factors are prime numbers. For example, although a factored form of 12 is 2×6, it is not the prime factorization of 12 because 6 is not a prime number. The prime factorization of 12 is $2 \times 2 \times 3$ or $2^2 \times 3$.

prime number—Any number that has only two factors, one and itself. For example, of the numbers 2, 9, 17, and 91, the only prime numbers are 2 and 17. Both 9 and 91 have more than two factors. The factors of 9 are 1, 3, and 9. The factors of 91 are 1, 7, 13, and 91.

prism—A space figure that has two parallel, congruent faces (designated as bases) and sides that are parallelograms (called lateral faces).

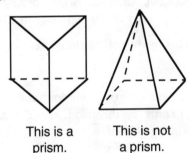

This is a
prism.

This is not
a prism.

probability—A measure of likelihood. For example, when you are flipping a coin, your probability of getting heads is 50%.

product—The answer to a multiplication problem. For example, the product of 2 and 3 is 6.

proper fraction—A fraction in which the numerator (the number above the line) is smaller than the denominator (the number below the line). For example,

$\frac{4}{9}, \frac{11}{13}$, and $\frac{23}{39}$ all are proper fractions.

proportion—An equation made up of two ratios.

For example, $\frac{9}{15} = \frac{15}{25}$ is a proportion.

protractor—An instrument for measuring angles.

quotient—The answer in a division problem. For example, in each of the following equations, the quotient is 13:

(a) $\frac{26}{2} = 13$ (b) $4 \overline{)52}^{\,13}$ (c) $143 \div 11 = 13$

radius—A line segment that connects the center of a circle or sphere with any point on the circle or sphere.

range—The difference found by subtracting the lowest data entry from the highest data entry in a frequency distribution. For example, if the data are 7, 19, 47, 47, 93, and 107, the range is obtained by taking 107 (the highest) and substituting 7 (the lowest). The range is 100.

rate—A ratio comparing two quantities expressed in different units of measure—for example, 217 miles in 7 hours.

ratio—A way to compare quantities. The ratio reflects the stated order of objects. For example, in a class of 13 girls and 11 boys, the ratio of girls to boys can be expressed as 13 to 11, 13:11, or $\frac{13}{11}$. The ratio of boys to girls can be expressed as 11 to 13, 11:13, or $\frac{11}{13}$.

ray—A portion of a line with only one endpoint. It extends, without end, in only one direction. Ray *JK* is expressed by using the following symbol: $\overrightarrow{JK}$.

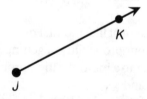

Note: When writing about rays with symbols, the first letter is *always* the endpoint. The symbol for the ray below is $\overrightarrow{RS}$ and is read "ray RS."

reciprocal—Either of two numbers that when multiplied together equal 1. For example,

$\frac{5}{9}$ and $\frac{9}{5}$ are reciprocals, because $\frac{5}{9} \times \frac{9}{5} = \frac{45}{45} = 1$.

rectangle—A parallelogram that has four right angles (that is, all angles are congruent).

regular polygon—A polygon that has all sides congruent.

repeating decimal—A decimal that is obtained when a fraction is changed to a decimal and the quotient does not come out exactly but has a recurring pattern. For example,

$\frac{1}{11}$ changed into a decimal results in $11 \overline{)1.00000}$ $^{.090909}$.

replacement set—the set of all the numbers that will be substituted for the variable.

rhombus—A parallelogram that has all sides congruent.

right angle—An angle with a measure of exactly 90°. The sides of right angles are said to be perpendicular.

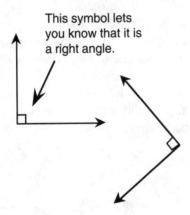

This symbol lets you know that it is a right angle.

right triangle—A triangle that contains a right (90°) angle.

round—To approximate the value of a number based on a stated place value. For example, 2,742 rounded to the nearest thousand is 3,000 and rounded to the nearest hundred is 2,700.

sample space—A listing that shows all the possible outcomes of a probability experiment.

scalene triangle—A triangle whose sides and angles are unequal.

scientific notation—A way to express very large or very small numbers in a more compact manner as a product of a number between 1 and 10 multiplied by the appropriate power of 10. For example, 624,000 written in scientific notation is 6.24×10^5.

set—A collection of objects. A set can be described using words or by listing all the things that are contained in the set.

signed numbers—The group of negative numbers and positive numbers.

simplify—Generally means to reduce a problem to its essentials. For example, the expression 5(4-3) simplified would be 5. Simplifying fractions means to reduce them to lowest terms; that is, to put the fraction in a form such that the numerator and the denominator have no common factors other than 1. For example,

$\frac{2}{3}$ is a simplified fraction; $\frac{14}{21}$ is not.

solution set—The numbers from the replacement set that "work" when substituted for the variable.

solve—To find the value of the variable in an equation. For example, if you were to solve $3z = 36$, the final step would read $z = 12$ (the letter would be alone on one side and everything else would be on the other side).

space figure—A figure that has points in more than one plane; sometimes called a solid or three-dimensional figure. Some examples appear below:

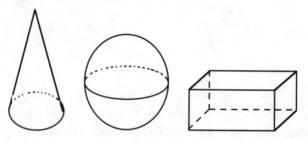

standard form—The regular way to write a number. For example, 17 is in standard form, whereas "seventeen" is not in standard form.

straightedge—Any rigid border used to draw a straight line.

substitute—To replace a variable with a number. For example, if 7 is substituted for *w* in the expression $3w + 3$, the expression would become $3(7) + 3$.

sum—The answer in an addition problem. For example, in $14 + 37 = 51$, the sum is 51.

supplementary angles—Two angles whose measures add up to 180°. For example, if m$\angle A = 114°$ and m$\angle B = 66°$, $\angle A$ and $\angle B$ are supplementary because $114° + 66° = 180°$.

surface area—The measure of the total outer surface of a solid. It is found by adding all the areas of the faces.

T table—A table of values. A place to display possible solutions to an equation. For example, a T table for $x + y = 5$ is

x	y
-1	6
0	5
1	4

terminating decimal—A decimal that is obtained when a fraction is changed to a decimal and the quotient comes out exactly. For example,

$\frac{3}{8}$ changed to a decimal results in a terminating decimal

because $8\overline{)3.000}$ $\overset{.375}{}$, with no remainder.

terms—Quantities separated by plus or minus signs. For example, in the expression $4m^2 - 3m + 2$, there are three terms. They are $4m^2$, $3m$, and 2.

transversal—A line that intersects two other lines. Example of a transversal

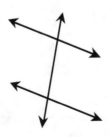

tree diagram—A drawing that shows all the possible outcomes of a probability experiment.

two-step equation—An open sentence involving two operations. For example, $x + 7 = 3$ would not be considered to be a two-step equation (it only involves addition). However, $2x + 7 = 3$ would be considered to be a two-step equation because it involves both multiplication and addition.

union—When the members of two or more sets are combined into one set. The symbol $\cup$ denotes union.

unit price—The rate for one portion of one item. For example, $1.20 per gallon.

variable—A letter that takes the place of a number. For example, in the equation $4x + 7 = m$, the variables are x and m.

vertical angles—The two pairs of nonadjacent angles formed when two lines intersect. Vertical angles are congruent.

volume—Measure of the inner space contained in a solid.

AT YOUR FINGERTIPS: CHARTS AND TABLES FOR QUICK REFERENCE

TEN QUICK TIPS FOR SOLVING WORD PROBLEMS

1. Know what you are looking for. Find the question.
2. Rewrite the problem in your own words.
3. Start with what you know; move toward what you do not know.
4. Draw a picture. Visualize the situation. Re-create the problem.
5. Get your facts organized. Make a table or a chart.
6. Look for a pattern in the data. Write down your observations.
7. Translate the words of the problem into symbols; write an equation.
8. Take a guess and check to see if it works.
9. Change the direction of your approach. Take a different viewpoint.
10. Talk it through with other people. Listen to and apply their suggestions.

TABLE OF MATHEMATICAL SYMBOLS

English Words	Mathematical Symbol(s)	English Words	Mathematical Symbol(s)
add	+	is similar to	~
angle	∠	line segment	—
braces	{ }	line	↔
brackets	[ ]	measure of an angle	m∠
centigrade	C	minus	-
degree	°	multiply	× • ( )
divide	÷ √	parallel	‖
does it equal?	?=	parentheses	( )
empty or null set	{ } φ	percent	%
Fahrenheit	F	perpendicular	⊥
intersection	∩	pi (3.14159)	π
is congruent to	≅	ray	→
is equal to	=	square root	√
is greater than	>	subtract	-
is less than	<	the quantity of	( )
is not equal to	≠	the set of	{ }
		triangle	Δ

METRIC TRANSLATIONS

Prefix	Meaning	Symbol	Relation to Standard
kilo-	thousand	k	1,000
hecto-	hundred	h	100
deka-	ten	da	10
deci-	tenth	d	$\frac{1}{10}$
centi-	hundredth	c	$\frac{1}{100}$
milli-	thousandth	m	$\frac{1}{1000}$

METRIC SENSE

TEMPERATURE

- Normal body temperature is 37°C.
- The freezing point of water is 0°C.
- The boiling point of water is 100°C.
- A temperature indicative of a fever is 41°C.
- Sweater/jacket weather might be 10°C.
- Picnicking weather might be 26°C.
- A moderately heated oven would be about 175°C.
- The inner temperature of a refrigerator is about 5°C.

VOLUME

- A bathtub holds about 400 liters of water.
- An aquarium holds about 17 liters.
- A teaspoon holds about 5 milliliters.
- A coffee mug holds about 200 milliliters.
- A car's fuel tank capacity is about 60 liters.
- The volume of an ice cream cone is about 24 milliliters.
- A juice glass holds about 250 milliliters.
- A gallon of milk is about 3.8 liters.

LENGTH

- The thickness of a dime is 1 millimeter.
- The length of a golf club is about 75 centimeters.
- The width of a paper clip is about 2 centimeters.
- Things that are approximately 1 meter: length of a baseball bat, height of a chalkboard, width of a door.
- The distance of 5 city blocks is about 1 kilometer.
- The length of a swimming pool is about 25 meters.
- The height of a basketball goal is about 3 meters.
- The length of a drinking straw is about 20 centimeters.
- The length of a bed is about 2 meters.

(continued)

MASS

- One liter of water weighs 1 kilogram.
- A paper clip weighs about 1 gram.
- A quarter weighs about 6 grams.
- A bicycle weighs about 11 kilograms.
- A pencil weighs about 5 grams.
- One drop of water weighs about 50 milligrams.
- A school bus weighs about 10 metric tons.
- The weight of a small whale is about 30 metric tons.

ALPHABETICAL LIST OF CONVERSIONS FOR UNITS OF MEASURE

UNIT	CONVERSION(S)
1 acre (a)	= 4,840 square yards (yd^2) = 43,560 square feet (ft^2)
1 centimeter (cm)	= 10 millimeters (mm)
1 century	= 100 years (yr)
1 cubic decimeter (dm^3)	= 0.001 cubic meter (m^3) = 1,000 cubic centimeters (cm^3) = 1 liter (l)
1 cubic foot (ft^3)	= 1,728 cubic inches (in^3)
1 cubic meter (m^3)	= 1,000,000 cubic centimeters (cm^3) = 1000 cubic decimeters (dm^3)
1 cubic yard (yd^3)	= 27 cubic feet (ft^3) = 46,656 cubic inches (in^3)
1 cup (c)	= 16 tablespoons (T) = 8 fluid ounces (fl oz)
1 day	= 24 hours (hr)
1 decade	= 10 years (yr)
1 dekameter (dam)	= 10 meters (m)
1 decimeter (dm)	= 10 centimeters (cm)
1 foot (ft)	= 12 inches (in)
1 gallon (gal)	= 16 cups (c) = 8 pints (pt) = 4 quarts (qt) = 128 fluid ounces (fl oz)

UNIT	CONVERSION(S)
1 gram (g)	= 1,000 milligrams (mg)
1 hectometer (hm)	= 100 meters (m)
1 hectare (ha)	= 0.01 square kilometer (km^2) = 10,000 square meters (m^2)
1 hour (hr)	= 60 minutes (min)
1 inch (in)	= 2.54 centimeters (cm)
1 kilogram (kg)	= 1,000 grams (g)
1 kiloliter (kl)	= 1,000 liters (l)
1 kilometer (km)	= 100 dekameters (dam) = 1,000 meters (m)
1 liter (l)	= 1,000 milliliters (ml) = 1,000 cubic centimeters (cm^3) = 1 cubic decimeter (dm^3) = 4 metric cups
1 meter (m)	= 10 decimeters (dm) = 100 centimeters (cm) = 1,000 millimeters (mm)
1 metric ton (t)	= 1,000 kilograms (kg)
1 mile (mi)	= 5,280 feet (ft) = 1,760 yards (yd) = 1.609 kilometers (km)
1 minute (min)	= 60 seconds (sec)
1 pint (pt)	= 2 cups (c) = 16 fluid ounces (fl oz)
1 pound (lb)	= 16 ounces (oz) = 453.59 grams (g)
1 quart (qt)	= 4 cups (c) = 2 pints (pt) = 32 fluid ounces (fl oz) = .9465 liters (L)
1 square foot (ft^2)	= 144 square inches (in^2)
1 square kilometer (km^2)	= 1,000,000 square meters (m^2) = 100 hectares (ha)
1 square meter (m^2)	= 100 square decimeters (dm^2) = 10,000 square centimeters (cm^2)
1 square mile (mi^2)	= 640 acres (a)
1 square yard (yd^2)	= 9 square feet (ft^2) = 1,296 square inches (in^2)
1 tablespoon (T)	= 3 teaspoons (t)

(continued)

UNIT	CONVERSION(S)
1 teaspoon (t)	= 5 milliliters (ml)
1 ton (T)	= 2,000 pounds (lb)
1 week	= 7 days
1 yard (yd)	= 36 inches (in) = 3 feet (ft)
1 year (yr)	= 52 weeks = 365 or 366 days

DECIMAL EQUIVALENTS OF SOME COMMON FRACTIONS

$\frac{1}{2}$	= .50		$\frac{5}{8}$	= .625
$\frac{1}{3}$	= .333...		$\frac{7}{8}$	= .875
$\frac{2}{3}$	= .666...		$\frac{1}{9}$	= .111...
$\frac{1}{4}$	= .25		$\frac{1}{10}$	= .10
$\frac{3}{4}$	= .75		$\frac{2}{10}$	= .20
$\frac{1}{5}$	= .20		$\frac{3}{10}$	= .30
$\frac{2}{5}$	= .40		$\frac{7}{10}$	= .70
$\frac{3}{5}$	= .60		$\frac{9}{10}$	= .90
$\frac{4}{5}$	= .80		$\frac{1}{12}$	= .0833...
$\frac{1}{6}$	= .166...		$\frac{1}{15}$	= .066...
$\frac{5}{6}$	= .8333...		$\frac{1}{20}$	= .05
$\frac{1}{7}$	= $.\overline{142857}$		$\frac{1}{25}$	= .04
$\frac{1}{8}$	= .125		$\frac{1}{100}$	= .01
$\frac{3}{8}$	= .375			

FRACTIONAL EQUIVALENTS OF SOME COMMON PERCENTS

1%	$=$	$\frac{1}{100}$	$37\frac{1}{2}\%$	$=$	$\frac{3}{8}$
4%	$=$	$\frac{1}{25}$	40%	$=$	$\frac{2}{5}$
5%	$=$	$\frac{1}{20}$	45%	$=$	$\frac{9}{20}$
$6\frac{2}{3}\%$	$=$	$\frac{1}{15}$	50%	$=$	$\frac{1}{2}$
$8\frac{1}{3}\%$	$=$	$\frac{1}{12}$	55%	$=$	$\frac{11}{20}$
10%	$=$	$\frac{1}{10}$	60%	$=$	$\frac{3}{5}$
$11\frac{1}{9}\%$	$=$	$\frac{1}{9}$	65%	$=$	$\frac{13}{20}$
$12\frac{1}{2}\%$	$=$	$\frac{1}{8}$	$66\frac{2}{3}\%$	$=$	$\frac{2}{3}$
$14\frac{2}{7}\%$	$=$	$\frac{1}{7}$	70%	$=$	$\frac{7}{10}$
15%	$=$	$\frac{3}{20}$	75%	$=$	$\frac{3}{4}$
$16\frac{2}{3}\%$	$=$	$\frac{1}{6}$	80%	$=$	$\frac{4}{5}$
20%	$=$	$\frac{1}{5}$	$83\frac{1}{3}\%$	$=$	$\frac{5}{6}$
25%	$=$	$\frac{1}{4}$	85%	$=$	$\frac{17}{20}$
30%	$=$	$\frac{3}{10}$	90%	$=$	$\frac{9}{10}$
$33\frac{1}{3}\%$	$=$	$\frac{1}{3}$	95%	$=$	$\frac{19}{20}$
35%	$=$	$\frac{7}{20}$	100%	$=$	$\frac{1}{1}=1$

ALL OF THE FACTORS OF COMPOSITE NUMBERS FROM 2 TO 100

NUMBER	ALL OF THE FACTORS
*4	1, 2, 4
6	1, 2, 3, 6
8	1, 2, 4, 8
*9	1, 3, 9
10	1, 2, 5, 10
12	1, 2, 3, 4, 6, 12
14	1, 2, 7, 14
15	1, 3, 5, 15
*16	1, 2, 4, 8, 16
18	1, 2, 3, 6, 9, 18
20	1, 2, 4, 5, 10, 20
21	1, 3, 7, 21
22	1, 2, 11, 22
24	1, 2, 3, 4, 6, 8, 12, 24
*25	1, 5, 25
26	1, 2, 13, 26
27	1, 3, 9, 27
28	1, 2, 4, 7, 14, 28
30	1, 2, 3, 5, 6, 10, 15, 30
32	1, 2, 4, 8, 16, 32
33	1, 3, 11, 33
34	1, 2, 17, 34
35	1, 5, 7, 35
*36	1, 2, 3, 4, 6, 9, 12, 18, 36
38	1, 2, 19, 38
39	1, 3, 13, 39
40	1, 2, 4, 5, 8, 10, 20, 40
42	1, 2, 3, 6, 7, 14, 21, 42
44	1, 2, 4, 11, 22, 44

* Indicates a perfect square

NUMBER	ALL OF THE FACTORS
45	1, 3, 5, 9, 15, 45
46	1, 2, 23, 46
48	1, 2, 3, 4, 6, 8, 12, 16, 24, 48
*49	1, 7, 49
50	1, 2, 5, 10, 25, 50
51	1, 3, 17, 51
52	1, 2, 4, 13, 26, 52
54	1, 2, 3, 6, 9, 18, 27, 54
55	1, 5, 11, 55
56	1, 2, 4, 7, 8, 14, 28, 56
57	1, 3, 19, 57
58	1, 2, 29, 58
60	1, 2, 3, 4, 5, 6, 10, 12, 15, 20, 30, 60
62	1, 2, 31, 62
63	1, 3, 7, 9, 21, 63
*64	1, 2, 4, 8, 16, 32, 64
65	1, 5, 13, 65
66	1, 2, 3, 6, 11, 22, 33, 66
68	1, 2, 4, 17, 34, 68
69	1, 3, 23, 69
70	1, 2, 5, 7, 10, 14, 35, 70
72	1, 2, 3, 4, 6, 8, 9, 12, 18, 24, 36, 72
74	1, 2, 37, 74
75	1, 3, 5, 15, 25, 75
76	1, 2, 4, 19, 38, 76
77	1, 7, 11, 77
78	1, 2, 3, 6, 13, 26, 39, 78
80	1, 2, 4, 5, 8, 10, 16, 20, 40, 80
*81	1, 3, 9, 27, 81
82	1, 2, 41, 82
84	1, 2, 3, 4, 6, 7, 12, 14, 21, 28, 42, 84
85	1, 5, 17, 85

* Indicates a perfect square

(continued)

NUMBER	ALL OF THE FACTORS
86	1, 2, 43, 86
87	1, 3, 29, 87
88	1, 2, 4, 8, 11, 22, 44, 88
90	1, 2, 3, 5, 6, 9, 10, 15, 18, 30, 45, 90
91	1, 7, 13, 91
92	1, 2, 4, 23, 46, 92
93	1, 3, 31, 93
94	1, 2, 47, 94
95	1, 5, 19, 95
96	1, 2, 3, 4, 6, 8, 12, 16, 24, 32, 48, 96
98	1, 2, 7, 14, 49, 98
99	1, 3, 33, 99
*100	1, 2, 4, 5, 10, 20, 25, 50, 100

* Indicates a perfect square

PRIME NUMBERS AND PRIME FACTORIZATION OF COMPOSITE NUMBERS FROM 2 TO 100

PRIME NUMBERS

2
3
5
7
11
13
17
19
23
29
31
37
41
43
47
53
59
61
67
71
73
79
83
89
97

COMPOSITE NUMBERS	FACTORIZATION
4	2 · 2
6	2 · 3
8	2 · 2 · 2
9	3 · 3
10	2 · 5
12	2 · 2 · 3
14	2 · 7
15	3 · 5
16	2 · 2 · 2 · 2
18	2 · 3 · 3
20	2 · 2 · 5
21	3 · 7
22	2 · 11
24	2 · 2 · 2 · 3
25	5 · 5
26	2 · 13
27	3 · 3 · 3
28	2 · 2 · 7
30	2 · 3 · 5
32	2 · 2 · 2 · 2 · 2
33	3 · 11
34	2 · 17
35	5 · 7
36	2 · 2 · 3 · 3
38	2 · 19
39	3 · 13
40	2 · 2 · 2 · 5
42	2 · 3 · 7
44	2 · 2 · 11
45	3 · 3 · 5
46	2 · 23
48	2 · 2 · 2 · 2 · 3
49	7 · 7
50	2 · 5 · 5

COMPOSITE NUMBERS	FACTORIZATION
51	3 • 17
52	2 • 2 • 13
54	2 • 3 • 3 • 3
55	5 • 11
56	2 • 2 • 2 • 7
57	3 • 19
58	2 • 29
60	2 • 2 • 3 • 5
62	2 • 31
63	3 • 3 • 7
64	2 • 2 • 2 • 2 • 2 • 2
65	5 • 13
66	2 • 3 • 11
68	2 • 2 • 17
69	3 • 23
70	2 • 5 • 7
72	2 • 2 • 2 • 3 • 3
74	2 • 37
75	3 • 5 • 5
76	2 • 2 • 19
77	7 • 11
78	2 • 3 • 13
80	2 • 2 • 2 • 2 • 5
81	3 • 3 • 3 • 3
82	2 • 41
84	2 • 2 • 3 • 7
85	5 • 17
86	2 • 43
87	3 • 29
88	2 • 2 • 2 • 11
90	2 • 3 • 3 • 5
91	7 • 13
92	2 • 2 • 23

(continued)

COMPOSITE NUMBERS	FACTORIZATION
93	$3 \cdot 31$
94	$2 \cdot 47$
95	$5 \cdot 19$
96	$2 \cdot 2 \cdot 2 \cdot 2 \cdot 2 \cdot 3$
98	$2 \cdot 7 \cdot 7$
99	$3 \cdot 3 \cdot 11$
100	$2 \cdot 2 \cdot 5 \cdot 5$

TEN HELPFUL CALCULATOR KEYS

KEY	FUNCTION

+/-   Changes the sign of a number from positive to negative (and vice versa).

√   Finds the square root of a number.

cons   Allows a number to be designated as a constant for use in repeated operations.

M+   **M-**   Stores a value in memory that can later be added to (M+) or subtracted from (M-).

MR   Recalls the value that has been stored in memory.

x^2   Squares the entered number.

y^x   Finds a specified power of an entered number.

C   Clear—clears the display, but not the memory.

AC   All Clear—clears everything, including the memory.

INDEX

A

abscissa (x-coordinate), 277, 278, 279
addends, 311
addition, 37, 54–60
  of algebraic fractions, 235, 237,
    266–68, 269–71
  of decimals, 88, 97–98
  of negative and positive numbers,
    234, 235, 246–48, 249
  of nonalgebraic fractions, 62, 63,
    66–67, 80–82
addition property of 0, 56, 59
algebra, *see* prealgebra
angles, 133–36, 145–49, 158–63
  acute, 131, 133, 139, 145, 146–47,
    148, 311
  adjacent, 131, 160–61, 185, 311
  alternate interior, 131, 160, 162,
    163
  bisection of, 132, 172, 183–85
  central, 131, 136, 163, 164
  complementary, 131, 135, 158–59,
    314
  congruent, 162, 165–66
  copying of, 131, 172, 180–83
  corresponding, 131, 160, 162, 163,
    168, 169, 171
  definition of, 145–46, 311
  degrees of, 315
  of intersecting lines, 159–63
  measurement of, 131, 134, 146–49
  naming of, 146, 312
  obtuse, 131, 133, 139, 145, 147,
    148, 320

  perpendicular, 153
  right, 131, 133, 139, 145, 147, 148,
    159, 160, 325
  straight, 159
  supplementary, 131, 135, 158–59,
    162, 327
  vertex of, 145, 146, 169
  vertical, 131, 160, 161, 162, 163,
    328
associative property, 37, 39, 56, 57, 60
axes, 276, 283–85

B

base systems, 17, 28–32, 312–13
British system of measurement,
    200–204, 332–34

C

calculators, 16, 214, 292, 343
canceling, 266, 272, 273, 274, 275
Celsius, 204
centi-, 195, 330
circles, 316, 163–64, 207, 222, 225
  arc of, 178
  area of, 132, 214–15, 227
  center of, 164, 313
  central angle in, 131, 136, 163,
    164
  chords of, 131, 136, 163, 164, 313
  circumference of, 132, 206,
    213–14, 313
  definition of, 131, 164
  diameter of, 131, 136, 163, 164,
    214, 315